Margins

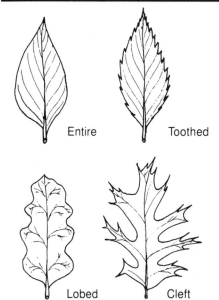

Entire

Toothed

Lobed

Cleft

Parts

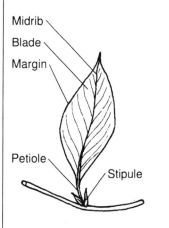

Midrib

Blade

Margin

Petiole

Stipule

Attachment

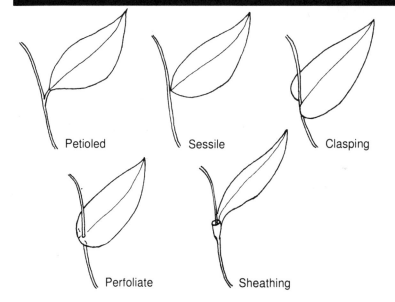

Petioled

Sessile

Clasping

Perfoliate

Sheathing

WILDFLOWERS *of* MAMMOTH CAVE NATIONAL PARK

WILDFLOWERS *of* MAMMOTH CAVE NATIONAL PARK

Randy Seymour

THE UNIVERSITY PRESS OF KENTUCKY

Publication of this book was assisted by a grant from the
Eastern National Park and Monument Association.

Scholarly publisher for the Commonwealth,
serving Bellarmine College, Berea College, Centre
College of Kentucky, Eastern Kentucky University,
The Filson Club, Georgetown College, Kentucky
Historical Society, Kentucky State University,
Morehead State University, Murray State University,
Northern Kentucky University, Transylvania University,
University of Kentucky, University of Louisville,
and Western Kentucky University.

Editorial and Sales Offices: The University Press of Kentucky
663 South Limestone Street, Lexington, Kentucky 40508-4008

01   00   99   98   97   5   4   3   2   1

Title page: left, EGGERT'S SUNFLOWER (*Helianthus eggertii*);
right top, JACOB'S LADDER (*Palemonium reptans*); right bottom,
BLACKBERRY LILY (*Belamcanda chinensis*)

Library of Congress Cataloging-in-Publication Data

Seymour, Randy, 1942–
     Wildflowers of Mammoth Cave National Park / Randy Seymour.
          p.   cm.
     Includes bibliographical references (p.   ) and indexes.
     ISBN 0-8131-0898-5
     1. Wild flowers—Kentucky—Mammoth Cave National Park.   I. Title.
QK162.S48   1997
582.13'09769'754—dc20   96-18727

Printed in Singapore

To the memory of my mother,
Myrtie Frances Barbour Seymour,
who walked in the woods and fields with me
when I was a child and showed me the
wildflowers. She believed with all her heart
that if people looked at the variety and beauty of
the wildflowers, they could not help but
believe in God. And so do I.

CONTENTS

■ ■ ■ ■ ■
ILLUSTRATIONS

ACKNOWLEDGMENTS

I am deeply indebted to Dr. Julian Campbell, botanist for the Kentucky Chapter of the Nature Conservancy, for sharing his love of botany, for his willingness to teach field botany to an amateur, and for his critical review of the photographs and descriptive text in this guide. For Dr. Campbell's generous gift of time, patience, and unfaltering encouragement, I shall be forever grateful.

Special thanks to Tres Seymour for helping to edit the manuscript and designing the word-processing formats used to record the data. His devotion to teaching his father enough about the use of a PC to allow the production of this guide is warmly appreciated.

My wife, Donna, deserves much of the credit for this guide. Her caring and understanding made it possible to put so much of our life on hold while this project was completed.

Although I have not made every suggested adjustment to the text, and any remaining errors are mine alone, the accuracy and quality of this guide have been immeasurably improved by the tenacious devotion and effort of Dr. John Thieret in reading and editing this manuscript.

It is with gratitude that I acknowledge the botanists and plant enthusiasts of the present and past for the wealth of information accumulated in books, without which I could not have completed this guide, and a small fraction of which is listed in the bibliography.

PREFACE

Mammoth Cave National Park, located in southcentral Kentucky, harbors within its 53,000 acres broad, dry upland forests; cool, damp ravines where surface streams suddenly disappear as the underlying rock changes from sandstone to limestone; and steep, precipitous bluffs at the boundaries of escarpments and along the deep gorge of the Green River. There are densely shaded slopes and narrow river bottoms that are often flooded in the spring. Heavily farmed prior to the beginning of land acquisition for the park in the late 1920s, much of the land is in successional growth, with visible reminders of its rich historic past. Scattered in small areas within the park are barrens, glades, meadows, ponds, marshy wetlands, hemlock gorges, and virgin hardwood forests. There are huge, deep sinkholes where the subterranean streams sometimes surface, and where temperatures may vary as much as 20 degrees from top to bottom during the summer. Adding even more variety to this mosaic of habitats is the geographic location of the park in a transitional area between the drier oak-hickory forests and open prairies to the west, and the more closed, damp, mixed-hardwood forests to the east. Prior to settlement the park lands and surrounding areas contained open glades and extensive prairies, probably maintained by naturally and aboriginally set fires. Temperatures may vary from over 100 degrees in summer to -25 degrees in winter. Rainfall, which averages about 50 inches annually, is seasonal with summer and fall drier than spring and winter.

The immense variety of habitats and seasonal climate changes provide the basis for the park's equally large and diverse plant community. Though limited, past botanical studies within the park officially list 866 species of plants. Recent investigations indicate that the true number of plant species may well be closer to 1,100. The Kentucky State Nature Preserves Commission lists 21 species in the park as threatened, endangered, or of special concern, with four of these under review by the United States Fish and Wildlife Service for possible threatened or endangered status. There are several plant species in the park that are rare in Kentucky because they are at the geographical extremes of their range, while others are rare because of the continuing shrinkage of suitable habitat.

Mammoth Cave National Park has the potential to become one of the greatest protectors of biological diversity in the eastern United States. Unfortunately, but perhaps understandably, past management and resource allocations have been devoted almost exclusively to the subterranean national treasure within the park, the world's longest cave system. After all, the cave is the primary reason the park was established. Management of the surface landscape has consisted primarily of fire suppression and maintenance of lawnlike, primary roadsides. Plant succession toward total parkland coverage by climax forests appears to be the unspoken goal for the surface.

Gone are the wolf, cougar, bear, and human predators that kept the deer herds in check. Absent are the naturally and aboriginally set fires that kept large areas open. Gone are the buffalo that created microhabitats with their trails, wallows, and eating habits. Vanished are numerous birds and smaller animals that affected the ecosystems and helped to create biodiversity. Numerous introduced plants have become established as dominant species. Most of these changes, which individually and collectively have adversely impacted the ecosystems promoting biodiversity in the park, are irreversible. There are only small remnants of some habitats still existing in the park, especially the barrens, glades, and other open-area habitats that contain a disproportionate number of the known plant species. Already a significant number of plants have been extirpated from the park and an even larger number are on the verge of extirpation. Passive, "noninterference" management methods are no longer acceptable.

Mammoth Cave National Park has been designated an International Biosphere Reserve, and National Park Service policies are changing toward total ecosystem management. Mammoth Cave National Park is extremely fortunate to have on its staff several dedicated professionals who demonstrate visionary, total ecosystem management philosophies. In my opinion, with increased public support and additional resources, these talented people can successfully continue the movement toward management for biodiversity. Mammoth Cave National Park could truly be a mecca for those who cherish wildflowers and the vibrant, healthy ecosystems that make their existence possible.

INTRODUCTION

This guide is designed for those who have little or no botanical training. It is for those who, by learning the identity and something about the folklore and history of the flowers they find growing wild, will leave enriched by the experience.

Mammoth Cave National Park is known around the world as the site of the world's longest cave system. More than two million people enter the park each year and more than 500,000 explore the cave environment. Most leave without ever knowing about or experiencing the wonder of the terrestrial surface above the caves.

Dramatic increases in the number of visitors to the cave in recent years have pressed the ability of the fragile cave ecosystem to accommodate the visitors with a high-quality experience. Often people face long waits and sold-out tours. Some, without the prospect of something enjoyable to do while they wait, leave without ever entering the cave. I hope that this guide will be instrumental in enticing many of the park's visitors out onto the trails, and that it will provide there the means to a lasting and memorable introduction to the wonderful world of wildflowers.

HOW TO USE THIS BOOK

This guide contains photographs and descriptions of 400 wildflowers, all found along the trails and roads within Mammoth Cave National Park. With a few showy exceptions, these are herbaceous plants. Most of the trees, shrubs, and woody-stemmed vines have been omitted.

As any botanist will tell you, the best way to identify plants is by the use of a botanical key. Though true, the use of such keys demands an intimate knowledge of botanical taxonomic terminology, which few of us possess.

Most find it simpler to match a flower in hand to a picture, and that is the method used in this guide. To locate a plant here requires only that you know the color of the flower and the time of year it blooms.

The photographs and descriptions are arranged first by time of year in flower. These time frames are spring (March 1–May 31), summer (June 1–July 31), and fall (August 1–October 22). Second, within each time section flowers are arranged by color. The color sections are white, yellow/orange, red/pink, blue/purple, and green/brown. Within each color, the plants are arranged by family so that all plants of similar appearance are together. Generally, just knowing the flowering time and color will allow the user to turn to within seven pages or less of an unknown plant's photograph and description.

As with any simplified artificial method for identification, this one has its faults. The most obvious is where a plant's flowering period overlaps into more than one time period. In this case, the plant photograph will be found in the earliest time category. If the user cannot locate the plant in the time category for the time the flower is found, the user should search the prior time period. A second major problem with this method is revealed when a plant produces flowers of two separate colors or when the colors tend to merge into other colors or become indistinct. In this case, the lighter of the two colors or shades of color should be searched first.

PLANT NAMES

Preceding the descriptive text for each species is, in order, the common name, scientific name, family common name, and family scientific name. Note that the scientific names for species are in italics.

The common names given are those believed to be of most frequent use locally, and the choices were certainly influenced by those I am most familiar with. In some instances, the common names were chosen from older references. For lack of published examples, however, I have made up common names for three of the species. Just because the name the user may know for a plant is not the one used in this guide does not mean that the user's name is not valid. Although sometimes confusing, common names often reflect some characteristic of the plant, superstition about the plant, past medical use, practical use, or other value of historical or human interest.

Many plants have more than one common name. For instance Cleavers, *Galium aparine,* has at least 55 common names in print, and the number of names are an indicator of the tremendous number of past uses for the plant.

For almost all species, the scientific names follow *Gray's Manual of Botany,* Eighth Edition, by M. L. Fernald. Scientific names are unique to each species, and their use removes any confusion about which species one is talking about. The nomenclature in *Gray's Manual of Botany* was chosen because it is the nomenclature most frequently used in the works cited in the bibliography. It is also closest to the nomenclature used in the few illustrated technical guides available, which are the logical next step for the novice. Also, *Gray's Manual of Botany,* in my opinion, is still the best technical manual available for our area.

Gray's Manual of Botany is 45 years old, however, and numerous changes in nomenclature have been necessary since its publication. Therefore, to keep this guide up to date with current science, the most recently accepted nomenclature, following *A Synonymized Checklist of the Vascular Flora of the United States, Canada, and Greenland* by John T. Kartesz, published in 1994, is included in parentheses below the scientific species and family names.

DESCRIPTIVE TEXT

I tried to use a simplified terminology in the descriptive text. Certain botanical terms, however, are unavoidable. For easier reference, every attempt was made to restrict these terms to those given in the illustrations of leaf structure and flower structure.

Associated with each photograph is a brief description of the plant's physical characteristics. When compared to an unknown plant, these should allow the user to confirm the identity. The content of the descriptive text was derived from observations in the field, herbarium specimens, photographs, and was widely drawn from particularly helpful, previously published work.

Noted in parentheses just following the descriptive text is whether the plant is a native of North America or a species introduced from another continent.

FLOWERING PERIOD

Following the descriptive text is the time period I *observed* the plant in flower during my study and data collection for this guide in 1992. Included also is an *appendix of observed flowering period,* a graphical illustration that assists in finding and identifying plants that flower during periods that overlap the three time frames. Also included is a *flower hunting planning guide,* which shows the number of species known to be in flower in any two-week period during the spring, summer, and fall.

Timing of survey trips and intervals between observations in any given area are the greatest cause of incompleteness in these records. Plants restricted to specific habitats with less than a 30-day flowering cycle were possibly missed or recorded disproportionately to their actual flowering period. Several years of observation would be necessary to provide an accurate and complete flowering period record in the park. These flowering period records are minimal and may be distorted by an early spring.

PLANT FREQUENCY

Following the flowering period dates, the relative abundance of the plant within the park is indicated. *Endangered* indicates the plant is not only rare, but is in danger of being extirpated from the park. *Rare* means there are only a few plants within the park and they should be zealously protected. *Infrequent* signifies you may expect to find the plant, but in limited numbers. *Frequent* indicates the plant may be found in large numbers, but not in all areas. *Abundant* means the plant is in very large numbers and can be found in most areas of the park.

FOLKLORE AND USES OF PLANTS

Since the dawn of time plants have sustained us. Not only are they as important as the air we breathe, they are responsible for that very air. Plants have provided our shelter, fed us, clothed us, cured our illnesses, and become a part of our religions and our superstitions. Nothing else on earth has so impacted our lives, our civilization, or our very existence. Yet we generally know little about the plants that daily surround us.

Included with each plant description is a short paragraph telling something of interest about the plant's history, its practical use, past herbal or medicinal use, food value, value to wildlife, name source, potential use in science or medicine, poisonous properties, relationship to religious practices, place in superstition, and a myriad of other facts and myths. Special emphasis has been given to plant uses by Native Americans.

WARNING: Although many plants have proven medicinal and culinary values, you should *not* follow the information, directions, or advice in this guide regarding the edibility of plants and you should *not* use the information relating to medical practices to treat illnesses. This information is provided as a source of interest only. Most plants can be harmful to you under certain circumstances, and only a doctor should prescribe medicines. Many plants that are perfectly safe to eat can be easily confused with others that are deadly poisonous. In addition, it is unlawful to pick flowers or collect plants or plant parts in the park.

TRAILS IN THE PARK

I have walked the park's backcountry trails from early morning until dark dozens of days without seeing or hearing another human being. I had for company only the deer, turkeys, squirrels, chipmunks, wood ducks, seemingly innumerable song birds, and an occasional raccoon, opossum, bobcat, or muskrat. The sounds were limited to the rustle of leaves from a foraging or frightened animal, the wind in the trees, the song of the birds, the gurgle of water in a small stream, the splash of a fish in the river, the cry of a hawk, or the occasional bark of a squirrel, snort of a deer, or gobble of a turkey. As pleasant as this company and these sounds were, it was always the bright, quiet beauty of the variety of wildflowers that most pleased my senses.

There are more than 60 miles of trails in the park, including easy and even handicapped-accessible trails. Some of the trails are strenuous and offer a near-wilderness experience. Some are more moderate and offer wide scenic vistas, education in the natural sciences, or historical perspectives on the area. Whichever your choice, you can be sure there will be a variety of wildflowers along the way.

The nature and scenic trails on the south side of the river are generally short and well marked. The backcountry trails on the north side of the river are lengthy and follow more rugged terrain. These trails cross steep ravines, switch back and forth, and up and down rugged hillsides and must be considered strenuous. Horseback riders as well as hikers use the backcountry trails. This multiple use, at times, leaves the trail surface rough. Depending on the season, the backcountry trails may not be as easy to follow as the south-side trails. Reflective markers have been placed at many of the trail intersections to lessen confusion. Armed with topographic maps, compass, and years of backcountry hiking experience, I have still gotten lost on the trails in the park.

When walking the backcountry, it is wise to stay on the trail. All of the wildflower records for this guide were taken from very near the trails. By venturing off, one risks getting lost, encountering the infamous ticks and chiggers of the region, getting infected with poison ivy, or falling and injuring oneself. Hiking off trail can also greatly damage the fragile environment.

Here are a few tips for walking the backcountry trails:

1. Sign the trail register and tell someone where you are going.

2. Stay on the trail.

3. Take maps, compass, and a light.

4. Take the water you will need with you. Do not drink from surface streams or springs.

5. Wear secure, protective footwear and loose, layered clothing adequate for the most severe weather.

Topographic maps are available for sale at the hotel gift shop and the park Visitor Center. Brochures detailing the trails of the park are provided free of charge by the Park Service at the information desk of the Visitor Center and the Headquarters Campground Entrance Station. The Park Service recommends the *Trails Illustrated Map*.

LOCATING WILDFLOWERS IN THE PARK

There is a joy of discovery and a very real sense of satisfaction that comes with identifying a flower or plant for the first time. The photographs and text in this guide should aid you in achieving this enjoyment. But an even greater thrill awaits you in the "challenge of the chase." My love affair with wildflowers has been enhanced through the years by the *search* for those flowers not before seen or recognized. To assist those who thirst for the excitement and adventure in such discovery, a part of this book is designed to tell you where each flower can be located in the park.

To present a comprehensive listing of areas where each species can be found, it was necessary to hike all the trails and travel all the roads in the park repeatedly at regular intervals during the flowering season. Due to greater visitor use of trails and roads on the south side of the river, these trails were walked and the roads were driven twice each month. Camping areas at Dennison Ferry and Houchins Ferry were walked but were included as part of the records on the respective roads. The longer backcountry trails and roads on the north side of the river were walked or driven once each month.

During the study year of 1992, I walked a little over 900 miles within the park and drove hundreds more. The bulk of the labor in writing this book, admittedly a labor of love, has gone into preparing the *index of flowers by trail* found at the end of the text. This index can be used in two ways. First, you can determine which trails or roads a flower can be found on by reading across from the flower name. Or you can see which flowers you can expect to find on a given trail or road by reading down from the trail or road name. This index is minimal and errors of omission can be expected, especially on roads, where it is very easy to miss a plant from a moving vehicle.

Following the *index of flowers by trail* is a *flower hunting planning guide,* which lists the trails and shows how many different species were found, as well as how many species were found only on that particular trail and on no other trail.

SPRING FLOWERS

March 1 – May 31

FOUR-LEAVED MILKWEED
Asclepias quadrifolia

MILKWEED FAMILY
Asclepiadaceae

Leaves at the middle of this slender, 1' to $2\frac{1}{2}$' plant are in whorls of 4. All leaves are petioled, broadly lanceolate, and above or below the whorls of 4, leaves are paired. Flowers are in from 1 to 3 terminal umbels. The 5 reflexed petals are pinkish and the 5 hoods are more whitish. (Native)

May 10–July 8   Infrequent

Native Americans used this plant to rid warts and as a laxative. Like other milkweeds, its milky sap contains resinoids that may be toxic.

WHITE MILKWEED
Asclepias variegata

MILKWEED FAMILY
Asclepiadaceae

This milkweed is mostly a dry woodland dweller and is from 2' to 3' tall with paired, opposite, and petioled narrow-ovate leaves. The flowers are in umbels and the individual $\frac{1}{4}$"-wide flowers have 5 reflexed petals and 5 incurved hoods. The flower is white with a purplish center. (Native)

May 28–June 21   Infrequent

The flower clusters, young shoots, and very young pods were reportedly boiled and eaten by Native Americans. Cooking may have destroyed the now known toxic resinoids in the raw plants.

TWINLEAF
Jeffersonia diphylla

BARBERRY FAMILY
Berberidaceae

An almost completely divided leaf, which seems to have 2 blades, distinguishes this plant. At flowering time, however, the leaves are only 6" to 8" tall and may still be partially folded. The 1"-wide solitary white flowers are on a leafless stalk and have 8 petals and 8 stamens in a single circle. This flower might be confused with Bloodroot, which has numerous conspicuous yellow anthers. (Native)

March 5–April 9   Infrequent

Sore throats, cramps, rheumatism, diarrhea, and urinary infections are just a few of the ills Native Americans treated with this plant. Note the pipelike seedcases with hinged covers that pop open when the seeds are mature.

MAY-APPLE
Podophyllum peltatum

BARBERRY FAMILY
Berberidaceae

Open woods and clearings may be carpeted in the spring with these 12" to 18" plants whose leaves are umbrella-like in shape. The leaves are deeply 5 to 7 lobed. Some stems have a single leaf, but only those with a pair of leaves bear flowers. The single, 1"-wide, waxy white flower has 6 to 9 petals and droops from a short stalk growing from the axil of the pair of leaves. (Native)

March 21–May 27   Frequent

The ripe fruits are used to make jelly, preserves, and a wonderfully cooling drink when mixed with lemonade or wine and sugar. Chemicals in the plant are being used experimentally to treat some cancers and were used by Native Americans as a cathartic, emetic, and purgative, as well as an insecticide. The plant, especially the root, is POISONOUS.

EARLY SCORPION-GRASS
Myosotis verna
Borage Family
Boraginaceae

This is a 4"- to 12"-tall, hairy plant with
flowering stems slightly arching above. Flowers are in a raceme, white, tubular, 5-lobed
and only about ¼" wide. Leaves are linear
oblong to spatulate, sessile, and short hairy.
Note the minute hooked hairs on the calyx
lobes. (Native)

April 28–April 30   Infrequent

Also called Forget-Me-Not, the scientific name
means mouse ear and is from the Greek *myos,*
meaning mouse, and *ous,* meaning ear, and is in
reference to the hairy, mouse-ear shaped leaves
of some species. Herbalists suggest this plant
may be effective in treating pulmonary affec-
tions.

BABY'S-BREATH
Arenaria patula
(*Minuartia patula* var. *patula*)
Pink Family
Caryophyllaceae

This dainty, airy, little plant is
from 4" to 10" tall. The almost
threadlike, mostly smooth stems
branch from the base. Leaves are
opposite and so narrow as to be needlelike. The ⅜"-wide flowers have 5
white, notched petals and 5 pale green sepals. (Native)

April 21–July 8   Infrequent

A similar cultivated plant, also called Baby's-Breath, is used extensively in floral
arrangements. The needlelike foliage of our wild plant is an indicator of the
harsh limestone barrens and cliffs on which this dainty little plant is found.

COMMON CHICKWEED
Stellaria media

PINK FAMILY
Caryophyllaceae

Because of its creeping nature, this 4"- to 16"-long plant may be taller than it first appears. The leaves are opposite, long petioled, and ovate. There are 5 white petals, but because the petals are so deeply notched the flower appears to have 10 petals. The sepals are longer than the petals in this chickweed. (Introduced)

March 9–May 29   Abundant

In Europe and Asia, where this plant originated, herbalists used it in ointments for skin irritations and sores. An herbal tea including this plant is available in specialty stores. Its abundance and large number of seeds make it a valuable plant for wild birds.

STAR CHICKWEED
Stellaria pubera

PINK FAMILY
Caryophyllaceae

The 6"- to 12"-long stem with opposite, paired, ovate, and ½"- to 2"-long leaves are mostly erect, but may occasionally seem to be horizontal to the ground. The flowers are white with 5 very deeply notched petals and 5 shorter green sepals. A row of very fine hairs grows on opposite sides of the stalk between pairs of leaves. (Native)

March 27–May 14   Frequent

The leaves of this native chickweed are eaten in salads and are quite palatable cooked as a substitute for spinach. The fact that the seeds are relished by numerous species of birds may account for its common name.

YARROW
Achillea millefolium

COMPOSITE FAMILY
Compositae
(Asteraceae)

Flowers on this 1' to 3' plant are in crowded, flat-topped clusters. What look like 4 to 6, (normally 5), very small, white to pinkish petals are really rays on this composite. Leaves are lanceolate in outline with the basal ones having short petioles and those above sessile. All leaves are extremely finely dissected into a fernlike appearance. (Introduced)

May 22–July 30   Frequent

Native Americans and settlers used Yarrow to soothe burns and bruises, to stop the flow of blood in cuts, to regulate menstruation, to soothe sore nipples of nursing mothers, and to relieve headache, stomachache, and fever. Modern experiments vindicate it as an anti-inflammatory and an astringent.

PLANTAIN-LEAVED PUSSYTOES
Antennaria plantaginifolia

COMPOSITE FAMILY
Compositae
(Asteraceae)

Flower heads are a fluff of white. In this species there are several heads on each plant. The stem is hairy and from 3" to 16" tall. Leaves are in a basal

rosette and are long petioled, ovate, and have 3 main veins. (Native)

March 9–May 14   Frequent

Often found in large colonies on poor ground, these plants produce chemicals that discourage other plant competitors. It was used by Native Americans as a tonic to revive mothers after childbirth and by early pioneers as a shampoo to get rid of lice and to mothproof clothing.

SOLITARY PUSSYTOES
Antennaria solitaria

COMPOSITE FAMILY
Compositae
(Asteraceae)

This 2" to 10" plant has a whitish downy stem and a single white flower head. There is a basal rosette of ovate, mostly 3-veined leaves tapering into a long-margined petiole. Upper leaves are tiny and somewhat like scales. Note the whitish runners. (Native)

March 26–April 23   Frequent

The common name refers to the fancied resemblance of the soft, fluffy, white head to a cat's paw. Although cattle reportedly will not eat this plant, it is of some value to wildlife, as grouse, quail, and deer all seem to relish the tender leaves.

OX-EYE DAISY
Chrysanthemum leucanthemum
(Leucanthemum vulgare)

COMPOSITE FAMILY
Compositae
(Asteraceae)

Twenty to 30 bright white, slightly notched rays surround an equally bright and slightly depressed, yellow center on this 2"-wide flower head. Flower heads are usually solitary on the thin, smooth, sparingly leafed stalk. Upper leaves are linear spatulate, small, somewhat clasping, and irregularly lobed. Lower leaves are much broader, deeply cut, toothed, and petioled. (Introduced)

May 9–August 3   Abundant

This weedy alien is an invaluable aid in determining the status of one's love affairs. This is accomplished by plucking the rays one at a time in rhythm to "she loves me, she loves me not." If you don't like the answer, try another flower—they don't all have the same number of rays.

COMMON FLEABANE
Erigeron philadelphicus

COMPOSITE FAMILY
Compositae
(Asteraceae)

This fleabane has a generally hairy 1' to 3' stem. The upper leaves are clasping and usually entire or only slightly toothed. The lower leaves are top shaped, narrowing to the stem, but not clasping, and are broadly toothed. Rays are very numerous, (100 to 150), are tinged with pink or lavender, and the $\frac{3}{4}$"-wide flower heads are at the tips of the several branches, with the buds nodding. (Native)

April 28–May 30   Abundant

This plant was used extensively by Native Americans as an astringent to stop both internal and external bleeding. A tea of this plant was a folk remedy for diarrhea, kidney stones, and diabetes. This plant may cause skin irritation in susceptible individuals.

ROBIN-PLANTAIN
Erigeron pulchellus

COMPOSITE FAMILY
Compositae
(Asteraceae)

Flower heads are about 1" wide with narrow, white rays and a yellow cluster of disk florets in the center. Rays on the newly opening buds of the few-headed cluster may be pink. The 1' to 2' plant is covered with soft hair. Basal leaves are spatulate with widely separated, shallow, blunt teeth. The few scattered stem leaves are lanceolate and nearly entire. (Native)

April 11–May 24   Frequent

Robin-Plantain has the largest flower heads of any of our *Erigeron* species and is the first to bloom. The genus name is from *eri,* meaning early, and *geron,* meaning old man, and is in reference to the thick, soft hair on some species. Medicinally, *E. pulchellus* is probably similar to *E. philadelphicus* and *E. annuus.*

STONECROP
Sedum ternatum

ORPINE FAMILY
Crassulaceae

The low, spreading stems of this plant lie horizontally on the ground or over rocks, sending up vertical, 3" to 6" stems. Leaves are fleshy, rounded on the ends, toothless, and in whorls of 3 except for a few solitary near the apex. The 4 or 5, tiny, white, pointed petals are on a 3-pronged inflorescence. The stamens are double the number of petals and the dark anthers are conspicuous. (Native)

April 11–May 16   Frequent

The young leaves in spring and the sliced roots in fall are reported to be fine additions to salads. Another common name, Pepper-and-Salt, refers to the small black anthers against the white background of the petals. This plant is an excellent ground cover for damp rock gardens.

GARLIC MUSTARD
Alliaria officinalis
(*Alliaria petiolata*)

MUSTARD FAMILY
Cruciferae
(Brassicaceae)

Growing from 1' to 4' tall, this plant has deeply veined, alternate, petioled, somewhat heart-shaped leaves with uneven, deep, sharp-toothed margins. The small, white, 4-petaled flowers are about ⅜" wide and are in terminal clusters. (Introduced)

April 20–May 10   Locally Abundant

This highly invasive plant from Europe has been the subject of special studies in the park because of its weedy nature. An old common name in England, where it was eaten by the impoverished, is Poor Man's Mustard. It is listed in modern herbals as being antiseptic and diuretic. When crushed, the leaves smell similar to garlic.

PURPLE CRESS
Cardamine douglassii

MUSTARD FAMILY
Cruciferae
(Brassicaceae)

Because the flowers are similar to the toothworts' and bloom at the same time, this flower may be overlooked. The 4" to 12" stems are lightly hairy and bear sessile, few-toothed, lanceolate, alternate upper leaves. The lower leaves are more ovate and the basal leaves are long petioled, and ovate to heart shaped. Flowers are ¼" wide, white to pinkish, and are in a loose raceme. (Native)

March 15–May 10   Infrequent

A very similar plant is *Cardamine bulbosa,* which has longer petioles and more rounded lower-stem leaves.

Purple Cress is found in low wet areas. For a spicy flavor, add the very young leaves to salads. The peppery roots can be grated and used to make a horseradishlike condiment.

TWO-LEAVED TOOTHWORT
Dentaria diphylla
(*Cardamine diphylla*)

MUSTARD FAMILY
Cruciferae
(Brassicaceae)

Like other toothworts, this plant has 4-petaled, white flowers in a terminal cluster on a solitary, 6" to 12" stem. The distinguishing characteristic is the pair of leaves about halfway up the stem, which are divided into 3 broadly ovate, wide-toothed leaflets. (Native)

March 20–April 24   Infrequent

The Two-Leaved Toothwort is the last of the toothworts to flower. The pungently peppery tuberous root from this plant, finely grated and added to your favorite cocktail dip, is guaranteed to leave a lasting impression on your guests.

SLENDER TOOTHWORT
Dentaria heterophylla
(*Cardamine angustata*)

MUSTARD FAMILY
Cruciferae
(Brassicaceae)

At first glance this plant might be confused with the Cut-Leaf Toothwort. However, this plant has only 2 stem leaves and the 3 narrow-lanceolate leaflets are not nearly as toothed. Also this plant has a 3-parted basal leaf whose leaflets are broad and deeply toothed. The 6"- to 15"-tall plant has a loose raceme of ½" long flowers with 4 white to pinkish petals. (Native)

March 8–May 2   Abundant

This plant is abundant in upland woods early in the spring and makes a refreshingly pleasant, if somewhat peppery, nibble for those hiking the backcountry trails or studying the flora in the park.

CUT-LEAF TOOTHWORT
Dentaria laciniata
(*Cardamine concatenata*)

MUSTARD FAMILY
Cruciferae
(Brassicaceae)

About halfway up this single, smooth, 6" to 12" stem is a whorl of 3 leaves. Each leaf is divided into 3 to 5 narrow, finely toothed segments. The small 4-petaled white to light pink flowers are in a raceme at the top of the stem. Basal leaves are seldom present at flowering time. (Native)

March 1–May 30   Abundant

This is the earliest flowering of the *Dentaria* species in the park. Its ancient use by Native Americans is indicated by the discovery of carbonized tubers at archaeological sites dating to 1100 A.D. The name toothwort is derived from the toothlike scales on the tubers.

TOOTHWORT
Dentaria multifida
(*Cardamine dissecta*)

MUSTARD FAMILY
Cruciferae
(Brassicaceae)

Of all the toothworts, *D. multifida* is closest in resemblance to the Cut-Leaf Toothwort. The 4" to 8" plant is shorter, however, and there are only 2 opposite leaves, which are toothless and so deeply cut that the segments are needlelike. There are no basal leaves and the 4-petaled white flowers are in a terminal raceme. (Native)

March 20–May 2   Locally Frequent

Not nearly as abundant as *D. laciniata* or *D. heterophylla,* this plant's strong, sharp, peppery tubers are recommended as a trail nibble, an addition to salads, a substitute for horseradish when mixed with vinegar, or an ingredient to meat sauces.

PENNYWORT
Obolaria virginica

GENTIAN FAMILY
Gentianaceae

A small, 3" to 5" plant with a fleshy, greenish to purplish stem. The ½"-long leaves are thick, opposite, and ovate. The flowers are white to pinkish, tubular, 4-lobed, and are borne in the leaf axils in numbers of 1 or 3. (Native)

March 8–June 4   Frequent

The genus name is from *obolos,* a small Greek coin, in reference to the small, thick, roundish leaves. This is a diminutive, often overlooked plant, desirable for wildflower gardens but extremely difficult to transplant.

WHITE BERGAMOT
Monarda russeliana

MINT FAMILY
Labiatae
(Lamiaceae)

In this species of *Monarda* the corolla is white to pale purple and the lip is dotted with purple. The plant is from 8" to 18" tall with a smooth stem. Leaves are sessile (or have very short petioles) and lanceolate with a few small teeth. Outer bracts may be tinged with purple. (Native)

May 14–June 12   Infrequent

The genus name is dedicated to Nicolas Monardes, a sixteenth-century author of many papers on medicinal and other useful plants, especially those of the New World. Native Americans used *Monarda* species to treat fever, chills, backache, stomach cramps, headache, and bronchial problems.

SYNANDRA
Synandra hispidula

MINT FAMILY
Labiatae
(Lamiaceae)

Bright white, hooded flowers with 3 flaring lip-lobes, which are veined with purple stripes on the middle lip and throat, grow from the axils of the upper, sessile, ovate, leaflike bracts. The lower leaves on this 8" to 18" plant are heart shaped, long petioled, and blunt toothed. (Native)

April 11–July 7   Locally Frequent

The biennial nature of this plant was obvious within the park in 1992 and 1993. In 1992 there were hundreds of plants in flower at the few sites where it was found. At the same sites in 1993, the number of flowering plants could be counted on one's fingers.

WOODS VETCH
Vicia caroliniana

PEA FAMILY
Leguminosae
(Fabaceae)

This 1' to 2½'–long, nearly smooth plant has tall, slender racemes of drooping, pealike, white flowers about ½" long. The ladderlike leaves have from 10 to 18 narrow, round-tipped leaflets. There is a tendril past the leaflets at the end of the leaf. (Native)

April 20–May 10　Infrequent

Woods Vetch was reported to be one of the Cherokees' most important medicinal plants. A principal use was to rub it in numerous, shallow cuts made in the flesh of ball players to toughen their muscles.

WILD GARLIC
Allium canadense

LILY FAMILY
Liliaceae

This is similar to the Wild Onion, *A. vineale,* a familiar backyard plant. It is 6" to 24" tall with an umbel of 6-petaled (actually with 3 petals and 3 sepals), pinkish to white flowers, which are often subtended by greenish, tiny bulblets. The stem is flat, not hollow as in *A. vineale.* Leaves are long, thin, and mostly basal. (Native)

May 22–July 7　Frequent

Two similar plants are *Allium vineale* with hollow leaves and a single clasping leaf on the stem, and *A. cernuum,* which has a distinctly nodding inflorescence.

An excellent wild food source. Recommended are the green bulbs pickled, the entire plant cooked as greens, the bulbs boiled, the leaves and bulbs in salads, and the boiled bulbs as a base for cream-of-onion soup. Native Americans dried the bulbs for winter cooking and seasoning.

WHITE TROUT-LILY
Erythronium albidum

LILY FAMILY
Liliaceae

Like the similar Yellow Trout-Lily, this plant has a pair of basal, spreading, fleshy, elliptical leaves. In this species, however, the leaves are less likely to be mottled with brown. The single, bluish white, bell-shaped flower has 6 sharply recurved perianth parts and is on a smooth, 4" to 8" stem. (Native)

March 27–April 9   Rare

It takes seven years for a seed to produce a flowering plant. The bulbs, which may be over 12" under the surface, are edible and are relished by Black Bears. If one wishes to go to the trouble of digging the small bulbs, they are quite palatable as a substitute for potatoes when boiled until soft and served with butter.

FALSE GARLIC
Nothoscordum bivalve

LILY FAMILY
Liliaceae

An umbel of small, white to greenish white flowers of 3 sepals and 3 petals adorn a smooth, leafless, 6" to 14" stalk. The leaves are linear, basal, and grasslike. The leaves do not grow above the flowering umbel. (Native)

April 21–May 10   Frequent

Worldwide there are about 10 species in this genus, all in North and South America except one, which is in China. It is a relatively common phenomenon for North American plants and their very close relatives to be found nowhere in the world except China.

STAR-OF-BETHLEHEM
Ornithogalum umbellatum

LILY FAMILY
Liliaceae

The 6 white, waxy perianth parts are distinctly ribbed on their backs with green. There are usually 5 to 6 flowers on short stalks ascending from the top of a smooth, 4" to 10" stem. The long, narrow leaves have a whitish midrib. (Introduced)

April 24–April 30   Infrequent

This plant is poisonous to cattle either green or cured in hay. Historically the plant was considered edible and is used as a nutritious food in Asia, where it is boiled or roasted. There are reports in this country, however, of children being poisoned by eating the plant. Symptoms include nausea, vomiting, and diarrhea.

FALSE SOLOMON'S-SEAL
Smilacina racemosa
(*Maianthemum racemosum spp. racemosum*)

LILY FAMILY
Liliaceae

The tiny white flowers are in a whorled, plumelike panicle at the end of an arching, $1\frac{1}{2}'$ to 3' stem. The leaves are alternate, sessile, heavily veined, ovate, and sharply pointed. The stem bends a little at each leaf axil, appearing to zigzag slightly. The flowers of the true Solomon's Seal dangle from the leaf axils. (Native)

April 11–May 30   Frequent

The ripe, red berries are eaten by grouse and other woodland birds and are edible by humans, though quite bitter tasting. Two medicinal uses by Native Americans were using the smoke from the root to treat insanity and to quiet a crying child. If the latter worked, one can understand its reputation for the former.

BENT TRILLIUM
Trillium flexipes

LILY FAMILY
Liliaceae

As in all *Trillium* species, the leaves, petals, sepals, and stamens are 3's or in multiples of 3. The 1" petals on this species may be white or maroon, but all have a white base. The flowers most often hang on a straight stalk below the leaves. Note that the pointed, broadly ovate leaves are sessile and somewhat coarse. (Native)

April 5–May 16   Infrequent

The young shoots are said to be edible in salads or as cooked greens. Native Americans used several *Trillium* species medicinally to treat menstrual problems, various types of hemorrhaging, nose bleeds, and other ills requiring an astringent.

DUTCHMAN'S-BREECHES
Dicentra cucullaria

POPPY FAMILY
Papaveraceae
(Fumariaceae)

Rising from a scaly bulb, the triangular leaves are divided into many narrow segments, giving a lacelike appearance. The smooth flowering stalk is from 4" to 10" long, and arches at the tip. The flowers are waxy white, with 2 distinct spurs above, suggesting pantaloons hanging upside down. (Native)

March 26–April 21   Locally Frequent

Another common name is Little Blue Staggers, possibly referring to the poisonous, though rarely fatal, effects of the alkaloids found in the plant. It is reported to have been an important love charm to some Native Americans.

SQUIRREL-CORN
Dicentra canadensis

POPPY FAMILY
Papaveraceae
(Fumariaceae)

Like Dutchman's-Breeches, the leaves are separate and deeply cut, appearing lacelike. The flowers growing on an arching stem are more greenish white and lack the obvious yellow tip of Dutchman's-Breeches. These flowers are somewhat heart shaped with no elongated spur and with small flaring lips. (Native)

April 9–April 17   Infrequent

Uses by Native Americans include treatment for syphilis and skin problems. Herbalists in the past recommended it for treating syphilis, swelling of the lymph nodes, and menstrual complaints. Like *D. cucullaria,* it is poisonous, especially to cattle.

BLOODROOT
Sanguinaria canadensis

POPPY FAMILY
Papaveraceae

When the 8 to 12 petals of the showy white flowers first emerge, a deeply lobed leaf, heavily veined beneath, envelops a single, 4"- to 8"-tall, smooth stem. The 20 or more bright yellow stamens are conspicuous in the center of the 1"- to 2"-wide, solitary blossom. The petals quickly fall, but the leaf continues to grow and may reach 6" to 8" in width. The flower grows from a thick rhizome that seeps an orange-red sap when broken or scraped. (Native)

March 9–April 11   Locally Frequent

Although the reddish sap contains a poisonous alkaloid, Native Americans made extensive use of the rhizome as a dye and paint for body, clothing, and basketry. It was also used for a variety of medical disorders such as colds and skin diseases. Modern experiments show it to have antiseptic, anesthetic, and anticancer properties.

SPRING BEAUTY
Claytonia virginica

PURSLANE FAMILY
Portulacaceae

A pair of long, narrow to ovate, opposite, fleshy leaves are located about halfway up on the smooth, 3"- to 6"-tall stem. Leaf shape is extremely variable. Several stems may arise from each deeply buried tuber. The diminutive, $\frac{1}{2}$"-wide, 5-petaled flowers are white or faintly pink with much darker pink veins. They are produced in a loose raceme at the top of the stem. (Native)

March 1–May 10   Abundant

Because it has an unstable number of chromosomes, this plant is important in the study of genetics. The small tubers were eaten both raw and boiled by Native Americans and settlers. Because of their small size, the considerable work needed to dig them hardly seems justifiable.

SHOOTING STAR
Dodecatheon meadia

PRIMROSE FAMILY
Primulaceae

A rosette of leaves varying in width, but somewhat spatulate in shape, forms a base for the smooth, 10"- to 20"-tall stem. The flowers droop from slender stalks at the tip of the stem. Each flower has 5 white petals that flare dramatically backward, and the stamens come together to form a beak pointing downward. (Native)

April 21–May 29   Rare

In ancient times a bouquet of the dart-shaped flowers of *Dodecatheon* carried the message "you are my divinity." Western Native Americans are reported to have eaten the roasted tubers of this genus. *Dodecatheon meadia* could probably also be used as an emergency food.

WHITE BANEBERRY
Actaea pachypoda

BUTTERCUP FAMILY
Ranunculaceae

Note the single, smooth, flowering stem and rounded terminal raceme of tiny, white flowers standing well atop the 1' to 2' plant. Look very closely to see the tiny, narrow petals and long, numerous stamens. Leaves are multiple compound with leaflets irregularly lanceolate and sharply toothed. (Native)

April 20–May 14   Infrequent

All parts of this plant are poisonous, and eating the white berries, locally called Dolls Eyes, has been reported fatal to children. Despite its violently purgative properties, Native Americans used the plant medicinally, especially in treating menstrual and postchildbirth problems and pain.

RUE ANEMONE
Anemonella thalictroides
(*Thalictrum thalictroides*)

BUTTERCUP FAMILY
Ranunculaceae

A thin, delicate, 4"- to 8"-tall stem is topped by 2 or 3, white, ¾"-wide flowers. The petal-like sepals are on short stalks above a whorl of small, 3-lobed, and rounded tip leaves (really bracts). There are usually 6 sepals, but from 7 to 10 may occur. (Native)

March 9–May 24   Frequent

The tuberous roots are edible when prepared like potatoes and are high in starch content. Native Americans reportedly used the roots medicinally to treat diarrhea and vomiting. However, caution is advised, as most members of the Buttercup Family contain toxins.

HEPATICA
Hepatica acutiloba
(*Hepatica nobilis* var. *acuta*)

Buttercup Family
Ranunculaceae

The ¾"-wide flowers have 6 to 10 petal-like sepals, varying in color from white to pink to blue. Below the sepals are 3 green, bract-like leaves on a 3" to 8" stem that are densely covered with soft hair. At flowering time, the previous year's mottled reddish brown leaves are still present. The older leaves are 3-lobed, pointed, and leathery. In a similar species, *H. americana,* the leaf lobes are rounded. (Native)

March 8–April 21   Locally Frequent

The genus name is from the Latin *hepaticus,* pertaining to the liver, and is in reference to the resemblance of the shape and color of the older leaves to the liver. True to the Doctrine of Signatures, ancient herbalists and Native Americans alike used this plant to treat liver diseases.

HEPATICA
Hepatica americana
(*Hepatica nobilis* var. *obtusa*)

Buttercup Family
Ranunculaceae

The densely hairy, leafless, 3" to 8" stems bear individual flowers with 6 to 10, ¾"-wide, white to pink to blue petal-like sepals above 3 round-lobed bracts. The older leaves are a mottled reddish brown and the 3-lobed segments have rounded tips. A very similar species, *H. acutiloba,* has pointed lobes and grows mostly along moist, limestone rock outcrops and along bluffs, whereas *H. americana* is found mostly in moist, sandy areas. (Native)

March 15–May 30   Infrequent

In addition to treating diseases of the liver, Native Americans and settlers used Hepatica to treat lung diseases, hemorrhoids, indigestion, sore throat, coughs, crossed eyes, and female maladies. The roots were also used to make a dye. Hepatica is the state flower of Missouri and Minnesota.

GOLDENSEAL
Hydrastis canadensis

BUTTERCUP FAMILY
Ranunculaceae

There are no petals on this flower. Since the sepals fall very early from the solitary blossom, usually only the showy white stamens around several pistils are observed. Plants are 8" to 14" tall and have a pair of maplelike, wrinkled, deeply cut, 5 to 7 lobed, sharply toothed leaves. The stem is hairy. (Native)

April 11–May 10   Infrequent

This plant should be zealously protected, as it has been collected to near extinction in many areas. Native Americans and folk medicine practitioners used it for uterine bleeding, ringworm, stomach disorders, cancer, tuberculosis, and as an astringent, laxative, tonic, mouthwash, and antiseptic. Scientists have confirmed a few of these uses.

FALSE RUE ANEMONE
Isopyrum biternatum
(*Enemion biternatum*)

BUTTERCUP FAMILY
Ranunculaceae

The slender, smooth stems may be from 8" to 16" tall and the leaves are compound with mostly 3-lobed leaflets. The $\frac{3}{8}$"- to $\frac{5}{8}$"-wide flowers are white and terminal on the branches. The similar Rue Anemone is much shorter, has larger flowers, and fewer and less deeply lobed leaves. (Native)

March 9–April 30   Locally Abundant

All species in the Buttercup Family contain acrid alkaloids and are toxic to some degree. These plants are especially poisonous to cattle when green, but lose their toxic properties in hay during the drying process.

EARLY MEADOW RUE
Thalictrum dioicum

BUTTERCUP FAMILY
Ranunculaceae

Distinct, conspicuous, bright yellow stamens dangle beneath the loose clusters of drooping flowers, which have 4 to 5 greenish white, petal-like sepals on the staminate plants. The purplish green flowers on the separate, pistillate plants do not droop. Growing 1' to 2' tall, the smooth stem has numerous divided leaves with generally 3 rounded lobes on each leaflet. (Native)

April 15–May 1   Infrequent

The seeds from *Thalictrum* were reportedly used as a love medicine by Native Americans to reconcile a quarreling couple. The Cherokee used the root of a *Thalictrum* species to treat diarrhea and vomiting. Male and female flowers are on separate plants and are probably pollinated by the wind.

WILD STRAWBERRY
Fragaria virginiana

ROSE FAMILY
Rosaceae

The plant is hairy and has 3 ovate, rounded-tipped, coarsely toothed leaflets terminal on the 2" to 6" stalks, which most often grow from runners. Flowers are white with 5 petals and are borne in clusters that do not exceed the height of the leaves. Note that the seeds are "embedded" in the strawberry. (Native)

April 11–May 29   Locally Frequent

In addition to a pleasant tea from the leaves, the berries can be used like cultivated berries but, in the author's opinion, are far superior in flavor. A host of wildlife actively seek the plant and berries. A rich source of vitamin C, Wild Strawberry has been used to treat scurvy and a wide variety of other medical disorders.

INDIAN PHYSIC
Gillenia stipulata
(*Porteranthus stipulatus*)

Rose Family
Rosaceae

Leaves on this 1' to 3' plant have 3 lanceolate, sharply toothed leaflets. However, they also have 2 sharply toothed leaflike stipules that make the leaves seem to have 5 leaflets. There are 5 narrow, somewhat wavy, white petals and a reddish calyx. (Native)

May 28–July 14   Infrequent

Indian Physic was used in folk medicine and by Native Americans and herbalists as a strong laxative and emetic. It was also used to treat indigestion, colds, asthma, and in a poultice for swellings, rheumatism, and bee stings. The plant is reported to be possibly toxic.

CLEAVERS
Galium aparine

Madder Family
Rubiaceae

Pointed-tipped and linear-lanceolate leaves in whorls of mostly 8 distinguish this species from other similar species. Its reclining, square stems may be up to 4' long and have stiff, downward-pointed bristles on the angles. Margins of the leaves are also bristle tipped. Very small, white, 4–petaled flowers are in 1 to 3–flowered cymes. (Native)

April 11–June 13   Abundant

Galium aparine has over 55 common names in print, which reflects its wide variety of uses. These include a caffeine-free coffee substitute, a filler for bedding, an agent to curdle milk in making cheese, an aid in treating bed wetting in children, a source of red dye from the roots, and as a wash to remove freckles. It can also be eaten in salads or as greens.

HOUSTONIA
Houstonia lanceolata
(Houstonia purpurea var. *calycosa)*

MADDER FAMILY
Rubiaceae

Easily confused with others of the same genus, *H. lanceolata* has slightly broadened, lanceolate, thick leaves with a single prominent central vein. Stem leaves are sessile, opposite, and numerous, and even the little calyx lobes are lanceolate. Flowers are only $\frac{1}{4}$" wide, white, tubular with 4 flaring lobes and are in a loose terminal cluster. The plant is from 6" to 15" high. (Native)

April 11–June 8   Infrequent

The Madder family is one of the largest families of flowering plants in the world with almost 500 genera and nearly 6000 species. *Gray's Manual of Botany,* however, lists only 9 genera and 47 species in the northeastern United States. The genus *Houstonia* is named for Dr. William Houstoun, 1695-1733, an English botanist. No medicinal or culinary uses are known for this plant.

LARGE HOUSTONIA
Houstonia purpurea

MADDER FAMILY
Rubiaceae

Small, whitish to pale blue, 4-lobed, tubular flowers are in small clusters on branching flower stems on this 4" to 18" plant. Leaves are opposite, sessile, toothless, ovate to oblong-ovate, and have 3 to 5 (mostly 3), prominent veins. (Native)

May 22–July 16   Frequent

Flowers in this genus may be dimorphic, which means that in some flowers the anthers are hidden in the corolla tube with the stigma protruding, and in others the stigma is hidden in the tube and the anthers protrude. This plant apparently has no medicinal uses.

PARTRIDGE-BERRY
Mitchella repens

MADDER FAMILY
Rubiaceae

A distinctive, little, forest-floor plant with twin, diminutive, 4-lobed, tubular, white flowers. This is a trailing plant with ovate, ½"- to ¾"-long pairs of shiny, evergreen leaves. The flowers are fringed on the inside and the twin flowers produce a single red berry. (Native)

May 16–June 30   Locally Frequent

Numerous Native American peoples greatly valued a tea made from the small, red berries to lessen the difficulties and pain of childbirth. The berries may be nibbled or used to make a colorful, but somewhat tasteless, addition to salads. Grouse, turkey, quail, and several small mammals regularly eat the berries.

BISHOP'S-CAP
Mitella diphylla

SAXIFRAGE FAMILY
Saxifragaceae

The delicate, white, and fringed petals on this 10" to 18" plant must be viewed with a hand lens to be truly appreciated. The tiny flowers are in a short-stemmed raceme. On the stem below the flowers are 2 sessile, sharply toothed leaves. The larger basal leaves are long petioled, somewhat heart shaped, and ragged toothed. (Native)

April 7–May 13   Infrequent

Both common and genus names have their origin in the shape of the young seed pods, which resemble a bishop's miter. The genus name *Mitella* is from *mitra,* a cap. Though reputed in folk medicine to be of medicinal value, there is no scientific evidence to substantiate the claims.

EARLY SAXIFRAGE
Saxifraga virginiensis

SAXIFRAGE FAMILY
Saxifragaceae

When this plant first begins to flower, identification may be difficult because of the near absence of the very short flower stem. Later in the season the hairy, branching stem may be 12" to 15" tall, growing from a basal rosette of overlapping, wide, toothed, oval leaves. The small, $\frac{1}{4}$"-wide flowers are white with 5 petals and 10 conspicuous, yellow anthers. (Native)

March 1–May 2   Frequent

The young leaves, preferably gathered before flowering, make interesting and nutritious additions to salads or may be boiled for 10 minutes and eaten as greens. Saxifrage soup has also been given favorable mention. This very early spring plant is a popular and easily grown plant for rock gardens.

FOAMFLOWER
Tiarella cordifolia

SAXIFRAGE FAMILY
Saxifragaceae

Each tiny flower has 5 petals and 10 very long stamens. The flowers are borne in a raceme on a 6"- to 12"-tall single stem. The flowers bloom from the base of the raceme upward, often giving the raceme a pointed-cone appearance. The leaves are basal, similar to maple leaves, roundish to heart shaped, and have from 3 to 7 heavily toothed segments. (Native)

March 27–May 27   Frequent

The high tannin content in this plant may account for its use by Native Americans and herbalists as a tonic, diuretic, and mouthwash. It was used to treat indigestion, diarrhea, mouth sores, eye ailments, kidney stones, and bladder diseases. It was also used in poultices for wounds.

FOXGLOVE BEARD-TONGUE
Penstemon digitalis

FIGWORT FAMILY
Scrophulariaceae

This is a tall, 2' to 4' plant with a smooth stem. The 1¼"-long, white, thin corolla tube opens into a wider tube, then into 5 flaring lobes of unequal length and may be tinged with lavender in the throat. The pointed, ovate, lower leaves narrow into winged petioles and the upper leaves are more lanceolate, sessile, almost clasping, and have small, sharp teeth. Flower stalks are in pairs from upper leaf axils. (Native)

May 14–July 2   Frequent

The genus name is from *pente,* meaning five, and *stemon,* as in stamen, and refers to the 5 stamens, 4 of which are fertile and 1 that is sterile and often conspicuously covered with dense hair.

SLENDER-FLOWERED BEARD-TONGUE
Penstemon tenuiflorus

FIGWORT FAMILY
Scrophulariaceae

This 15" to 30" plant is soft hairy, especially on the leaf surfaces. Leaves are lanceolate and sparsely toothed, or in some cases, smooth margined. The flowers are white and the thin corolla tube abruptly expands into a much larger tube. A distinguishing feature is the curling of the lower lip upward to nearly close the throat. (Native)

May 22–June 16   Infrequent

The small irregular seeds of the genus *Penstemon* are of little value to most wildlife, but are eaten by some rodents. There are virtually no known medicinal or culinary uses for the approximately 250 species of *Penstemon* in the United States. The majority of species are found in the western states.

HONEWORT
Cryptotaenia canadensis

Parsley Family
Umbelliferae
(Apiaceae)

The tiny, white, 5-petaled flowers in branching umbels on this 1' to 3' plant are rather inconspicuous. Examination with a hand lens reveals no sepals on the flowers. Basal leaves are long petioled and divided into 3 pointed-ovate, irregularly sharp- toothed segments. Upper stem leaves are sessile. (Native)

May 22–July 18   Frequent

Honewort can be prepared as a root vegetable, as cooked greens, as an ingredient to salads, or used in soups and for seasoning. In Japan, where this species is also native, it is cultivated as an important garden vegetable.

HARBINGER-OF-SPRING
Erigenia bulbosa

Parsley Family
Umbelliferae
(Apiaceae)

Because of its 2" to 4" size, its tiny, white flowers, and its scarcity of foliage when the flowers first appears, *E. bulbosa* is easy to overlook. The flowers are in umbels and the dark anthers are conspicuous. The 1 or 2 leaves are divided and deeply lobed. (Native)

March 1–April 7   Frequent

The common name refers to the time of flowering, as it is one of the very first spring flowers. The small, bulblike tuber can be eaten raw or as a cooked vegetable after boiling for 10 to 15 minutes.

CICELY
Osmorhiza longistylis

PARSLEY FAMILY
Umbelliferae
(Apiaceae)

Minute, white flowers with protruding stamens are in a terminal umbel on this 1' to 3' plant. The stem is nearly hairless and the compound leaves are multiple pinnate. The leaflets are lanceolate and toothed. (Native)

April 11–June 13   Frequent

A very similar plant is *Osmorhiza claytoni,* which is very soft hairy.

The roots make an exceptional aniselike seasoning. There are numerous records of Native Americans using the roots in washes and medications for the eyes. Cicely was also used to treat gas, coughs, and stomachaches and as a poultice to treat wounds and boils.

SWEET WHITE VIOLET
Viola blanda

VIOLET FAMILY
Violaceae

This very small, delicate, white violet is only 2" to 5" high, with leaves and flowers on separate stems. The 3 lower petals are veined with purple and the 2 upper petals often curve sharply backward at the tips. Basal leaves are rounded, heart shaped, and the lobes are so close together they sometimes overlap. Flower and leaf stems may have reddish bases. (Native)

April 13–May 1   Infrequent

This violet is infrequent in the park and is very environment specific. A gardening periodical reported that this plant did not transplant well. *Viola blanda* demands cool, moist ravines to thrive, and the cause of difficulty in transplanting was probably an unsuitable site.

LANCE-LEAVED VIOLET
Viola lanceolata

VIOLET FAMILY
Violaceae

The leaves and flowers are on separate stems and are from 3" to 6" tall. The leaves are narrow lanceolate, long petioled, and toothed. The flowers are white with the 3 lower petals heavily veined with purple. (Native)

May 24–May 29   Rare

This violet is relatively rare in the park and requires a wet, boggy habitat. Violet is the state flower for Illinois, New Jersey, Rhode Island, and Wisconsin.

PALE VIOLET
Viola striata

VIOLET FAMILY
Violaceae

Stipules on this 6"- to 12"-long, leafy-stemmed violet are ragged toothed and very noticeable. The flowering stems angle somewhat at the leaf axils. Leaves are broad, heart shaped, and toothed. Flowers are creamy white with purple veins on the lower 3 petals, with heavier veins on the central petal. (Native)

April 9–June 16   Frequent

The leaves of violets are high in vitamins A and C and can be eaten raw in salads or cooked like greens. The seeds of violets are eaten by several upland game birds and turkeys enjoy the tuberous roots. Medicinal uses for violets are quite ancient, often being mentioned by Homer and Virgil.

YELLOW STARGRASS
Hypoxis hirsuta

AMARYLLIS FAMILY
Amaryllidaceae
(Liliaceae)

The 6 bright yellow "petals" actually consist of 3 sepals and 3 petals. The grassy-looking, hairy, linear leaves are erect and taller than the 3" to 6" flower stems. The flowers are only about ½" wide. (Native)

April 23–May 30   Infrequent

Unless in flower, this plant is likely to be mistaken for a grass. The Amaryllidaceae Family includes several cultivated ornamental plants such as daffodils. Like some of its relatives, yellow stargrass, with its bulblike corms, is easily grown in wildflower gardens.

LANCE-LEAVED COREOPSIS
Coreopsis lanceolata

COMPOSITE FAMILY
Compositae
(Asteraceae)

The tips of the 6 to 10 (usually 8) bright yellow rays on the 2"-wide flower heads are noticeably notched, usually into 4 lobes. Upper stem leaves on this 12" to 24" plant are narrow lanceolate, toothless, and sessile. Lower leaves are slender petioled and may have 1 to 2 narrow lobes below the primary leaflet. (Native)

May 1–June 21   Infrequent

Lance-Leaved Coreopsis is a native plant commonly cultivated in flower gardens. Native Americans reportedly used *Coreopsis* medicinally to cure diarrhea and to induce vomiting.

DWARF DANDELION

Krigia biflora

COMPOSITE FAMILY
Compositae
(Asteraceae)

This 1' to 2' plant has a completely smooth, sometimes waxy-white, branching stem. The $1\frac{1}{4}$"-wide flower heads are yellow, dandelion-like, and are terminal on the few branching, leafless stems. Small stem leaves are clasping at each branch axil. The much larger basal leaves may have smooth margins or be wavy toothed. (Native)

April 11–June 28 Frequent

Finding this plant in a field guide may depend on which name is chosen. None seem to fit the plant, as it isn't a dwarf, nor does it resemble another common name, Goat's Beard. *Gray's Manual of Botany* lists *Adopogon virginicum, Cynthia virginica,* and *K. amplexicaulis* as previous scientific names.

DWARF DANDELION

Krigia dandelion

COMPOSITE FAMILY
Compositae
(Asteraceae)

This plant has a solitary, yellow, 1"-wide, dandelion-like flower head, and is from 6" to 20" tall. It has no stem leaves and the flowering stem does not branch. The 3"- to 6"-long basal leaves are variably wavy lobed and may even be entire. (Native)

April 24–June 5 Infrequent

A similar plant is *Krigia virginica,* which is much smaller, only reaching 2" to 10" in height.

Another common name for this plant is Potato Dandelion, probably in reference to the tuberous root, although there is apparently no literature indicating that the root is eaten. This and other *Krigia* species have a bitter, milky juice that may account for it not being eaten.

GOLDEN RAGWORT
Senecio aureus

COMPOSITE FAMILY
Compositae
(Asteraceae)

The numerous, yellow flower heads on this 1' to 2½' plant are ¾" wide, with from 8 to 12 rays. The flowering stems are often branched. Upper leaves are few, narrow, and deeply incised. Basal leaves are usually numerous, long petioled, broadly toothed, and may be somewhat purplish beneath. (Native)

May 13–May 28   Frequent

This plant was esteemed by Native Americans and nineteenth-century herbalists to treat menstrual problems, leukorrhea, problems with menopause, and to speed difficult childbirth. It is also reported to have been used to induce abortion.

BUTTERWEED
Senecio glabellus

COMPOSITE FAMILY
Compositae
(Asteraceae)

The 2' to 3' stem on this species of *Senecio* is succulent, fleshy, and hollow. Flower heads are in a tight, almost rounded, dense terminal cluster. There are 6 to 12 yellow rays on the ¾"-wide blossoms. Stem leaves are sessile and deeply cut into lobed, wrinkled segments, with the terminal segment the largest. Basal leaves are similar, but much larger and petioled. (Native)

May 9–July 30   Infrequent

This species of *Senecio* is most often found in wet or even swampy areas in the park. All *Senecio* species contain the highly toxic alkaloid, pyrrolizidine, and livestock are often poisoned by the plants.

ROUNDLEAF RAGWORT
Senecio obovatus

COMPOSITE FAMILY
Compositae
(Asteraceae)

When fully in bloom, the flower heads are mostly in a flat-topped, 12" to 18" cluster. There are from 8 to 12 yellow rays on the small, ½" to ¾" heads. Most leaves are basal, toothed, and spatulate, tapering to the stem. Occasional upper leaves are more narrow, with the lower half deeply incised. (Native)

March 8–May 14   Frequent

Medical uses of various *Senecio* species in folk medicine and by Native Americans included treatment of kidney stones, urinary problems, lung ailments, and tuberculosis. They were also reportedly used as a diuretic and astringent.

SMALL'S RAGWORT
Senecio smallii
(*Senecio anonymus*)

COMPOSITE FAMILY
Compositae
(Asteraceae)

Lower portions of both the long-petioled basal leaves and the flowering stem have dense, woolly hair. Basal leaves are 3" to 6" long, lanceolate, and toothed. Upper stem leaves are much smaller, very deeply cut, and short petioled. Flower heads are yellow, ½" wide, have 8 to 10 rays, and are in large clusters on stems 18" to 30" high. (Native)

May 14–July 9   Rare

The Latin name is from *senex,* meaning old man, and refers to the hoariness of many species, or to the white hairs of the heads. *Senecio* is a very large genus of plants with more than 2000 species. Many contain alkaloids that are toxic and reportedly caused cancer in laboratory animals.

DANDELION
Taraxacum officinale

COMPOSITE FAMILY
Compositae
(Asteraceae)

There are few wildflowers as well known as the Common Dandelion. The 2"- to 18"-tall weed has 1" to 2" wide, showy heads of tiny, yellow flowers, very ragged sharp-lobed leaves that are linear lanceolate in outline, a hollow milky stem, downward dropping outer bracts, and a round, fluffy seed ball. (Native)

March-September   Frequent

Wine made from the petals, a coffeelike drink from the roots, spring greens rich in vitamin A from the leaves, and fritters from the flower heads are some of the attributes of this often-cursed plant. Not the least of its values are the pleasure and wonder of a child blowing on the seed heads and watching the tiny parachutes float away on the wind.

WINTERCRESS
Barbarea vulgaris

MUSTARD FAMILY
Cruciferae
(Brassicaceae)

This mostly smooth plant is 1' to 2' tall. Lower leaves are petioled and pinnatifid, with the terminal lobe rounded and much larger than the lateral lobes. Upper leaves are sessile or clasping and broadly toothed instead of lobed. Flowers are yellow, 4-petaled, and in a raceme. Note the rounded, linear, appressed seedpods. (Introduced)

April 23   Infrequent

The seeds of this weedy invader are used significantly by Mourning Doves. Once widely eaten as a fresh green, it has recently been discovered to be quite harmful and should be avoided. In Europe, it has historically been used as a poultice for wounds.

SMOOTH ROCK CRESS
Arabis laevigata

MUSTARD FAMILY
Cruciferae
(Brassicaceae)

Leaves on this 1' to 3'–tall, smooth plant are alternate, entire or sparsely toothed, and clasp the stem. Basal leaves are more ovate, toothed, and petioled. The 4-petaled, tubular flowers are greenish yellow in a loose raceme. (Native)

March 20–April 29   Infrequent

The Smooth Rock Cress is probably more easily recognized by the 3" to 4" arching or down-curving seed pods than by its flowers. This plant generally requires a calcareous (limestone) environment. Given the right soil, this can be an excellent rock garden plant.

EARLY SPURGE
Euphorbia commutata

SPURGE FAMILY
Euphorbiaceae

Leaves on this 8" to 18" plant are sessile, broader than long, semicircular in shape, and the upper leaves are often overlapping to form a notched circle around the stem. The clusters of minute, yellow flowers are without

petals and are borne in a cuplike arrangement of the terminal leaves. (Native)

April 3–May 13   Infrequent

Several species of *Euphorbia* have been used in herbal medicine, primarily as an agent to induce vomiting and to empty the bowels. Because of possible poisoning, modern herbalists do not recommend their use. The milky sap in the plants has been reported to cause skin irritations.

HOP CLOVER
Trifolium agrarium
(Trifolium aureum)

PEA FAMILY
Leguminosae
(Fabaceae)

This is a mostly roadside, 6" to 18" clover with ½"-tall, oval heads of yellow flowers. Mature flowers turn brown and downward with age. The 3-part leaflets grow from the same point, are oblong-ovate, sessile, and though toothed, the teeth are extremely small. (Native)

May 14–July 23   Abundant

The common name refers to the apparent similarity of the withered flowers to hops. This weedy plant can be used as a forage crop. Like other clovers, the foliage is edible and a tea can be made from the flower heads.

YELLOW TROUT-LILY
Erythronium americanum

LILY FAMILY
Liliaceae

The name Trout-Lily, and sometimes Fawn-Lily, is derived from the brown splotches on the pair of broad, pointed, bladelike basal leaves. These splotches resemble the markings on a trout or baby deer. A single, 4"- to 8"-tall stem, rises from between the 2 leaves and bears a single, drooping, yellow, bell-shaped flower with the 3 petals and 3 sepals sharply recurved. (Native)

March 21–April 21   Locally Abundant

Much more abundant than *E. albidum,* Yellow Trout-Lily bulbs make an excellent potato substitute, although uncooked they may be mildly emetic. Native Americans used the leaves in a poultice to treat ulcers and tumors. Native American women are reported to have eaten the raw leaves to prevent pregnancy.

LARGE-FLOWERED BELLWORT
Uvularia grandiflora

LILY FAMILY
Liliaceae

This plant, which may reach 24" in height, arches at the top and has a wilted appearance because of the partially unfolded leaves that clasp and surround the stem. The flowers are 1" to 2" long, drooping, yellow, and bell shaped. Unlike the similar *U. perfoliata,* this flower is smooth inside and the leaves are whitish and slightly hairy beneath. (Native)

April 15–May 27   Rare

This species of *Uvularia* was used extensively by Native Americans as a sedative and tonic and to treat sore throat, sores, wounds, snake bite, and sore muscles. The young shoots were reportedly eaten and used to prepare a drink.

BELLWORT
Uvularia perfoliata

LILY FAMILY
Liliaceae

A single, yellow, 1"- to 1¼"-long, bell-shaped flower droops from an arching, 6" to 18" stem. The petals and sepals are indistinguishable and the flower appears unfolded. The identifying characteristic, however, is the way the stems appear to pierce the base of the leaves. A coarse texture and orangish granules on the inside of the petals differentiate this flower from the larger *U. grandiflora.* (Native)

April 15–May 29   Abundant

Stripped of their leaves, the young shoots can be boiled for about 10 minutes and are a reasonable substitute for asparagus. Native Americans are reported to have used a tea made from the roots to treat sore throats and as a cough medicine.

YELLOW LADY'S-SLIPPER
Cypripedium calceolus* var. *pubescens
(Cypripedium pubescens)

ORCHID FAMILY
Orchidaceae

There are 4 to 5 ovate to lanceolate, clasping, parallel-veined, alternate, entire leaves on the 8"- to 18"-tall stem. The moccasin or pouch shape is distinctive on this beautiful yellow orchid. Note the 2 twisted lateral petals. (Native)

April 21–May 27   Endangered

This is the rarest of the park's orchids and finding it is a wildflower enthusiast's dream. Besides its rarity, another good reason not to disturb this plant is that its hairs may cause a dermatitis in some individuals. Native Americans commonly used it as a sedative.

LARGE YELLOW WOOD-SORREL
Oxalis grandis

WOOD-SORREL FAMILY
Oxalidaceae

The margins of the heart-shaped, cloverlike leaflets are edged with purple on this 1' to 2' plant. Close examination will reveal that the bases of the 5 yellow, $\frac{3}{4}$"-wide petals are tinged with pink. (Native)

April 30–June 21   Frequent

Children like to chew the sour, tangy-tasting leaves on this easily identified plant. The leaves are a refreshing addition to salads, but should not be eaten in large quantity because of the concentrations of oxalic acid in the plant. This acid is reported to prevent the absorption of calcium.

YELLOW WOOD-SORREL
Oxalis stricta

WOOD-SORREL FAMILY
Oxalidaceae

Heart-shaped, cloverlike leaves and pretty yellow flowers with 5 petals make this genus easy to identify. Distinguishing between species is much more difficult. In *O. stricta* the ⅔"-wide petals are often reddish at the base and the pod stalks bend at a sharp angle. Seed pods are mostly vertical. This plant is from 4" to 8" tall. (Native)

April 23–June 24   Frequent

High in vitamin C, this plant is used in salads, as a lemonade-like drink, and is also simply chewed for the refreshing taste, but it should be used sparingly because of the oxalic acid in the plant. *Oxalis stricta* was used in folk medicine to treat cancer. Native Americans made an orange dye from the plant.

YELLOW CORYDALIS
Corydalis flavula

POPPY FAMILY
Papaveraceae
(Fumariaceae)

The foliage is similar to Dutchman's-Breeches and Squirrel-Corn in having very deep and finely cut compound leaves. The ½"-long, yellow flowers have a slightly down-curved, short, saclike spur and the larger upper and lower petals are crested or fringed at their tips. This plant is from 5" to 12" tall and the flowers are in a raceme at the end of many-branched stems. (Native)

March 8–April 23   Frequent

Though not known to be fatal, the toxic alkaloids in this plant can cause serious trembling and convulsions. It is used in folk and herbal medicine for dysentery, diarrhea, and menstrual irregularities. The Chinese also use roots of closely related species to treat menstrual irregularities.

CELANDINE POPPY
Stylophorum diphyllum

POPPY FAMILY
Papaveraceae

Almost as conspicuous as the 4 bright yellow petals on this 10" to 20" plant are the densely hairy, oval buds. Most of the deeply pinnatified leaves are basal. The flowering stems usually have a pair of deeply lobed leaves below the flower stalk. (Native)

April 5–May 9   Infrequent

This is a great wildflower garden plant with lush foliage and a long flowering period. Provided with an ideal environment, the Celandine Poppy has become extremely invasive and weedy in the wildflower garden of my friend Nevellen Craddock.

WHORLED LOOSESTRIFE
Lysimachia quadrifolia

PRIMROSE FAMILY
Primulaceae

Very short-petioled or sessile leaves on this slender 1' to 2½'plant are usually in whorls of 4. Very thin, long flower stalks grow from each of the 4 leaf axils. Flowers are yellow with a splotched red center and have 5 petals. (Native)

May 28–June 18   Infrequent

It has been suggested that the dried leaves can be used to make a tea. Native Americans used a root tea as an emetic and a leaf tea to treat kidney and bowel problems.

KIDNEYLEAF BUTTERCUP
Ranunculus abortivus

BUTTERCUP FAMILY
Ranunculaceae

The plant is mostly smooth and from 6" to 20" tall. The flowers are about $\frac{1}{4}$" wide with 5 tiny, yellow petals and 5 often-drooping, greenish sepals. Petioled basal leaves are roundish heart or kidney shaped and round toothed. Stem leaves are variably segmented into 3 to 5 parts. (Native)

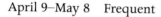

April 9–May 8   Frequent

A very similar and often difficult to separate species is *Ranunculus micranthus,* which is generally more hairy than *R. abortivus.*

Farmers do not want buttercups in their pastures since they are quite poisonous to cattle. The toxic alkaloid, however, loses its potency in the drying process and is harmless in cured hay. Cattle that have eaten buttercups produce bitter-tasting milk with a reddish tinge.

EARLY BUTTERCUP
Ranunculus fascicularis

BUTTERCUP FAMILY
Ranunculaceae

This buttercup may be easily confused with *R. hispidus* and flowers at about the same time. In this plant the 5 waxy, yellow petals are narrow and oblong and the silky-hairy leaves are incised into 3 to 5 very blunt lobes. The plant is 3" to 8" tall and the stems are mostly hairy at the base. It generally grows on dry hillsides, whereas *R. hispidus* prefers moist areas. (Native)

April 20–April 21   Infrequent

Buttercups contain the toxic alkaloid protoanemonine, which taken internally may cause kidney damage and convulsions. Externally it will cause blisters and serious skin irritation. In ancient times beggars were said to have used the plant's juice to cause ugly blisters on their skin to gain sympathy.

HISPID BUTTERCUP
Ranunculus hispidus

BUTTERCUP FAMILY
Ranunculaceae

This somewhat reclining, 8" to 24"
plant has hairy stems and petioles,
especially below and when young.
Note that there are no runners.
Leaves are mostly 3-divided with
the leaflets pointed, deeply lobed,
and toothed with the terminal segment the largest. Flowers are about ¾"
wide with 5 shiny, yellow, ovate petals. (Native)

March 27–May 14   Frequent

Although known by them to be poisonous, Native Americans used buttercups
to cure headache, as an astringent, and to treat wounds. Because of the known
caustic properties of the plants, their use was restricted to exterior treatments
or, if taken internally, only in highly diluted mixtures. Smoke from the plants
was most often the prescription.

HOOKED CROWFOOT
Ranunculus recurvatus

BUTTERCUP FAMILY
Ranunculaceae

This is a quite hairy, 1' to 2' plant.
The tiny, yellow petals are subtended by longer, green, down-
curved sepals and the center of the
¼"- to ⅜"-wide flowers are greenish, giving the entire flower a
greenish appearance. Leaves are
cleft nearly to the stem, are 3-
lobed, and toothed. (Native)

April 16–May 14   Frequent

The buttercups have been used as a poison to tip arrows, to make both yellow
and red dyes, and as a pain killer, under the premise that the pain from the
medicine would be greater than the pain of the injury. Though poisonous to humans and cattle, the plant is of value to several species of birds and rodents.

COMMON CINQUEFOIL
Potentilla simplex

ROSE FAMILY
Rosaceae

The ½"-wide flowers, with 5 yellow petals, grow on prostrate runners that may be up to 18" long. The hairy stems often root at the nodes. Leaves have 5 toothed leaflets and the leaves and flowers are on separate stalks. The middle leaflet is the largest of the 5 lanceolate leaflets. (Native)

April 11–June 4   Frequent

The tannic acid in cinquefoils may be the reason for their use medicinally by herbalists to treat fever and hemorrhaging and as an astringent. The genus name is from *potens,* in reference to its reputedly strong medicinal powers.

BARREN STRAWBERRY
Waldsteinia fragarioides

ROSE FAMILY
Rosaceae

This 2"- to 6"-tall plant has no runners. The long-petioled leaves are divided into 3 wedge-shaped, deeply toothed leaflets. The ½"-wide flowers have 5 yellow petals and are on leafless stalks. (Native)

April 17   Rare

The species name *fragarioides* means "like the wild strawberry." Though similar in structure to Wild Strawberry, *Fragaria virginiana,* this plant forms no fleshy berries.

GROUND-CHERRY
Physalis virginiana

TOMATO FAMILY
Solanaceae

Another common name, Chinese-Lantern, refers to the thin, bladderlike capsule formed by
the sepals around the ripe, red berry. In this
species the "lantern" is very deeply indented at
the top. The tubular, pale yellow flowers, with
purple spots in their throats, hang below the
leaves from short stalks growing from the leaf
axils. This hairy plant is 1½' to 2½' tall, with
ovate, sparingly wavy-toothed leaves that taper at both ends. (Native)

May 28–October 4   Frequent

If you can beat the quail, turkey, opossums, mice, and other critters to the ripe
cherries, they make wonderful pies, jam, preserves, and syrup. They are also
very good raw. A word of caution though: the unripe fruit and the leaves are
poisonous as are so many plants in the Tomato Family.

CLUSTERED SNAKEROOT
Sanicula gregaria
(*Sanicula odorata*)

PARSLEY FAMILY
Umbelliferae
(Apiaceae)

This is a smooth, 1' to 3'–tall,
branching plant. Leaves are 5-
parted palmate, sharply
toothed with bristles on the
teeth, and the leaflets are lanceolate to spatulate in outline. Note the hooked
hairs on the burrlike calyx and the tiny, yellowish petals overtopped by the
exerted anthers. (Native)

May 10–June 27   Frequent

This plant is used internally by Native Americans to treat sore throats and fevers and externally to treat skin diseases. Many members of the *Umbelliferae* are
violently poisonous, while others are known for their use as food and spices.
This plant is easily confused with other similar species.

GOLDEN ALEXANDER
Zizia aptera

PARSLEY FAMILY
Umbelliferae
(Apiaceae)

Tiny, yellow flowers are in small umbels atop a primary umbel on this smooth, 1' to 2½' plant. Basal leaves have heart-shaped bases, and the upper leaves are short-petioled, 3-parted, lanceolate, and toothed. This flower may be easily confused with *Thaspium trifoliatum* but the central flower (seen with a magnifying glass) does not have a stalk. (Native)

April 23–June 17   Frequent

Native Americans are reported to have used species of *Zizia* for insomnia, fevers, and to heal wounds. It was also thought to aid in the treatment of syphilis. Identification of plants in this family can be confusing and many members of this family are highly poisonous.

HOARY PUCCOON
Lithospermum canescens

BORAGE FAMILY
Boraginaceae

The orange-yellow flower color is unusual and distinctive. Covered with fine, soft hair, the plant is from 5" to 12" tall with narrow, alternate, and toothless leaves. Flowers are in clusters and there are 5 petal-like lobes to the tubular corolla. The stamens are hidden in the corolla tube. (Native)

April 20–May 29   Frequent

Native Americans valued this plant and used a red dye made from the roots to paint their bodies. It is said that they also used the leaves to make a mixture that was applied externally to cure fevers and convulsions.

BLACKBERRY-LILY
Belamcanda chinensis

The flowering stem of this 1½' to 3' plant grows from a clasping, spathelike leaf axil and branches above. Note the swordlike leaves. The 6 perianth parts (3 sepals and 3 petals) are yellow-orange, spotted with crimson-purple dots, and are 1½" to 2" wide. (Introduced)

May 28–August 16   Infrequent

This plant is not really a lily, but instead a member of the Iris Family, as can be noted from the basal fan of swordlike leaves. It is a native of Asia and an escape from cultivated flower gardens. The common name refers to the clusters of fleshy, shiny black seeds that resemble blackberries. It is perhaps our most beautiful import.

HORSE-GENTIAN
Triosteum angustifolium

HONEYSUCKLE FAMILY
Caprifoliaceae

The 1' to 2' stem is bristly hairy, and the hairs are tinged reddish brown. Leaves are opposite, entire, rough-hairy, sessile, and lanceolate, tapering from the middle to the base. Flowers are solitary in the upper leaf axils, tubular, about ½" long, and yellowish red. The orange-red fruits are more conspicuous than the flowers. (Native)

May 14   Infrequent

Settlers are said to have dried and roasted the berries of this plant to grind and use as a coffee substitute. Native Americans considered the plant emetic and cathartic, using it primarily to treat fevers.

FIRE PINK
Silene virginica

PINK FAMILY
Caryophyllaceae

The 5 petals of this $1\frac{1}{2}$"-wide flower are notched at the tips into 2 lobes and are a showy, fire-engine red. The loose clusters of flowers grow on sticky-hairy, 1' to 2' stems and the leaves are narrow and opposite. The sepals form a 5-pointed, sticky, calyx tube. (Native)

April 7–June 5   Frequent

Another common name for this plant, Catchfly, refers to the sticky hairs that prevent insects from obtaining nectar without pollinating the flowers. Fire Pink was reported to have been used as a worm medicine, although some Native Americans considered the plant to be poisonous.

ROCK-MOSS
Sedum pulchellum

ORPINE FAMILY
Crassulaceae

Leaves on this succulent, 4" to 12" plant are short, fleshy, needlelike, sessile, and closely crowded on the stem. The pointed-tipped, 5-petaled, white to pink, sessile flowers are on 4 to 7 forking, flat-topped or slightly downward-arching branches. (Native)

May 14–July 8   Infrequent

Widow's-Cross is another common name for this diminutive plant. This *Sedum* grows exclusively on limestone rocks, and the height of the plant is dependent on how wet or dry the rocks are.

PURPLE ROCKET
Iodanthus pinnatifidus

MUSTARD FAMILY
Cruciferae
(Brassicaceae)

The 4 pale lavender to pinkish white petals narrow sharply at the base. The numerous flowers are in a spreading panicle on this 1' to 3' plant. Upper leaves are lanceolate, clasping, and sharply toothed. Lower leaves have winged petioles, are clasping, sharply toothed, and deeply cut on the lower part into 2 to 6 pairs of toothed segments. (Native)

May 9–June 5   Infrequent

The genus name for this native perennial is from the Greek *iodes,* meaning violet colored, and *anthos,* meaning flower. It is the only really pink member of *Cruciferae* in the park during the spring. The plant is found almost exclusively around springs or along the river.

RED DEAD-NETTLE
Lamium purpureum

MINT FAMILY
Labiatae
(Lamiaceae)

This is a short, 4" to 10" plant with dark pink, hooded, tubular flowers. The leaves are heart shaped, opposite, toothed, petioled, few below, and numerous, drooping, and overlapping above. The leaves may be reddish or purplish on top and light green beneath. (Introduced)

April 13–April 29   Infrequent

This weedy import from Europe is found in disturbed areas. It was reported to have been eaten as a potherb in certain parts of Europe, and herbals recommended it in a mixture to help stop bleeding.

VIOLET WOOD-SORREL
Oxalis violacea

WOOD-SORREL FAMILY
Oxalidaceae

The cloverlike, 3-parted leaves with heart-shaped leaflets are basal, shorter than the flowering stems, purplish beneath and may have stained brown spots above. Flowers are loosely clustered on smooth, 4"- to 8"-tall stems and have 5 flaring pinkish purple petals. (Native)

April 11–May 16   Frequent

The small bulbs, leaves, and seeds of the Violet Wood-Sorrel, also called Wild Shamrock, are eaten by numerous birds and other wildlife. Hikers chew the leaves and a rejuvenating drink is made by brewing the leaves and adding a sweetener. As with other *Oxalis* species, use of large amounts should be avoided due to the presence of oxalic acid.

COLUMBINE
Aquilegia canadensis

BUTTERCUP FAMILY
Ranunculaceae

The flowers are mostly red outside and yellow inside, $1\frac{1}{2}$" to 2" long, and hang from the tips of small, smooth, branched stems on this 1' to 2' plant. The shape is distinctive with 5 long, curving spurs pointed upward and the yellow stamens hanging conspicuously below. The leaves are in threes and each leaflet is 3 lobed. (Native)

March 23–June 15   Infrequent

Columbine was a powerful "love medicine" for some Native Americans and was used medicinally for stomach problems, uterine bleeding, headaches, and fevers. Seeds are reported to have been rubbed into the hair to expel lice. The plant may be poisonous and narcotic to some people.

VALERIAN
Valeriana pauciflora

VALERIAN FAMILY
Valerianaceae

The filaments and threadlike tips of the stigma extend beyond the 5 small, pinkish white, flaring petals on a long, thin corolla tube. Flowers are terminal in a cyme. Basal leaves are long petioled and heart shaped. Stem leaves on this 12" to 30" plant are opposite and divided into 3 to 7 broadly lanceolate and toothed leaflets, with the terminal leaflet being the larger. (Native)

May 2–June 13   Infrequent

Native Americans used a *Valeriana* species as an antiseptic by grinding the roots and applying the powder to cuts and wounds. A closely related European species, *V. officinalis,* is sold in Europe as a sedative. The strong-smelling herb is also said to attract both cats and rats.

PERIWINKLE
Vinca minor

DOGBANE FAMILY
Apocynaceae

Note the 5-pointed-star shape formed at the mouth of the corolla tube. The 5 blue-violet, flaring petals seem to twist slightly counterclockwise. The plant is an evergreen vine with opposite, glossy, ovate leaves. Flowers are about 1" wide. (Introduced)

March 9–May 24   Frequent

Periwinkle is found at cemeteries and old home sites and is used as a ground cover and for erosion control. Scientific evidence tends to confirm its use by herbalists as an agent to retard the flow of blood.

WILD COMFREY
Cynoglossum virginianum
BORAGE FAMILY
Boraginaceae

Small, pale blue, 5-lobed flowers about ¼"
wide are in often drooping, short racemes
at the top of this 1½' to 2' plant. The entire
plant has stiff hairs. Stem leaves are lanceolate and clasping. Basal leaves are much
larger, oblong ovate, petioled, and pointed.
Both stem leaves and basal leaves are toothless. (Native)

April 11-May 22   Frequent

Young plants can be cooked as greens and a
tea can be made from the dried leaves. The
Cherokee used the root medicinally to treat
cancer and kidney problems. They also used
the plant in preparation of love charms.

BLUEBELLS
Mertensia virginica
BORAGE FAMILY
Boraginaceae

The blue flowers resemble
small bells with long, stout
handles. They hang in
loose terminal clusters on 1'
to 2'-tall, smooth, fleshy
stems. Leaves are light
green, alternate, ovate and
elongated at the bases.
Note that the unopened flowers are a distinct pink instead of blue. (Native)

March 21–May 1   Infrequent

Also known as Virginia Cowslip and Roanoke-Bells, this was one of the first
plants sent back by early explorers to England, where it was treasured as a garden plant. In actuality, the "bells" look more like a trumpet.

VENUS' LOOKING-GLASS
Specularia perfoliata
(*Triodanis perfoliata* var. *perfoliata*)

BLUEBELL FAMILY
Campanulaceae

This plant has a very finely hairy, usually unbranching, 6" to 20" stem. Leaves are alternate, roundish, clasp the stem with heart-shaped bases, and are wavy toothed on the edges. The $\frac{1}{2}$"-wide flowers are solitary in the leaf axils and are violet-blue with 5 spreading corolla lobes. (Native)

May 16–July 23   Infrequent

Specularia perfoliata is somewhat unusual because of the flowers on the lower part of the stem that do not open, and which are self pollinating and seed producing. Also the seed capsules split in three places to expel the seeds.

EARLY SPIDERWORT
Tradescantia virginiana

SPIDERWORT FAMILY
Commelinaceae

Although varying from deep purple to light blue, the flower color is quite bold. Borne in a terminal cluster, the flowers have 3 symmetrical petals and showy yellow

anthers. Leaves are long-linear and sharply folded at the midrib. Plant height is 10" to 18" and flowers are approximately $1\frac{1}{2}$" wide. (Native)

April 11–May 14   Infrequent

Early Spiderwort is valuable to those studying cell structure and function because of its abnormally large chromosomes. It is also of value in the study of pollution because of the apparent frequency with which the cells undergo mutation when exposed to various levels of pollution.

PURPLE CONEFLOWER
Echinacea pallida

COMPOSITE FAMILY
Compositae
(Asteraceae)

Rose-pink or lavender rays droop downward around a rust-colored center on this 18"- to 36"-tall, solitary, hairy-stemmed plant. The rays become lighter in color with age. Leaves are linear lanceolate, parallel veined, entire, and the lower leaves have long petioles. Petioles become shorter on the upper leaves. (Native)

May 22–July 20   Infrequent

Native Americans, especially in the plains, used *Echinacea* for snake and spider bites, toothaches, sores, wounds, sore throats, colds, and numerous other ailments. Scientists have confirmed its use as an external antiseptic. A large number of medicines using *Echinacea* are manufactured and sold commercially in Europe.

WILD GERANIUM
Geranium maculatum

GERANIUM FAMILY
Geraniaceae

The long, beak-shaped seed capsule is the source of another common name, Cranesbill. The plant is 1' to 2' tall, has 5 pink to purple, 1"-wide petals and the paired leaves are deeply cleft into 5 heavily toothed parts. There are 10 stamens and the flower and leaf stems are moderately hairy. (Native)

March 27–May 14   Frequent

A smaller species is *Geranium carolinianum,* which has finely divided leaves and smaller flowers in clusters.

The plant was valued by Native Americans for its astringent and styptic properties and for treatment of diarrhea. They also ate the young leaves. Wild Geranium cannot self-pollinate since the stamens and pistil mature at different times. It has a unique system of dispersing its seeds by an explosive contraction of the seed capsule.

APPENDAGED WATERLEAF
Hydrophyllum appendiculatum

WATERLEAF FAMILY
Hydrophyllaceae

The filaments and anthers protrude past the 5 somewhat bell-shaped flowers with their pale purple petals. The leaves are large, alternate, deeply cleft into 5 lobes, sharply toothed, and are somewhat maplelike. Note the dense, soft hair covering this 1' to 2' plant. Minute reflexed appendages appear between the sepals. (Native)

April 11–May 30   Infrequent

The species name, *appendiculatum,* means having appendages. It is the key to identification of this plant and refers to the tiny reflexed appendages between the calyx lobes. The young leaves of other species of *Hydrophyllum* are said to be used as a cooked green.

PURPLE PHACELIA
Phacelia bipinnatifida

WATERLEAF FAMILY
Hydrophyllaceae

The 5 petals on the tubular flowers have a white center and are more violet-blue than purple. The hairy filaments extend far past the petals. Dense, soft hair covers the stems on this 12" to 24" plant. The leaves are once to several times twice divided into 3 to 7 sharp-toothed segments. (Native)

April 30–May 10   Infrequent

Although there is little recorded use of eastern species of *Phacelia,* they are related to the waterleafs, which may be eaten as a cooked green. There are more than 20 species of this genus in the western United States, where they are reported to have been eaten by Native Americans as well as by numerous wildlife species.

PHACELIA
Phacelia purshii

WATERLEAF FAMILY
Hydrophyllaceae

Edges of the 5 pale blue petals are delicately fringed on this 8" to 18" plant. The blue fades to white at the center of the ½"-wide blossoms. Its leaves are deeply cut into 9 to 15 pointed segments. Upper leaves are sessile and the lower leaves are petioled. (Native)

April 30–May 10   Infrequent

This is a desirable and easily cultivated wildflower garden plant. Another common name is Miami Mist, which is derived from the Miami Valley in Ohio where it is especially abundant. In the park it is found almost exclusively along the river.

BLUE-EYED GRASS
Sisyrinchium angustifolium

IRIS FAMILY
Iridaceae

The "eye" in the name refers to the yellow center of the ½"-wide, bright blue flowers. There are 3 petals and 3 similar sepals, which have a sharp point at the tip. In this species the winged stem is slightly taller than the erect, narrow, grasslike, 6" to 15" leaves. The flower stem may be forked and angled near the tip. (Native)

April 11–May 30   Infrequent

A similar plant is *Sisyrinchium albidum,* which has white perianth parts.

Eaten by Wild Turkey and Ruffed Grouse, this is not a grass but a member of the Iris Family. Native Americans used a root tea made from the plant to treat worms and stomachaches and as a laxative.

CRESTED DWARF IRIS
Iris cristata

IRIS FAMILY
Iridaceae

The 3 largest down-curved segments of the flower are the sepals. On each sepal there is a small, 3-ridged crest on a yellow patch bordered with white. The 3 petals and 3 petal-like stigmas above are solid blue. Leaves clasp the 3"- to 8"-tall flowering stems and the wide, grasslike leaves grow from the rhizome and arch above the flowering stems. (Native)

April 20–May 14   Frequent

It is reported that Native Americans used the plant as an ointment for sores and in a tea for hepatitis. However, modern evidence indicates that the resinous substance in the plant can cause purging, burning, and severe digestive tract upset. It may also cause serious skin irritation.

GROUND-IVY
Glechoma hederacea

MINT FAMILY
Labiatae
(Lamiaceae)

This is a small, creeping plant with blunt-toothed, roundish leaves that are somewhat heart shaped at the base. The $\frac{1}{2}$"-long, blue flowers are tubular and grow in whorls from the leaf axils. (Native)

March 9–May 24   Abundant

Ground-Ivy was replaced by hops in the making of beer and ale. It was also used to treat lead poisoning, measles, influenza, toothaches, wounds, ringing in the ears, colic in babies, lung and kidney ailments, backaches, cancer, hives, and various other aches and pains. It does make a superb herbal tea.

HEAL-ALL
Prunella vulgaris

MINT FAMILY
Labiatae
(Lamiaceae)

Heal-All is quite variable in color, height, and flowering period. It may be from 3" to 30" tall and the flowers range from light purple to almost white. It can flower from May through September. It usually has a single stem, but it may be branched. Leaves are pointed ovate with midstem leaves more toothed than upper or basal leaves. The $\frac{1}{2}$"-long, tubular flowers have a finely hairy hood and a slightly fringed lip below and are in a dense, rounded spike of green to purplish tinged, hairy, ovate-pointed bracts. (Native)

May 22–September 30   Abundant

The common name indicates how widely this plant was used medicinally. Its uses included treatment for sore throats, mouth sores, internal bleeding, and external wounds. Although its use has been mostly discontinued in modern herbals, very recent scientific accounts exonerate some of its uses.

LYRE-LEAVED SAGE
Salvia lyrata

MINT FAMILY
Labiatae
(Lamiaceae)

Bright blue, tubular, 1"-long flowers, with the lower lip larger than the upper lip, are in whorls on this 1' to 2' plant. Stem leaves are merely bractlike. Leaves in the basal rosette are petioled, 2" to 8" long, and very irregularly cleft with relatively smooth margins. The plant is slightly hairy. (Native)

April 11–May 30   Abundant

Modern herbals list this plant as effective treatment for sore throat and bleeding gums. Native Americans made a salve from the roots to treat sores, and a tea made from the whole plant was used to treat colds and coughs.

LEONARD'S SKULLCAP
Scutellaria parvula var. *leonardi*

MINT FAMILY
Labiatae
(Lamiaceae)

This mostly smooth, square-stemmed plant is only 4" to 8" tall. The middle and upper leaves are opposite, lanceolate, sessile, and entire. Lower leaves are short petioled and more ovate. The lipped, tubular, single, purplish flowers grow from the upper leaf axils. (Native)

May 14–May 29   Infrequent

This is the smallest of our *Scutellaria* species and is found mostly in limestone-barren areas. The genus *Scutellaria* has been widely used to treat a variety of nervous disorders.

SAMPSON'S SNAKEROOT
Psoralea psoralioides
(*Orbexilum pedunculatum* var. *psoralioides*)

PEA FAMILY
Leguminosae
(Fabaceae)

Narrow-lanceolate, untoothed, 2"- to 3"-long leaflets are in threes on this 1' to $2\frac{1}{2}$' plant. The pealike blossoms are in a dense spike on a long, smooth, slender stem above the leaves. The flowers are pinkish purple. (Native)

May 22–July 9   Infrequent

There is an account of people in the Appalachians using a tea made from the ground root of "sampson's snakeroot" to treat colic. Like so many other plants used in folk remedies, only the common name was given in the report and one cannot be certain it is *P. psoralioides* that was used.

WILD HYACINTH
Camassia scilloides

LILY FAMILY
Liliaceae

Pale blue to almost white flowers with 6 pointed "petals" (really 3 petals and 3 sepals) are in a loose raceme on a smooth stem that is from 1' to 2' tall. Leaves are basal, wide, long, and grasslike. There is a distinct crease down the center of each leaf. (Native)

April 11–April 29   Rare

Eastern Native Americans are reported to have eaten the onionlike bulbs of this species, but it apparently was not an important part of their diet. In the West, Native Americans fought extended wars over the right to harvest areas abundant in another species of *Camassia, C. quamash.*

SESSILE TRILLIUM
Trillium sessile

LILY FAMILY
Liliaceae

Like all *Trillium* species, this plant has 3 leaves, 3 sepals, and 3 petals. The leaves of this 4" to 10" plant are heavily mottled with different shades of green. The petals, which are most often maroon but may be greenish yellow,

are sessile and grow from the bases of the 3 leaves. The sepals are usually semierect. (Native)

March 1–April 21   Frequent

The plant and its roots were used by Native Americans as an eye medicine and for labor pains. It was also used as a red dye and as a love potion. One account says the leaves were eaten as greens and the roots are emetic.

SHOWY ORCHIS
Orchis spectabilis
(Galearis spectabilis)

ORCHID FAMILY
Orchidaceae

The flowers of this diminutive orchid are distinctly bicolored with a rose-purple hood above and a white-spurred lip beneath. There are 2 wide, bladelike, smooth, basal leaves. A single, small, green bract is attendant to each flower. (Native)

May 1   Rare

Not the rarest of our orchids, but still a delight to find for any wildflower enthusiast. A unique feature of this little orchid is that only the female bumblebee pollinates the flowers, whose structure requires the smooth cheeks of the female.

BLUE PHLOX
Phlox divaricata

PHLOX FAMILY
Polemoniaceae

The blue and sometimes lavender 1"-wide flowers are on a hairy, 1' to 1½' stem. The leaves are opposite, widely spaced, and narrow lanceolate. Flowers radiate from the tip of the plant and have long, thin tubes spreading into 5 flaring, wedge-shaped lobes that are sometimes notched at the centers. The stamens are completely hidden. (Native)

March 27–May 14   Frequent

This is the earliest flowering of our several *Phlox* species. *Phlox* was reported to have been used medicinally to treat digestive ailments and skin problems. They have also been used as a mild purgative.

JACOB'S-LADDER
Polemonium reptans

PHLOX FAMILY
Polemoniaceae

This plant has branched, loose clusters of ½"- to ¾"-wide, blue, bell-shaped flowers with 5 petals on the stems, which are 6" to 15" tall. The common name is derived from the shape of the leaves, which have from 5 to 15 paired leaflets on a long petiole. Stamens are white and do not project beyond the petals. (Native)

March 1–May 14   Frequent

Uses by herbalists, Native Americans, and in folk medicine include treatment for coughs, colds, fevers, bronchial problems, hemorrhoids, and tuberculosis and for the bites of poisonous snakes and insects. Folk medicinal uses most often advised mixing with copious amounts of white whiskey.

LARKSPUR
Delphinium tricorne

BUTTERCUP FAMILY
Ranunculaceae

Flowers of the Larkspur are bilaterally symmetrical with the uppermost of the 5 showy sepals elongated into an upward-pointing spur. The 4 petals are very small. The dark blue blossoms are 1" to 1½" long and in a loosely spaced cluster. The leaves are 5 parted and each part is deeply cut. (Native)

April 9–May 10   Locally Frequent

The seeds and young plants can be fatal if eaten in large quantities. This plant contains several toxic alkaloids and is a real danger to cattle. Some commercial medicines for lice include preparations from the seed of *Delphinium*.

BLUETS
Houstonia caerulea

MADDER FAMILY
Rubiaceae

Often found in large bunches, this tiny flower grows on thread-thin, 2" to 6" stems. The 4 petals are blue, but the center of the corolla has a yellow dot encircled by a white ring. There is a basal rosette of leaves with a few smaller, alternate leaves on the stems. (Native)

March 26–June 8   Frequent

Bluets, also called Eyebright, Quaker Ladies, and Innocence, are sometimes used in rock gardens and for borders. The Cherokee are reported to have used a tea made from the leaves to stop bed wetting.

SMALL BLUET
Houstonia patens
(Houstonia pusilla)

MADDER FAMILY
Rubiaceae

Small Bluets are truly small, growing only 2" to 4" tall. The basal leaves are larger than the few, tiny stem leaves. The $\frac{1}{4}$"-wide, deep blue, 4-petaled, tubular flowers have a very noticeable red or wine-colored throat. (Native)

April 6–April 11   Rare

Here is your chance to find a flower not previously listed by any professional botanist who has studied plants in the park. Around the beginning of April look for the plant in closely mowed areas of cemeteries.

WOOD-BETONY
Pedicularis canadensis
FIGWORT FAMILY
Scrophulariaceae

This low plant is 5" to 15" tall, with narrow, hairy leaves so deeply cut as to be fernlike. Flowers are tubular with long, arching hoods, which are in a conspicuously bracted, hairy, terminal, whorled cluster. The color is quite variable, usually yellow or brownish red. (Native)

March 20–May 10   Frequent

Another common name, Lousewort, comes from the erroneous belief that cattle and sheep get lice from the plant. Herbalists believe the tannin in the plant makes it useful to treat cuts and wounds. It has been used as snuff and Native Americans thought it a powerful aphrodisiac. Rabbits relish the leaves.

MARSH BLUE VIOLET
Viola cucullata
VIOLET FAMILY
Violaceae

Flowering stems are 5" to 10" tall and stand well above the heart-shaped, smooth, and toothed basal leaves. Leaves are more narrowly triangular than most other blue violets. Flowers are blue with darker centers. The shorter central petal is veined and each of the 2 side petals bear a tuft of hair. (Native)

April 13–May 14   Rare

As its common name indicates, this plant lives in moist places and is often found in dry or seasonal stream beds. Like other violets, it is high in vitamins A and C and is an excellent addition to salads or can be used as a cooked green or thickening agent for soup.

FIELD PANSY
Viola kitaibeliana
(Viola bicolor)

<small>VIOLET FAMILY</small>
Violaceae

The large, deeply cut, round-tipped stipules on this 3" to 8" branching plant are so conspicuous they may be mistaken for the leaves. The small leaves are top shaped and long petioled. The 5 petals are pale lavender and the 3 lower petals are veined with purple. Flowering stems are smooth and branch from the leaf axils. (Introduced)

April 6–April 23   Locally Frequent

This is a plant of fields and waste places and therefore is not abundant in the heavily forested areas of the park. Field Pansy was reported to have been used by Native Americans for numerous skin ailments. The practice may have been borrowed from settlers who used *V. tricolor,* another European pansy, in similar ways.

COMMON BLUE VIOLET
Viola papilionacea
(Viola sororia)

<small>VIOLET FAMILY</small>
Violaceae

Flowers are on smooth, 3" to 6" stalks, which are generally equal in length to the toothed, rough-veined, broadly heart-shaped leaves. The 2 side petals are bearded and all 3 lower petals of this violet-blue flower are veined. (Native)

March 8–May 10   Abundant

Violets can be used in sauces and soups as a thickening agent. The flowers make splendid jam, jelly, syrup, candy, and even wine. They are used to make a healthful herbal tea, and the vitamin-rich foliage is often used in salads.

BIRDFOOT VIOLET
Viola pedata

VIOLET FAMILY
Violaceae

Unlike the broad, arrow-shaped leaves of the more common violets, the leaves of this flower are finely divided into narrow segments. The segmented leaf is said to resemble a bird's foot. Also, the 5 blue, 1"- to 1 $\frac{1}{4}$"-wide petals are larger than in most other violets. The plant is 4" to 8" tall with the flower stem rising above the leaves. (Native)

April 21–May 9   Infrequent

Native Americans used violets extensively in their medical treatments to cause vomiting, as a laxative, and as a remedy for chest diseases. Their most widespread use was as an ointment for treatment of bruises, sores, and wounds.

THREE-LOBED VIOLET
Viola triloba
(*Viola palmata* var. *triloba*)

VIOLET FAMILY
Violaceae

A blue violet very easily confused with *V. palmata*. This species has deeply incised 3-parted and 5-parted leaves, but also may have heart-shaped leaves. The plant is slightly hairy. A distinguishing feature is that all 3 lower petals have tufts of hair at their bases. (Native)

April 21–May 8   Frequent

Ancient herbalists and folklore afforded violets the ability to cure a hangover, to protect one from wicked witches, and to clear the complexion. The juice can be used as a simple litmus test: an acid makes it red and a base makes it green.

JACK-IN-THE-PULPIT
Arisaema atrorubens
(Arisaema triphyllum)

ARUM FAMILY
Araceae

"Jack" is the clublike spadix encased in the "pulpit," which is an encircling spathe with a pointed hood over the pulpit. The spathe is usually striped to some degree, and the stripes may be green, white, or purplish. There are 1 or 2 distinctly 3-parted leaves. (Native)

April 4–May 30   Frequent

Native Americans sliced and thoroughly dried the bulblike corms and ground them into flour. Raw or even boiled corms will cause intense pain in the mouth because of the presence of calcium oxalate crystals. Preparations from the corms were also used as an insecticide. The red berries are relished by Wild Turkey.

GREEN DRAGON
Arisaema dracontium

ARUM FAMILY
Araceae

What is actually a single, 1' to 3' leaf is divided into 5 to 15 ovate, pointed leaflets, which are often arranged in an arch above the solitary stem. A pointed, pale-greenish spadix protrudes well beyond the pointed spathe growing under the single leaf. (Native)

May 10–June 21   Infrequent

Like the closely related Jack-in-the-Pulpit, the corm of this plant can be used for flour when prepared properly, but the needlelike crystals will injure the mouth if the corms are not properly dried. Native Americans reportedly used the corm medicinally for female ailments.

WILD GINGER
Asarum canadense

BIRTHWORT FAMILY
Aristolochiaceae

The plants are often found in dense colonies growing from shallow, creeping rootstocks that have a gingerlike odor and taste. Small, maroon, petalless, cup-shaped flowers with 3 slightly recurved and pointed sepals, appear at ground level. Shiny, heavily veined, heart-shaped leaves are borne in pairs on densely hairy 4" to 10" stems. Flowers grow from between the 2 leaf stems. (Native)

April 7–May 30   Frequent

The dried and powdered rhizome may be used as a substitute for ginger or the fresh rhizome can be candied. Native Americans used it medicinally as an antiseptic, a contraceptive, and to treat colds and coughs. A young park ranger, who shall remain anonymous, can readily confirm the emetic powers of a tea made from the roots.

BLUE COHOSH
Caulophyllum thalictroides

BARBERRY FAMILY
Berberidaceae

Botanists say the 3 compound leaves halfway up the chalky blue, 18" to 36" stem constitute a single leaf. To the layperson they appear more like 3 separate leaves. Each leaf part has Meadow-Rue-like, 3-lobed leaflets. The ½"-wide, yellowish green to purplish flowers are in a cluster. There are 6 sepals and 6 yellowish, reduced petals. The flowers are replaced by deep blue, conspicuous, berrylike seeds (Native)

March 26–May 14   Infrequent

The roots were widely used by Native Americans as an indispensable aid to childbirth and for menstrual problems. It was also used to treat rheumatism. The foliage may cause skin irritation and there are reports of children being poisoned by the pretty blue "berries."

SICKLEPOD
Arabis canadensis

MUSTARD FAMILY
Cruciferae
(Brassicaceae)

Long, down-curving seed pods are more noticeable on this 1' to 3' plant than the small clusters of
4-petaled, greenish white flowers. The flowering
stem may be lightly hairy below and smooth
above. The basal leaves are petioled, lanceolate,
and wide toothed. Upper leaves are sessile but not
clasping, tapering at each end, widely toothed,
and finely hairy. (Native)

May 16–July 7   Infrequent

Although the new growth of this plant has a noticeably disagreeable smell, the
scent is dispelled by cooking. The young shoots are supposed to be quite good when
boiled for 10 to 15 minutes in several changes of water and served like asparagus.

WILD YAM
Dioscorea quaternata

YAM FAMILY
Dioscoreaceae

In this species of Wild Yam the lower parallel-
veined, heart-shaped, and pointed leaves are in
a whorl of 4 to 7. The plant is erect below and
twining above, with upper leaves alternate. The
tiny, greenish, male and female flowers grow
from the leaf axils and are on separate plants.
The plant, including its twining upper portion,
may be from 3' to 6' tall. (Native)

April 11–June 15   Frequent

A similar species known to occur in the park,
Dioscorea villosa, has most leaves alternate, or at most, in a whorl of 3.

Dioscorea species contain the chemical diosgenin, which is used to make drugs
that treat numerous problems related to the sexual organs and to make birth
control pills. Native Americans used the plant to relieve the pain of childbirth
and for rheumatism. There is some evidence in modern science that substantiate
these uses.

AMERICAN COLUMBO
Swertia caroliniensis
(Frasera caroliniensis)

GENTIAN FAMILY
Gentianaceae

When in flower, the stem, which grows from a basal rosette of leaves, is from 4' to 7' tall with whorls of mostly 4 shiny, long-lanceolate leaves. The flowers are in a tall, pyramid-shaped panicle. There are usually 4 greenish yellow petals spotted with brownish purple. There is a conspicuous gland on each petal. (Native)

April 28–July 8   Locally Frequent

This plant is mostly a triennial, meaning it flowers in its third year. There is a report of its roots being made into a tea to treat lower abdominal ailments.

SOLOMON'S SEAL
Polygonatum biflorum

LILY FAMILY
Liliaceae

Stems of this plant are from 1' to 3' long, unbranched, gracefully arching, and have sessile, alternate, pointed-ovate leaves with a corrugated appearance. The

small, bell-shaped, greenish yellow flowers hang below the arching stem from the leaf axils in clusters of from 1 to 3. (Native)

April 20–May 30   Frequent

The early spring sprouts can be cooked like asparagus. There are accounts of the rhizome being eaten or made into a flour. Native Americans reportedly used the roots as an aphrodisiac and a contraceptive, as well as in the treatment of bruises.

CARRION-FLOWER
Smilax ecirrata

LILY FAMILY
Liliaceae
(Smilacaceae)

This Carrion-Flower is from 18" to 30" tall, erect, and has no tendrils. The long-petioled leaves are parallel veined, ovate, smooth, sharp pointed, and are in a whorl at the summit. The greenish flowers are on a separate stalk below the leaves and the umbel of flowers is usually globular in shape. Long, loose, pale bracts clasp the stem. Male and female flowers are on separate plants. (Native)

April 30–May 30   Infrequent

This plant is truly deserving of its common name. The noxious odor of the flowers attract carrion flies for pollination. Considering the smell, it is difficult to imagine using the plant for food, but the rhizomes are said to make a reasonable flour when crushed and dried.

CARRION-FLOWER
Smilax herbacea

LILY FAMILY
Liliaceae
(Smilacaceae)

Long-stemmed, ball-shaped umbels of small, greenish white flowers grow from the leaf axils on this tall, tendril-climbing vine. Leaves have 7 to 9 parallel veins, are ovate with pointed tips, and are petioled. Male and female flowers are on separate plants. (Native)

May 10–June 28   Infrequent

The flowers of this carrion flower smell even worse than those of *S. ecirrata*. Since the foul odor is present only during flowering, it is possible to understand the use of the young shoots as a substitute for asparagus.

PUTTY-ROOT ORCHID
Aplectrum hyemale

ORCHID FAMILY
Orchidaceae

In late summer, fall, and winter a single, dull green, slightly pleated 4"- to 6"long leaf with faint whitish stripes locates where this orchid will flower in the spring. The flowers are in a 8" to 16" raceme on a pale, leafless stem. The flowers are greenish yellow with a whitish, lightly toothed lip spotted with purple. (Native)

May 2–May 9   Infrequent

Upon killing a deer, Cherokee hunters are reported to have placed a piece of the root in the wound to insure that the animal would be exceptionally fat. Other Native Americans used the corms in poultices, on boils, and for respiratory problems. The common name refers to the puttylike contents of the normally paired corms.

CORAL-ROOT ORCHID
Corallorhiza wisteriana

ORCHID FAMILY
Orchidaceae

This 4" to 12" orchid has no green parts and is saprophytic. The stem and small, scalelike leaves are purplish. Flowers are in a spike and are purplish with a white lower lip, which is spotted with purple. A similar species, *C. odontorhiza,* flowers in the fall. (Native)

April 16   Infrequent

Because its color makes it extremely difficult to locate, the plant may be more abundant than believed. Native Americans used it as a sedative and herbalists used it to treat various inflammatory ailments.

LILY-LEAVED TWAYBLADE
Liparis lilifolia

ORCHID FAMILY
Orchidaceae

A 5" to 10" raceme of dainty, orchid flowers on a fleshy stem grows from between 2 clasping, glossy, oval-shaped basal leaves. Each flower is on a slim, maroon stalk and has 2 dangling threadlike sepals. The lip is a semitransparent brownish green and the spur is whitish. (Native)

May 10–June 22   Infrequent

The genus name *Liparis,* from the Greek *liparos,* meaning fat or shining, refers to the glossy, oval-shaped leaves. Any economic use of this little orchid should be precluded by its infrequency and beauty.

SQUAWROOT
Conopholis americana

BROOM-RAPE FAMILY
Orobanchaceae

A yellowish brown, unbranched, thick, fleshy stem that is from 3" to 8" tall and covered with scale-like, brownish leaves gives the young Squawroot somewhat of a pine-cone appearance. The numerous, yellowish tubular flowers are hooded and lipped and grow from the leaf axils. (Native)

April 11–June 4   Frequent

Squawroot has no green parts and is parasitic. It gets its food from the roots of trees, especially oaks. It can be grown in a wildflower garden with some difficulty and must be started from seeds sown close to oak roots.

ALUM-ROOT
Heuchera americana

<small>SAXIFRAGE FAMILY</small>
Saxifragaceae

The slim flowering stem is 1' to 3' tall, smooth, and many-branched. Tiny, green or reddish tinged, bell-like flowers with 3 minute petals hang suspended from the thin, loose branches. The stigma and the orange anthers extend beyond the sepals and petals. Leaves usually have long, smooth petioles, are mainly basal, heart shaped, and are broadly blunt toothed. (Native)

April 11–June 28   Frequent

A tea made from the leaves of this Alum-Root is reported to have been used to treat diarrhea and dysentery and as an effective gargle for sore throats.

SUMMER
FLOWERS

June 1 – July 31

SUMMER

SPIDER LILY
Hymenocallis occidentalis
(Hymenocallis caroliniana)

AMARYLLIS FAMILY
Amaryllidaceae
(Liliaceae)

This large, white flower is 3" to 5" wide. The thick flowering stem is $1\frac{1}{2}$' to 2' tall, bearing an umbel of 3 to 6 flowers. The slender, green perianth tube spreads into 6 narrow, 3"- to 4"-long "petals" (really 3 petals and 3 sepals). In the flower center there is a continuous, showy white, funnel-like membrane connecting the bases of the filaments. The leaves are basal, 1' to 2' long, and sword shaped. (Native)

July 29–September 14   Infrequent

The genus name is from the Greek *hymen,* meaning membrane, and *callos,* meaning beauty, and refers to the thin membrane connecting the filaments. Endangered in most areas because of removal for gardens, its recovery here is one of the success stories of park protection.

GINSENG
Panax quinquefolium
(Panax quinquefolius)

GINSENG FAMILY
Araliaceae

Standing strictly erect, this plant is 8" to 16" tall. The long-petioled leaves are in a whorl of 3 and are divided into 5 pointed-ovate, toothed, and petioled leaflets with the 2 lowest being smaller. The tiny, greenish white flowers are in a single, small umbel growing above the whorl of leaves and are not nearly as conspicuous as the red berries. (Native)

July 2 -   Endangered

The Chinese ascribe great medicinal and aphrodisiac properties to this plant. The extremely high prices paid for the roots have caused it to be collected to near extinction in most areas. Though most medicinal claims have no scientific basis, it may be helpful in stress-related illnesses.

WHORLED MILKWEED
Asclepias verticillata

MILKWEED FAMILY
Asclepiadaceae

Leaves on the mostly solitary, finely hairy, 1' to 2½' stems are in whorls of 3 to 7. The leaves are linear, sessile, and entire. Small umbels of numerous flowers are on short, finely hairy stalks in the leaf axils. The reflexed lobes are greenish white and the hoods are white. (Native)

July 8–August 23   Infrequent

This milkweed was reported to have been used in folk medicine in the southern states as a remedy for snake and insect bites. Native American medicine claims the milky juice of *Asclepias* will rid warts when applied to the wart only.

PALE SPIKE LOBELIA
Lobelia spicata

LOBELIA FAMILY
Campanulaceae

Lower leaves on this 1' to 2½' plant are ovate, short petioled, and somewhat wavy on the edges. Upper leaves are more linear lanceolate, sessile, and toothless. Flowers are in a long, dense, single spike, which is somewhat hairy at the base and smooth above. The blossoms are white to occasionally pale blue, tubular, sessile, and with 5 unequal lobes. (Native)

June 20–October 7   Locally Frequent

A tea made from this plant was used by Native Americans to induce vomiting. In small doses, herbalists say it is a stimulant and in large doses it is a relaxant.

JAPANESE HONEYSUCKLE
Lonicera japonica

Honeysuckle Family
Caprifoliaceae

The fragrance of the flowers is almost worth the weedy nature of this climbing vine. The plant has a hairy stem. The leaves are ovate, short petioled, opposite, and toothless. Lower leaves may be lobed. Flowers are white to pink to yellow, tubular, and 2 lipped, with long, curved stamens extending beyond the flaring lips. The upper lip is 3 lobed and the lower 2 lobed. (Introduced)

May 30–July 23   Abundant

Another honeysuckle, *Lonicera sempervirens,* has long, tubular, red flowers and perfoliate leaves.

Introduced from Asia, this invasive plant provides good cover and food for numerous wildlife species during critical winter months. In Asia it is widely used medicinally to treat colds, fevers, rheumatism, sores, and tumors. It has been proven to have antiviral and antibacterial properties. Children may enjoy sucking the nectar from the tube.

STARRY CAMPION
Silene stellata

Pink Family
Caryophyllaceae

White, 5-petaled, ¾"-wide flowers, with the tips of the petals deeply fringed are in a loose panicle on this very finely hairy, 2' to 3' plant. Upper leaves are lanceolate, pointed, sessile, and in whorls of 4. Occasional lower leaves are opposite. Note the bell-shaped calyx. (Native)

July 14–August 29   Infrequent

According to Cherokee legend, even the most venomous snake will avoid people who carry a piece of the root of this plant in their mouths. The juice was believed by both Native Americans and mountain settlers to cure snakebites.

WESTERN DAISY
Astranthium integrifolium

COMPOSITE FAMILY
Compositae
(Asteraceae)

At a distance this flower might be mistaken for the Ox-Eye Daisy, but close examination reveals many differences. This plant has spatulate leaves with smooth margins and is only 6" to 16" tall. The flower heads are about 1" wide and the yellow center is concave. Also, the white rays may be tinged with pink. (Native)

June 12–July 12   Rare

This is our only representative of the genus *Astranthium* and it is quite rare in the park. The genus name is from the Greek *astron,* meaning star, and *anthos,* meaning flower. The species name refers to the smooth margins of the leaves.

GREAT INDIAN PLANTAIN
Cacalia muhlenbergii
(*Arnoglossum muehlenbergii*)

COMPOSITE FAMILY
Compositae
(Asteraceae)

This very large plant is 3' to 9' tall, with a grooved and angled stem. Leaves are 3" to 10" wide, roundish in outline, unevenly lobed, toothed, and petioled. Flower heads are in wide, flat-topped clusters and are greenish white. It is similar to *C. atriplicifolia,* but leaves and stem do not have a whitened gloss and leaves are larger and less angular on the lobes. (Native)

June 15–August 25   Locally Frequent

Great Indian Plantain was highly treasured by Native Americans to treat cuts, bruises, wounds, and cancers. A poultice made of the leaves was plastered over the effected area to draw out the "poisons."

DAISY FLEABANE
Erigeron annuus

COMPOSITE FAMILY
Compositae
(Asteraceae)

A terminally branched plant, 1' to 4' tall, with numerous (40 to 70) thin, white to purplish tinged rays on the ½"-wide flower heads. Stems are hairy, as are all leaves except those on the flowering stem. Basal leaves are ovate, long petioled, coarsely toothed, and sessile. Flowering stem leaves are linear lanceolate, mostly toothless, and sessile. (Native)

May 28–September 10   Abundant

A very similar plant, *Erigeron strigosus,* is shorter, less hairy, and has linear, almost toothless, middle and upper leaves.

A local farmer whose Orchard Grass hayfield was badly infested with "white top" was overheard to say in resignation, "It'll beat a snowball I reckon." In fact, it is reported to be a preferred forage for sheep.

GREEN-STEMMED JOE-PYE-WEED
Eupatorium purpureum

COMPOSITE FAMILY
Compositae
(Asteraceae)

This Joe-Pye-Weed has a smooth, sometimes purplish stem, which is from 4' to 10' tall. The stem is not hollow, is mostly green, and has a purplish ring at the leaf junctions. Leaves are ovate lanceolate, toothed, petioled, 4" to 12" long, and are in whorls of 3 or 4. Flowers heads are pinkish, with 5 to 8 tubular flowers in the heads that are arranged in a branching terminal cluster. (Native)

July 19–October 5   Infrequent

One group of Native Americans believed that if a man carried a piece of this plant in his mouth when he went courting, he was certain of gaining the favor of the lady. Herbalists use the plant to treat urinary infections and kidney stones.

ROUND-LEAVED THOROUGHWORT
Eupatorium rotundifolium

<small>COMPOSITE FAMILY</small>
Compositae
(Asteraceae)

The stem is finely hairy and from 1' to 3' tall. Leaves are opposite, toothed, sessile, and broadly ovate, with the lower leaves being almost heart shaped and clasping. Flowering stems branch at the summit and have 5 or more white florets in the heads. There are usually 3 rows of bracts, with the outer ones being the shortest. (Native)

July 3–September 18   Infrequent

Two similar plants are *Eupatorium sessilifolium,* which has a smooth stem and lanceolate, sessile leaves, and *E. perfoliatum* with rough, deeply veined, perfoliate leaves.

The uses of this plant in folk medicine are probably hidden in the numerous and confusing common names of the several *Eupatorium* species. A reported use of this particular *Eupatorium* was to treat tuberculosis. Moonshine was often used in medicinal preparations of this plant, which may explain its widespread use and effectiveness.

GALINSOGA
Galinsoga ciliata
(Galinsoga quadriradiata)

<small>COMPOSITE FAMILY</small>
Compositae
(Asteraceae)

This is a branching, 4" to 15" plant with hairy stems. Leaves are ovate, short petioled to sessile, and toothed. Flower heads are very small, being only about $\frac{1}{4}$" to $\frac{3}{8}$" wide. Note the 5 very tiny, 3-lobed, white rays. (Introduced)

June 30–July 17   Infrequent

Although uncommon in the park, this plant can become a serious weed in gardens. In southeastern Asia, however, it is welcomed and has become an important part of the people's diet as a cooked green.

WILD QUININE
Parthenium integrifolium

COMPOSITE FAMILY
Compositae
(Asteraceae)

Flower heads are numerous in a terminal cluster on this 1' to 4' plant. There are usually 5 notched, white rays in each head, but they are relatively minute, and several times smaller than the subtending bracts. Leaves are lanceolate, toothed, and hairy on both surfaces. Upper leaves are sessile, while those below are increasingly petioled. (Native)

June 16–September 3   Locally Frequent

Native Americans used the roots for kidney and urinary tract problems, the leaves to treat burns, and the flowers to treat fever. Wild Quinine may cause allergies and skin irritation in susceptible individuals.

NARROW-LEAF WHITE-TOP ASTER
Sericocarpus linifolius
(Aster solidagineus)

COMPOSITE FAMILY
Compositae
(Asteraceae)

Note that the heads have only 4 to 5 white rays. The plant is 1' to 2½' tall and hairless. Leaves are linear, rounded at the tips, and narrowed at the base. The leaves are smooth margined. Outer bracts have somewhat reflexed, green tips. (Native)

June 21–September 4   Infrequent

Although the common name indicates this plant is an *Aster,* it is not a member of this genus. The true genus name is from the Greek *sericos,* meaning silky, and *carpos,* meaning fruit, and refers to the very silky achenes.

WILD POTATO-VINE
Ipomoea pandurata

MORNING-GLORY FAMILY
Convolvulaceae

This Morning-Glory has a usually smooth, trailing vine, which is 2' to 12' long. Its leaves are broadly ovate, pointed at the tip, and heart shaped at the base. The leaves are single, petioled, entire, and up to 6" long. The flowers are 5-lobed, white, tubular, and have a purple throat. (Native)

May 30–August 23   Frequent

The main root of this plant can be enormous, often weighing over 25 pounds. Native Americans found the difficulty of digging the huge roots worth the effort and, despite a slightly bitter taste, ate them baked or boiled. The roots were also used medicinally for coughs, asthma, headache, and as a laxative.

FLOWERING SPURGE
Euphorbia corollata

SPURGE FAMILY
Euphorbiaceae

This is a slim, 1' to 3' plant with alternate stem leaves and a whorl of smaller leaves above, from which the flowering stems branch. Leaves are oblong, sessile, and entire. The white "petals" look like a tiny, 5-petaled flower but are really bracts with the true flowers inside. Note the milky sap of the broken stem. (Native)

June 20–September 10   Frequent

The seeds are eaten by doves, quail, and other birds. The milky sap may cause skin irritation, although herbalists have suggested that the sap can be used to treat warts. Native Americans used a root tea as a laxative and to treat pinworms.

BROADLEAF WATERLEAF
Hydrophyllum canadense

WATERLEAF FAMILY
Hydrophyllaceae

This is a low, 6" to 20" plant with broad, 3"- to 10"-wide, long-petioled, and sharply toothed leaves that have 5 to 9 deep lobes. Upper and lower leaves are similar, with the upper being smaller. Flowers are white and in loose cymes below the leaves. The filaments noticeably exceed the length of the petals. (Native)

June 15–July 19   Frequent

Several early writers report that Native Americans ate the leaves both raw and as a cooked green. There are also reports that the plant was used to treat snakebite and poison ivy.

WHITE BERGAMOT
Monarda clinopodia

MINT FAMILY
Labiatae
(Lamiaceae)

This mostly smooth-stemmed plant is about 2' tall. The corolla tubes are white and do not have purple spots on the lower lip. Also note the tufts of hair on the distinct, $\frac{1}{4}$"-long petioles on the opposite, lanceolate, toothed leaves. Bracts subtending the heads have mostly whitish centers. (Native)

May 30–July 23   Infrequent

As with other *Monarda* species, the leaves steeped for 5 to 10 minutes make a passable tea. Characteristics of the leaves and corolla are somewhat variable, making this species of *Monarda* difficult to identify with certainty.

SLENDER MOUNTAIN-MINT
Pycnanthemum flexuosum

MINT FAMILY
Labiatae
(Lamiaceae)

Leaves on the mostly smooth, $1\frac{1}{2}$' to $2\frac{1}{2}$' stem are linear and sharp pointed with leafy branches growing from the upper leaf axils. Clusters of minute, 5-lobed, tubular, white flowers are terminal on the plant. (Native)

June 30–August 10   Frequent

Slender Mountain-Mint has an exceptionally strong minty smell. Although either the fresh or dried leaves of this plant are recommended for making tea, the minty flavor is very pungent and may be an acquired taste.

HOARY MOUNTAIN-MINT
Pycnanthemum incanum

MINT FAMILY
Labiatae
(Lamiaceae)

Terminal flower clusters on this mostly smooth, or very finely haired, $1\frac{1}{2}$' to 3' plant are subtended by leaves that are distinctly white. Other leaves may be whitish below and are lanceolate, toothed, and petioled. The small flowers are tubular, $\frac{1}{4}$"-long, white to pinkish, and have purple spots. (Native)

July 16–September 10   Frequent

All of the mountain mints have similar properties and were used by Native Americans to relieve gas, promote sweating, ease cramps, and as a stimulant. They were reported to have used the plants also to treat headaches, fevers, and colds.

WHITE TICK-TREFOIL
Desmodium pauciflorum

PEA FAMILY
Leguminosae
(Fabaceae)

This is a somewhat reclining plant with 1' to 2' long stems. The 3-parted leaves are alternate with pointed-ovate leaflets. The terminal leaflet is slightly wider and larger. Leaves are entire and long petioled. The pealike, white flowers are in few-flowered terminal racemes. (Native)

July 20–September 10   Frequent

Tick-Trefoils get their name from the leaves, which are divided into 3 leaflets. This species is our only truly white tick-trefoil. Bobwhite quail are about the only wildlife known to make any considerable use of this plant.

WHITE SWEET CLOVER
Melilotus alba
(Melilotus officinalis)

PEA FAMILY
Leguminosae
(Fabaceae)

This plant is 3' to 10' tall, smooth stemmed, and branching. Leaves are long petioled and divided into 3 short-stalked, tapered, blunt-tipped, narrow, finely toothed, and finely hairy leaflets. Flowers are white and are in long-stalked, slender racemes. (Introduced)

May 30–August 23   Frequent

A very similar plant is *Melilotus officinalis,* which has yellow flowers.

First introduced in the eighteenth century as bee forage, *M. alba* is now a hay crop for cattle. It can be eaten in salads, as a cooked green, or as a flavoring. The protein-rich seeds may be used in soups. It is of considerable value to wildlife, especially game birds. The plant is commonly used in commercial potpourri mixtures.

WHITE CLOVER
Trifolium repens

PEA FAMILY
Leguminosae
(Fabaceae)

Branches of this plant are 4" to 12" long and are creeping, often rooting at the nodes. The leaves are on long petioles and the 3 very short-stalked leaflets are somewhat inversely heart shaped and very finely toothed. Flowers are white, or white tinged with pink, and arranged in heads on tall, thin, flowering stems. (Introduced)

May 30–July 19   Frequent

A similar, but extremely rare, native clover is *Trifolium reflexum,* which has a red standard and white wings and keel.

This is an important food plant for birds and mammals. The dried flowers and seeds can be used to make flour. The dried flowers make a healthful tea and the foliage can be boiled and eaten as a cooked green. It is an important hay, pasture, and lawn plant.

RAMP
Allium tricoccum

LILY FAMILY
Liliaceae

Early in the spring, the long-lanceolate, 8" to 10" leaves appear and have a strong onionlike odor when bruised. By flowering time, however, the leaves have completely disappeared. The umbel of $\frac{1}{4}$"-long, greenish white flowers are on a completely naked, 6" to 12" stalk. The flowering stalk grows from an onionlike bulb. (Native)

June 22   Rare

This plant is celebrated at the Ramp Festival in Cosby, Tennessee, each spring where the faithful gather to consume large quantities. The odor of the cooking plants is overwhelming and eating them will provide a "true test of friendship." Ramps are said to prevent colds. (Eat them and people with a cold won't get close enough to give it to you.)

YUCCA
Yucca filamentosa

LILY FAMILY
Liliaceae
(Agavaceae)

Another common name, Needle-and-Thread, refers to the 1'- to 2½'-long, linear, sharply pointed, thick basal rosette of rough, evergreen leaves that have curling, threadlike hairs on the smooth margins. The flowers are borne on a single, woody, 2' to 10' stem and are in a large panicle with numerous cup-shaped, 1½"-long, white blossoms with 3 petals and 3 nearly identical sepals. (Native)

June 15–July 7   Infrequent

Native Americans are said to have powdered the roots and used the powder to stun fish. They used the roots to treat skin sores and the juice from the stems as a soap. A strong fiber can be made from the leaves and the flowers are said to be good in salads.

ENCHANTER'S NIGHTSHADE
Circaea quadrisulcata
(*Circaea lutetiana* ssp. *canadensis*)

EVENING-PRIMROSE FAMILY
Onagraceae

The flower has 2 sepals, 2 petals, and 2 stamens on this smooth, 1' to 2' plant. The tiny petals are white, deeply notched at their tips, and only about ¼" wide. Note the tall racemes. Leaves are opposite, broadly lanceolate, pointed, petioled, and irregularly pointed-toothed. (Native)

June 21–July 14   Frequent

The genus name is from Circe, the enchantress in Greek mythology who turned Ulysses' men into pigs. However, Mercury gave Ulysses a magic herb that protected him from Circe's power. The reason why the plant is named after Circe has been lost. Could this be the magic herb?

RATTLESNAKE-PLANTAIN
Goodyera pubescens

ORCHID FAMILY
Orchidaceae

A distinctive identifying feature of this flower is the basal rosette of 1"- to 3"-long, seemingly evergreen leaves with white veins running in both directions. The solitary flowering stalk is hairy and from 6" to 20" tall with a long, dense, terminal spike of tiny, dull white, orchid flowers. (Native)

July 16–August 29   Infrequent

There are accounts of Native American women rubbing themselves with this plant as a love charm. Herbalists and Native Americans have recommended the root to treat sores, burns, skin problems, and insect bites.

EARLY LADIES'-TRESSES
Spiranthes vernalis

ORCHID FAMILY
Orchidaceae

This little orchid is about 12" tall and the leaves are few, mostly basal, and linear lanceolate. The creamy white flowers are in a spike and are arranged in a single spiral. The lower lip is crisped and has yellowish ribs along the center. (Native)

July 10–July 23   Rare

This is the earliest flowering of the five *Spiranthes* species in the park. *Vernalis* in the specific name, meaning of the spring, implies that it flowers much earlier than it actually does. Although there are over 30,000 species of orchids known worldwide, we have fewer than two dozen different orchids in the park.

LOPSEED
Phryma leptostachya

LOPSEED FAMILY
Phrymaceae
(Verbenaceae)

The common name comes from the way the calyx, after flowering, bends to lie against the flowering stem. Flowers are purplish, about $\frac{1}{4}$" long, and tubular with lobed lips. They appear in pairs on 1 or more thin, 3" to 6" stems branching from the upper leaf axils. The plant is $1\frac{1}{2}$' to 3' tall and the leaves are pointed ovate, coarsely toothed, sessile above, and short petioled below. (Native)

July 7–August 19   Frequent

Lopseed is somewhat unusual in that this is the only species in the family *Phrymaceae* and is found both in Asia and North America. It has reportedly been used as an insecticide. Touch mature seed cases still attached to the plant and watch how far the seed are thrown.

VIRGINIA KNOTWEED
Tovara virginiana
(*Polygonum virginianum*)

BUCKWHEAT FAMILY
Polygonaceae

Note the sheaths at each leaf junction on this 2' to 4' plant. Leaves are broad, pointed ovate, short petioled, alternate, entire, and often somewhat crowded together just under the flowering stem. Flowers are inconspicuous, greenish white, generously spaced, and in a tall, flexible spike. (Native)

July 5–September 30   Frequent

Another common name is Jumpseed, referring to the fancied way the mature seeds "jump" from the plant when touched. This species is our only representative of the genus, which is also found in Asia.

SPOTTED WINTERGREEN
Chimaphila maculata

WINTERGREEN FAMILY
Pyrolaceae

This little 4" to 8" plant has somewhat leathery, evergreen leaves in whorls on its stem. The leaves are conspicuously marked with white on the midrib and along the beginnings of the lateral veins. Leaves are lanceolate and 1" to 3" long, with sharp but widely separated teeth. The waxy white or whitish pink, $\frac{1}{2}$"-wide, recurved, 5-petaled flowers are nodding in a sparse terminal cluster. (Native)

June 12–July 6   Frequent

The genus *Chimaphila* is best known as an ingredient in root beer. Native Americans used, and modern herbalists continue to use, Spotted Wintergreen to treat colds, urinary ailments, and the aches and pains of rheumatism.

INDIAN PIPE
Monotropa uniflora

WINTERGREEN FAMILY
Pyrolaceae
(Monotropaceae)

A single, nodding, white flower on this 3" to 10" plant, which has no green parts, gives it the appearance of a pipe. The stem is white and the leaves are reduced to white, somewhat transparent, scalelike structures clasping the stem. The flower stands erect and may turn blackish as it matures. (Native)

July 12–August 13   Rare

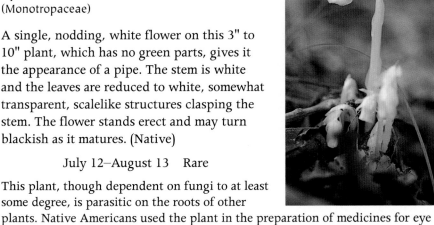

This plant, though dependent on fungi to at least some degree, is parasitic on the roots of other plants. Native Americans used the plant in the preparation of medicines for eye ailments. Its use was probably influenced by the fact that the juice is clear.

TALL ANEMONE
Anemone virginiana

BUTTERCUP FAMILY
Ranunculaceae

Basal leaves on this hairy, 2' to 3' plant are long petioled and 3-divided to the midrib. The lobes are irregularly cleft and sharp toothed. Stem leaves are similar with shorter petioles. Flowering stems branch at the whorl of stem leaves and the individual flowering stems are exceptionally tall with a single, 1¼"-wide, greenish white, 5-petaled flower. The "petals" are really sepals. (Native)

June 21–August 17   Frequent

Tall Anemone is poisonous to livestock. However, as in other members of the Buttercup Family, its taste is so violently bitter that cattle probably won't eat it. Native Americans used the plant to drain mucus from respiratory passages, to induce vomiting, and as an astringent.

TALL MEADOW RUE
Thalictrum polygamum
(*Thalictrum pubescens*)

BUTTERCUP FAMILY
Ranunculaceae

Growing from 3' to 10' tall, this is a smooth, branching plant with large, plumelike, leafy panicles of tiny, white flowers. The bushy, white, threadlike stamens provide the plume effect. The leaves are twice divided into rounded, 3-lobed leaflets. The plant has both staminate and pistillate flowers. (Native)

July 19–August 11   Infrequent

Thalictrum revolutum is a similar plant, which is mostly shorter, and has a purplish stem and minute, glandular hairs beneath the leaves.

Native Americans had many medicinal uses for *Thalictrum* species, among them the cure of snakebite, reduction of fever, cure of cramps, and as a diuretic. It was also smoked to bring luck in hunting and romance.

GOAT'S-BEARD
Aruncus dioicus

ROSE FAMILY
Rosaceae

No goat's beard ever looked like this very large, plumelike panicle of tiny, almost sessile, 5-petaled, white flowers on a branching 3' to 5' plant. The leaves are twice pinnately compound; the leaflets are pointed-ovate and toothed, and the paired ones are more rounded on one side than on the other. (Native)

May 30–June 30   Infrequent

Note that there are both male and female flowers on the same plant. It is reported that Native Americans found for this plant such diverse uses as an herbal bath for swollen feet and a compress for insect stings.

WHITE AVENS
Geum canadense

ROSE FAMILY
Rosaceae

This avens is hairy, branching, and from $1\frac{1}{2}$' to $2\frac{1}{2}$' tall. Terminal on the branches are $\frac{1}{2}$"-wide flowers with 5 downward-curving sepals and 5 white petals. Basal leaves are long petioled, 3-parted with 2 pairs of small, narrow leaflets and a single, much larger, terminal leaflet. Stem leaves are nearly sessile, lanceolate, and more equal in size. All leaves are sharply toothed. (Native)

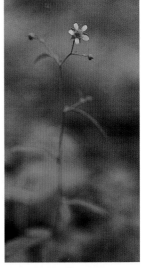

June 21–August 29   Frequent

A somewhat similar plant is *Geum vernum,* which is shorter, has yellow flowers, and less divided basal leaves.

The fruits of this plant are covered with hooked appendages that adhere to fur or clothing. Those who have had to pick the burrs from their socks know how effective this dispersal mechanism is. Native Americans used the plant for such things as dysentery, colic, asthma, sore throat, and uterine hemorrhage.

SHINING BEDSTRAW
Galium concinnum

MADDER FAMILY
Rubiaceae

This low, branching plant is 6" to 18" tall, with the edges of stems and leaves slightly rough. Leaves are in whorls of 6, linear, narrowed at the base, and blunt at the apex. The minute flowers are numerous, white, and in wide cymes. The fruit is smooth. (Native)

June 22–August 19   Frequent

Native Americans used this plant in a tea to treat urinary ailments and to treat the sickness known to white settlers as the "ague," which is marked by attacks of chills, fever, and sweating.

FRAGRANT BEDSTRAW
Galium triflorum

MADDER FAMILY
Rubiaceae

This species of *Galium* is more re-clining than *G. concinnum,* but leaf margins and petioles are also slightly rough. Leaves are in whorls of 6, lanceolate, and sessile. This plant is 3-branched with 3 flowers on each stem. Flowers are greenish white. The fruit has hooked hairs. (Native)

June 22–July 16   Frequent

A similar plant is *Galium tinctorium,* which has 3-lobed flowers.

The hooked hairs catch on the fur of passing animals for dispersal. The name "bedstraw" is from a quite old use of *Galium* as a mattress filler, and this species is especially sweet scented when dried.

ALUM-ROOT
Heuchera parviflora
var. *rugelii*
(*Heuchera parviflora*
var. *parviflora*)

Saxifrage Family
Saxifragaceae

Basal leaves on this 5" to 20"
plant are round in outline with
a somewhat heart-shaped base.

They are also widely shallow lobed with sharp teeth that come to a needlelike point. Petioles and stems are hairy. The tiny flowers have 5 white petals
and the styles protrude outward. (Native)

July 29–August 25   Rare

This particular species of *Heuchera* is found only on the sandstone bluffs along
the Pottsville escarpment. The "Devil's Den" area on the McCoy Hollow Trail is
such a place. Native Americans used the roots of *Heuchera* as a poultice on
wounds and sores.

ALUM-ROOT
Heuchera villosa

Saxifrage Family
Saxifragaceae

The 1' to 2½' stem on this Alum-
Root is very brown-hairy. The
leaves are oval, deeply 7- to 9-
lobed, toothed on the lobes,
hairy on the margins and veins
beneath, mostly basal, and long
petioled, and the lobes often
overlap at the petiole. The long,
thin flowering stem has a panicle of tiny, whitish flowers whose stamens extend beyond the corolla. (Native)

May 30–July 20   Locally Frequent

The common name of Alum-Root probably came from the similar uses of this
plant and those of Alum. The root of *Heuchera* was used as a styptic, an agent
that stops bleeding by constricting the blood vessels.

WILD HYDRANGEA
Hydrangea arborescens

<small>SAXIFRAGE FAMILY</small>
Saxifragaceae
(Hydrangeaceae)

This is a common, showy, 4' to 10' shrub. The leaves are very broadly ovate, but pointed, and have slender petioles and sharp teeth. Flowers are in 2"- to 5"-wide, umbrella-shaped corymbs. The showy, greenish white flowers have 3 to 4 petals and may be few or may cover the entire cluster. (Native)

June 13–September 6   Frequent

Appalachian folk medicine prescribes the bark from this plant for a poultice to treat "risins." Herbalists and Native Americans considered this an excellent plant to treat kidney stones. Wild Hydrangea is reported to be toxic under certain conditions.

MOTH MULLEIN
Verbascum blattaria

<small>FIGWORT FAMILY</small>
Scrophulariaceae

Although the raceme of flowers may be from 1' to 2' long on this 2' to 4' plant, only a few of the 1"-wide blossoms are mature at any one time. The flowers may be white or yellow with brownish purple marks on the back sides. Stamens have noticeably purplish hairs and the styles are extended and curved. Leaves are almost triangular and the smaller upper leaves seem to clasp. (Introduced)

June 13–July 19   Infrequent

This is but one of five species of *Verbascum* that have found their way here from Europe. Old herbal remedies use *Verbascum* to treat numerous cold and respiratory problems and as a poultice for wounds.

HAIRY ANGELICA
Angelica venenosa

<small>PARSLEY FAMILY</small>
Umbelliferae
(Apiaceae)

A tall, 3' to 6' plant with the upper parts having dense, very short, whitish hairs. The very lowest leaves are compound, 2- or 3-divided into lanceolate, finely toothed leaflets. The long leaf petioles are thick and the petioles clasp the stalk. Leaf size is reduced upward until the uppermost may consist of only a stemmed sheath. Tiny flowers are white and in flat-topped umbels. (Native)

July 14–August 17   Infrequent

Although one should be wary of any member of *Umbelliferae,* this species was cultivated by some Native Americans and used to relieve intestinal gas, for colic, to kill lice, and for excessive menstruation. It is also said to improve the taste of hams when hogs feed on it.

WATER HEMLOCK
Cicuta maculata

<small>PARSLEY FAMILY</small>
Umbelliferae
(Apiaceae)

Water Hemlock is a 3' to 6' branching plant whose stems are usually streaked with purple. Its leaves are twice or three times divided and petioled, with sheaths

on the petioles. The leaflets are lanceolate and sharp toothed. Tiny, white flowers are in umbels, and under a hand lens the 5 petals can be seen to be broad at the tips and slightly notched. (Native)

June 30–August 15   Infrequent

POISONOUS! Water Hemlock is probably our most violently poisonous plant. A single mouthful can be lethal. Symptoms of poisoning include violent convulsions, frothing at the mouth, blindness, vomiting, diarrhea, hard breathing, and extreme pain.

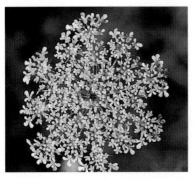

QUEEN ANNE'S LACE
Daucus carota

PARSLEY FAMILY
Umbelliferae
(Apiaceae)

The stem on this 1' to 4' plant is very coarsely hairy. The leaves are very finely divided and deeply cut into a lacy appearance. The name, however, comes from the broad, flat-topped, 2" to 4" umbels of innumerable, tiny, white flowers forming an intricate lace appearance. A freshly blossomed umbel has a single small reddish purple flower in its center and an older umbel folds upward from the outside to form a "bird nest." (Native)

June 18–September 13   Abundant

The name comes from its use in fashionable headdresses and bouquets in the seventeenth and eighteenth centuries. There is supporting evidence for its use as a poultice for burns, as an aid for intestinal gas, and as a source of vitamin A. It is also reported to rid worms. Contact with the wet leaves may cause skin irritation. Its roots are edible and the cultivated carrot is derived from this species.

BUTTON-SNAKEROOT
Eryngium yuccifolium

PARSLEY FAMILY
Umbelliferae
(Apiaceae)

Sometimes called Rattlesnake-Master, this is a distinctive, stiff, smooth plant, reaching 4' to 5' in height. There is a cluster of 1'- to 2½'-long, parallel-veined leaves at the base with spaciously separated spinelike teeth. Upper leaves are similar but few, shorter, and clasping. Flowers are whitish and in dense rounded heads, which are about 1" in diameter. (Native)

July 2–July 29   Rare

White settlers borrowed the use of this plant for treatment of venereal disease from the Native Americans, who also used it to treat snakebite, worms, impotence, and to cause vomiting, perhaps in their ceremonial cleansing. Woodland period moccasins found in Mammoth Cave were made from the fibers of this plant.

WOOD-NETTLE
Laportea canadensis

NETTLE FAMILY
Urticaceae

Bearing both male and female flowers, this plant has the stinging hairs common on other nettles. The plant is 2' to 3' tall with tiny, white to pinkish flowers growing in loose compound cymes from the leaf axils. Leaves are heavily veined, 2" to 5" wide, sharp-pointed ovate, sharp toothed, and petioled. (Native)

July 14–August 17   Infrequent

There is archaeological evidence that Native Americans used fiber from this and other *Urticaceae* to make thread and fabric dating back nearly 2000 years. The leaves are high in vitamins and minerals, and cooking renders them suitable for greens, soups, and a passable tea.

WHITE VERVAIN
Verbena urticifolia

VERVAIN FAMILY
Verbenaceae

The stem is somewhat fine-hairy, 4-angled, 3' to 5' tall, and terminally branched. Flowers are very small, tubular, white to pale blue, and clustered in tight spikes. Leaves are opposite, toothed, pointed lanceolate, with rounded bases and short petioles. (Native)

July 6–August 26   Frequent

Native Americans, settlers, and herbalists agree on the use of this plant to counteract the effects of poison ivy. The seeds are eaten by several song and game birds and the plant is plentiful enough to be of significant value to wildlife.

YELLOW TOUCH-ME-NOT
Impatiens pallida

TOUCH-ME-NOT FAMILY
Balsaminaceae

Very similar to the Spotted Touch-Me-Not, but flowers are yellow, sometimes spotted with reddish brown, and they are larger, up to 1¼" long. Also, the spur is shorter on the "windsock"-shaped flowers. The branching plant is up to 5' tall, with a smooth, watery stem and alternate, ovate, and toothed leaves. (Native)

June 30–August 15   Infrequent

Both *I. pallida* and *I. capensis* were widely used by Native Americans and in folk medicine to prevent and treat poison ivy. They also used it to relieve the discomfort of insect bites, nettle stings, and various skin problems of fungal origin. The name refers to the audibly violent bursting of the mature seedpods, which expel the seeds when touched.

PRICKLY PEAR CACTUS
Opuntia humifusa

CACTUS FAMILY
Cactaceae

Our only cactus. The stems are flattened, fleshy, jointed pads and the terminal pad is usually more oval in shape. Its leaves are the fleshy-based spines. Large, showy, 2½"- to 3½"-wide flowers have 10 to 12 yellow petals, often with a reddish orange center. (Native)

June 16–July 6   Infrequent

Though our cactus is not very appealing, it is quite edible. The pads can be deep fried or roasted and the fruit pulp can be dipped out to be eaten raw or made into a jelly. The seeds may be used to thicken soup or ground to make a usable flour. Native Americans are said to have used the juice to treat warts.

SPANISH NEEDLES
Bidens bipinnata

COMPOSITE FAMILY
Compositae
(Asteraceae)

This plant is 6" to 30" tall. The petioled leaves are so deeply incised into toothed segments that they appear somewhat fernlike. The numerous heads may have 3 or 4 short, yellow rays. Note that the rays may be absent. The linear seedlike fruits are tipped with 4 sharply barbed spines. (Native)

July 29–September 19   Frequent

Another common name, Beggar-Lice, refers to the barbed seeds, which are eaten by Wood Ducks, quail, and numerous song birds. Native Americans used the plant as an antiworm medicine.

LARGE COREOPSIS
Coreopsis major

COMPOSITE FAMILY
Compositae
(Asteraceae)

There are opposite, sessile leaves, each with 3 lanceolate, untoothed leaflets on this 1' to 3' plant. Flower heads are 1" to 2" wide with 6 to 10 bright yellow rays and a yellow disk. Inner and outer bracts are of equal length. (Native)

June 13–July 27   Infrequent

The leaves appear to be in whorls of 6, but close examination shows there are really only 2 sessile leaves, each divided into 3 leaflets. Native Americans are reported to have used some *Coreopsis* species to treat diarrhea and to induce vomiting.

PURPLE-HEADED SNEEZEWEED
Helenium nudiflorum
(*Helenium flexuosum*)

COMPOSITE FAMILY
Compositae
(Asteraceae)

The yellow rays on the 1½"-wide heads, which droop from the dark brown cone of florets, are wedge shaped and 3-toothed at their tips. Lower leaves are pointed spatulate and toothed, and petioles are winged. Upper leaves are narrow lanceolate, entire, and sessile. Note the wings on the 1½' to 3' stems. (Native)

July 16–October 2   Infrequent

The common name may have come from a reported use by Native Americans as an agent to cause sneezing to treat inflammation of the nose and air passages. Scientists have some interest in this genus because of reported antitumor properties.

WOODLAND SUNFLOWER
Helianthus divaricatus

COMPOSITE FAMILY
Compositae
(Asteraceae)

This is a slender, smooth-stalked, 2' to 5' plant with 2"-wide flower heads on sparingly branched terminal stems. There are 8 to 15 yellow rays. Leaves are 3-veined, opposite, nearly sessile or short-petioled, lanceolate, tapering evenly to a point, and rounded at the base. The leaves are shallow toothed, rough-hairy above, and short soft-hairy below. (Native)

July 10–September 6   Infrequent

A more abundant but similar sunflower is *Helianthus hirsutus,* which has a rough, stiff-hairy stem.

Though much smaller than the seeds of commercial sunflowers, the seeds of this species are relished by numerous song and game birds. The sunflower was the Incan symbol of the sun and is the national flower of Peru.

FALSE SUNFLOWER
Heliopsis helianthoides

COMPOSITE FAMILY
Compositae
(Asteraceae)

Flower heads are 1½" to 2½" wide. The 10 or more rays are yellow and slightly notched at the tips. The plant is 3' to 5' tall and smooth with branching flowering stems. Leaves are opposite, coarsely toothed, petioled, and pointed ovate to lanceolate above. (Native)

July 16–October 2   Frequent

This woodland plant is easily mistaken for a sunflower. The scientific name comes from the Greek *helios,* meaning sun, and *opsis,* meaning appearance, and refers to this plant's likeness to the sunflowers. Unlike the true sunflowers, the rays of *Heliopsis* do not drop off in age but remain, dry and papery, in the head.

WILD LETTUCE
Lactuca canadensis

COMPOSITE FAMILY
Compositae
(Asteraceae)

Leaf shape on this 3' to 10' plant is extremely variable. The stem is smooth and may have a whitish film. The numerous yellow, dandelion-like flower heads are in a long panicle. Generally, the basal leaves are long and narrow lanceolate in outline, deeply and widely cut, toothed and tapering to the stalk. Upper leaves are less cut as they ascend the stem until those just below the panicle are small, entire, lanceolate, and sessile. (Native)

July 3–August 16   Infrequent

The young leaves of Wild Lettuce are good in salads and even the older leaves are said to be superb cooked as a potherb. The seeds are eagerly sought by both game and song birds. Native Americans used the plant as a pain reliever and sedative, and the sap was used to treat skin ailments.

SMALL-FLOWERED LEAFCUP
Polymnia canadensis

COMPOSITE FAMILY
Compositae
(Asteraceae)

This is a sticky-hairy plant, growing up to 5' tall and branches at
the top. Its leaves are up to 10"
long and deeply cut into angular
and toothed lobes, with the upper
being arrow shaped and toothed. All leaves are petioled. Flower heads are
few and only about ½" wide with few, whitish yellow rays, though rays are
often absent. The plant has a heavy odor. (Native)

July 19–August 25   Infrequent

The genus is named for the muse Polyhymnia. This species probably shares
those properties that caused its close relative, *P. uvedalia,* to be widely used to
treat noncancerous breast maladies by Native Americans.

BEAR'S FOOT
Polymnia uvedalia
(Smallanthus uvedalia)

COMPOSITE FAMILY
Compositae
(Asteraceae)

This is a large, rough-
hairy, branching plant
from 3' to 9' tall. Its leaves,
which may be up to 1'
long, are opposite, broadly ovate in outline, angularly lobed, slightly hairy
on both surfaces, wing petioled below, and sessile above. The few, 1½"- to
3"-wide flower heads have 10 to 15 yellow rays, which often have 3-toothed
tips. (Native)

July 16–August 23   Infrequent

Bear's Foot is reported to be valuable as a treatment in medical conditions in-
volving the spleen. Its greatest potential, however, may be as an ingredient in
preparations to promote the growth of hair when applied externally.

PRAIRIE CONEFLOWER
Ratibida pinnata

COMPOSITE FAMILY
Compositae
(Asteraceae)

Four to 10 yellow rays, which are up to 3" long
and toothed at the top, hang downward from the
cone. The cone is gray when young, turning
brown with age. The plant is hairy and up to 4'
tall. Its leaves are extremely deeply cut into 3 to 7
lobes. Lower lobes may be toothed or cleft and
upper lobes are nearly smooth margined. (Native)

June 17–August 10   Infrequent

Most species of this genus are found in the plains,
often being confused with members of the genus
Rudbeckia. The bruised receptacle of a fresh plant emits an aniselike odor.
Leaves of some western species were reported to have been used by Native
Americans to make a tea.

BLACK-EYED SUSAN
Rudbeckia hirta

COMPOSITE FAMILY
Compositae
(Asteraceae)

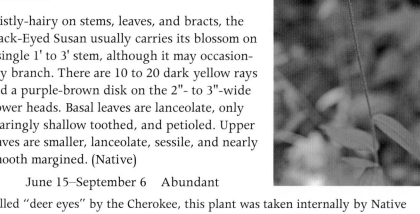

Bristly-hairy on stems, leaves, and bracts, the
Black-Eyed Susan usually carries its blossom on
a single 1' to 3' stem, although it may occasionally branch. There are 10 to 20 dark yellow rays
and a purple-brown disk on the 2"- to 3"-wide
flower heads. Basal leaves are lanceolate, only
sparingly shallow toothed, and petioled. Upper
leaves are smaller, lanceolate, sessile, and nearly
smooth margined. (Native)

June 15–September 6   Abundant

Called "deer eyes" by the Cherokee, this plant was taken internally by Native
Americans to treat worms, and the root juice was reportedly used to treat earaches. Because this plant does not compete well and cattle won't eat it, it is an
indicator of poor soil or overgrazing. It is the state flower of Maryland.

TALL CONEFLOWER
Rudbeckia laciniata

COMPOSITE FAMILY
Compositae
(Asteraceae)

This plant is 3' to 10' tall, has a usually smooth stem and numerous branches above. Flower heads are $2\frac{1}{2}$" to 4" wide with 6 to 10 yellow, slightly notched rays. The center is greenish yellow, concave, and elongates with age. Lower leaves are petioled, up to 1' long, and incised into 5 to 7 lobed or toothed segments. Upper leaves are mostly 3-parted or lobed with segments, lanceolate, and toothed. Terminal leaves may be unlobed and toothless. Leaves are mostly very fine-hairy. (Native)

July 27–September 4   Frequent

Although suspected of being poisonous to hogs, this plant was used by Native Americans, usually in combination with other plants, to treat burns and to relieve indigestion. It is also said to be a beneficial cooked spring green.

ROSINWEED
Silphium integrifolium

COMPOSITE FAMILY
Compositae
(Asteraceae)

This is a rather hairy plant with stems, leaves, and bracts all hairy to some degree. Leaves are opposite, pointed lanceolate, rounded at the base, usually toothed, sessile, and rough-hairy above. The plant branches at the top and the $1\frac{1}{2}$"-wide flower heads have 15 to 25 yellow rays. Note the broad, stiff, green outer bracts on unopened flower buds. (Native)

July 14–October 3   Infrequent

The park is on the very eastern edge of this species range; it is mostly a western plant. Several species of the genus *Silphium* were made into a tea or tonic by Native Americans to treat what settlers called "debility."

INDIAN-CUP
Silphium perfoliatum

COMPOSITE FAMILY
Compositae
(Asteraceae)

The smooth stem is 4' to 8' tall and 4-angled. The flower heads are 2" to 3" wide with 20 to 30 yellow rays that are toothed at their tips. Lower leaves are toothed, opposite, 6" to 12" long, and 4" to 8" wide. They are broadly pointed ovate with a wide base narrowing into a wide winged petiole. Most noticeable are the uppermost leaves, which are lanceolate, entire, and joined around the stem to form a cup that will actually hold water. (Native)

July 19–September 4   Infrequent

For a pleasant breath-freshening gum that won't decay your teeth, try breaking off the top of this plant and gathering the sap, as Native Americans did. Indian-Cup was also used by Native Americans to treat liver problems, back pain, profuse menstruation, rheumatism, and fever. Smoke of the root was inhaled to treat head colds.

WHORLED ROSINWEED
Silphium trifoliatum

COMPOSITE FAMILY
Compositae
(Asteraceae)

There is sometimes a whitish film on this smooth, 3' to 7' plant. Its leaves are pointed lanceolate, only slightly toothed, rough above, soft-hairy or smooth below, short petioled, and those in the center of the stem are in whorls of 3 or 4. Flower heads are terminal on branching stems, are up to 2" wide, and have 15 to 20 slightly notched, yellow rays. Note the stiff, green bracts on the unopened buds. (Native)

July 16–September 13   Frequent

Linnaeus used an ancient Greek name for a resinous plant to derive the genus name for this group. Like other *Silphium* species, the Whorled Rosinweed secretes a gumlike resin when broken.

EARLY GOLDENROD
Solidago juncea

COMPOSITE FAMILY
Compositae
(Asteraceae)

Flower heads are in a plumelike arrangement with 7 to 12 yellow rays. The plant is smooth, $1\frac{1}{2}'$ to 4' tall, and leaves have branching veins. Lower leaves are up to 1' long, pointed lanceolate, toothed, and rough, and taper into margined petioles. Leaves decrease in size upward. Leaves above are narrow lanceolate, sessile, and untoothed. Note the very small leaves in the upper leaf axils. (Native)

July 19–September 18   Abundant

This particular goldenrod was reported to have been used medicinally by several Native American tribes. The roots were soaked in water and taken internally as an aid in treating convulsions.

CROWNBEARD
Verbesina helianthoides

COMPOSITE FAMILY
Compositae
(Asteraceae)

The hairy stem on this 2' to 4' plant is 4-winged. Leaves are lanceolate, toothed, sessile, rough above, alternate, and 2" to 4" long. The few heads are $1\frac{1}{2}$" to $2\frac{1}{2}$" wide and have 8 to 15 yellow rays. (Native)

June 15–August 15   Infrequent

This is one of the first of the large, yellow-rayed composites, collectively called "sunflowers" by most people, to flower in the summer. In fact, the second part of the scientific name is taken from *Helianthus,* the genus name for the "true" sunflowers.

ST. ANDREW'S CROSS
Ascyrum hypericoides
(*Hypericum hypericoides*)

St. John's-Wort Family
Guttiferae

Stems on this low plant are 5" to 10" long, but because of its somewhat reclining nature the plant seems shorter. The ⅝"-wide, yellow flowers have 4 petals and 4 sepals but 2 of the sepals are very small. Leaves are opposite and ovate, tapering to the base and nearly sessile. (Native)

June 28–August 25 Frequent

Like some other members of *Guttiferae,* this plant may cause skin sensitivity to susceptible individuals. Native Americans reportedly used this plant to treat such ailments as fever, diarrhea, and kidney and bladder problems.

ST. JOHN'S-WORT
Hypericum dolabriforme

St. John's-Wort Family
Guttiferae

Small branchlets grow from the leaf axils on this 8" to 20" plant. Leaves are linear to linear lanceolate. The 1"-wide, 5-petaled, yellow flowers are in terminal cymes. The numerous stamens provide a broad bushy center. (Native)

June 16–August 15   Infrequent

Native Americans used a St. John's-Wort species to treat respiratory diseases. There are recent reports that indicate some species of *Hypericum* may be beneficial in the treatment of tuberculosis.

ORANGE-GRASS
Hypericum gentianoides
ST. JOHN'S-WORT FAMILY
Guttiferae

This wiry-looking plant is from 4" to 15" tall, with numerous alternating branches. Leaves are so small as to be scalelike and are opposite. The small flowers have 5 yellow petals, 5 to 10 anthers, and 5 sepals, which are shorter than the petals. (Native)

July 6–August 19   Infrequent

Looking nothing like our other members of *Hypericum,* this plant's principal claim to fame is its ability to thrive where virtually no other plants can grow. It is found on exposed sandstone, often with only a film of soil or sand covering the threadlike roots.

COMMON ST. JOHN'S-WORT
Hypericum perforatum
ST. JOHN'S-WORT FAMILY
Guttiferae

This species of St. John's Wort is best distinguished by the black dots on the edges of the 5 yellow petals. The plant is 1' to 2½' tall, has multiple branches and paired, opposite, narrow oblong, translucent dotted, toothless leaves. Note the bushy stamens and 3 styles. (Introduced)

June 17–August 23   Frequent

Naturalized from Europe, this species has a long history of use by herbalists in the treatment of wounds, bruises, and insect bites. Native Americans are reported to have used the plant for treatment of similar maladies.

SHRUBBY ST. JOHN'S-WORT
Hypericum spathulatum
(*Hypericum prolificum*)

St. John's-Wort Family
Guttiferae

Woody stems on this 3'- to 5'-tall, branching shrub are 2-edged. Leaves are somewhat glossy, narrow lanceolate, and smooth. Flowers have 5 petals, and are yellow, centered with a fluffy mass of yellow stamens. (Native)

July 6–August 23   Locally Frequent

Cattle that eat this and other *Hypericum* species are in danger of becoming highly sensitized to the sun. Cattle find the plants unpalatable, however, and will not likely eat enough to harm themselves if other forage is available. St. John's-Wort was considered an effective charm against evil spirits in medieval times.

PENCIL-FLOWER
Stylosanthes biflora

Pea Family
Leguminosae
(Fabaceae)

The ⅓"-wide, yellow, pealike flowers are borne terminally on stems branching from the base of this low, 6"- to 18"-long, mostly spreading plant. Leaves are very short petioled and the 3 leaflets are somewhat glossy, narrow ovate, and rounded at the tips with a stiff point. Note the tiny sheathing stipules. (Native)

June 30–September 6   Infrequent

This is the only yellow, "pea-shaped" flower found in the park. The genus name is from the Greek *stylos,* meaning column, and refers to the long, thin calyx tube. Though quite a stretch of the imagination, the common name is probably a comparison of the long, yellow tube to a pencil.

INDIAN CUCUMBER-ROOT
Medeola virginiana

LILY FAMILY
Liliaceae

A distinctive, 1' to 2' plant with 2 whorls of leaves. A midstem whorl has 4 to 10 lanceolate, smooth-margined, parallel-veined leaves. The terminal whorl has 3 to 4 similar, smaller, sessile leaves. The small flowers, which dangle from the stem tip on thin stalks, have 6 yellow, recurved petals, and the stamens are red. Fruits are blue berries and nonflowering individuals do not have the terminal whorl of leaves. (Native)

May 30–June 28   Rare

The little, blue berries are not edible. The roots look and taste like cucumbers, and are quite good, but the plants are now far too rare to destroy. Native Americans are said to have eaten the roots regularly, and there is one report that they chewed the root and spit it on their fishhooks to make the fish bite.

SEEDBOX
Ludwigia alternifolia

EVENING-PRIMROSE FAMILY
Onagraceae

Leaves are alternate, very short petioled or appearing sessile, linear lanceolate, tapering at each end, and toothless. Flowers are solitary in the leaf axils on very short stems. There are 4 yellow petals on each ⅝"-wide flower. Note the square-shaped capsule below the 4 persistent sepals on this smooth, 2' to 3' plant. (Native)

July 15–August 25   Locally Frequent

The 4 yellow petals quickly fall from this plant, leaving the 4 sepals on top of the ovary, which becomes a sharply angled four-sided, boxlike capsule full of minute seeds. This is a plant of wet areas.

SUNDROPS
Oenothera fruticosa

EVENING-PRIMROSE FAMILY
Onagraceae

At first glance, Sundrops may be confused with the Evening-Primrose. However, this somewhat branching, nearly hairless, 1' to 3' plant, flowers during the daytime. It has 4 yellow petals, which are slightly indented at the apex, and a short, slender corolla tube. The flower is about 1½" wide. Stamens are orange and the stigma forms a cross. Although leaves are variable they are generally narrow lanceolate, sessile, and smooth margined above, and short petioled and widely wavy toothed below. (Native)

June 15–   Endangered

Native Americans ate the seeds of several species of *Oenothera,* especially in the west. The crisp tuberous roots are also said to be edible.

FRINGED LOOSESTRIFE
Lysimachia ciliata

PRIMROSE FAMILY
Primulaceae

Stem leaves are broad lanceolate, entire, opposite, and petioled with a fringe of hair on the petiole. The plant is 1' to 3' tall and the yellow, ¾"-wide flowers hang downward. The 5 petals are yellow and their tips are finely toothed with a sharp point between the minute teeth. (Native)

June 30–July 14   Infrequent

Some loosestrifes were supposed to have a magical calming effect on animals. The plant may have some repellent properties toward gnats and other insects, which may account for this calming effect.

LANCE-LEAVED LOOSESTRIFE
Lysimachia lanceolata

<small>PRIMROSE FAMILY</small>
Primulaceae

This is a slender, erect, smooth, 1'- to 2½'-tall plant. It has long, linear lanceolate, and smooth-margined upper leaves, with very small leaves often in the axils. Basal leaves are wider and shorter. Note the runners at the base. The ½"-wide flowers have 5 abruptly pointed, yellow petals and their long stalks grow from the leaf axils. (Native)

June 15–July 16   Infrequent

Although *Lysimachia* is unlikely to be found at your local hairdresser, it has been used to dye hair blonde. It has also been used to make a tea.

AGRIMONY
Agrimonia parviflora

<small>ROSE FAMILY</small>
Rosaceae

This is the largest of our *Agrimonia* species, reaching 4' or more. It also has the largest number of leaflets, from 9 to 17. The stem is very hairy, and the tiny, 5-petaled, yellow flowers are on a long, curving, slender spike. Note the large, deeply cut stipules and the paired, very small leaflets between the primary leaflets. Primary leaflets are narrow lanceolate, toothed, and fine-hairy beneath. (Native)

July 27–September 10   Infrequent

Members of *Agrimonia* contain tannin, which is the probable reason for its herbal use as an antibiotic and astringent. It has also been used to treat asthma, coughs, and sore throat.

AGRIMONY
Agrimonia rostellata

ROSE FAMILY
Rosaceae

Stems on this *Agrimonia* are about 2' tall, and mostly smooth or with a few scattered hairs. Note that this species has tuberous roots. The leaves have mostly 5 to 7 leaflets, are ovate in outline, broadly toothed, and have paired, very small, smooth-margined leaflets between the primary leaflets. The small, yellow, 5-petaled flowers are in a long, narrow spike. (Native)

July 14–September 14   Frequent

A similar plant is *Agrimonia pubescens,* which has densely short-hairy stems.

Plants of *Agrimonia* are probably best known for their little seed burrs that cling so tenaciously to one's socks after a walk in the woods. The leaves and flowers also make a fragrant and spicy addition to herbal teas.

FALSE FOXGLOVE
Gerardia virginica
(*Aureolaria virginica*)

FIGWORT FAMILY
Scrophulariaceae

This species of False Foxglove has a downy whitish stem up to 4' tall and is sparingly branched at the top. Leaves are lanceolate in outline, abruptly tapering into petioles, very deeply lobed, and downy. Flowers are tubular, 1½" to 2" long, yellow, growing from the leaf axils, and have 5 wide lobes. (Native)

July 27–August 25   Infrequent

A similar plant is *Gerardia flava,* which is more deeply lobed and has nearly smooth leaves.

Gerardia virginica and *G. flava* are parasitic on the roots of oak trees. Specimens collected and pressed for herbarium use turn black.

COMMON MULLEIN
Verbascum thapsus

FIGWORT FAMILY
Scrophulariaceae

This tall, 2' to 7' plant is densely wooly-hairy on the stem and leaves. The leaves, which decrease in size toward the summit, are pointed, ovate, and narrow into winged petioles that may be more clasping above. The yellow, 5-petaled flowers are in a long, extremely dense terminal spike. (Introduced)

June 4–August 23   Infrequent

Common Mullein has been used for lamp wicks, to make a bright yellow dye, as a charm against demons, a love potion, a hair tonic, and a substitute for tobacco. Medicinally it was used to treat sore throats, the pain of rheumatism and headache, respiratory problems, and earaches. Laboratory tests indicate an effectiveness as an anti-inflammatory agent.

BUTTERFLY MILKWEED
Asclepias tuberosa

MILKWEED FAMILY
Asclepiadaceae

Our only bright orange milkweed, this is a hairy, terminally branching, 1' to 2' plant. The clusters of flowers have the usual 5 downward-curving corolla lobes and circle of 5 erect hoods. Leaves are alternate, lanceolate, sessile, and entire. Note the near absence of white sap when the stem is broken. (Native)

June 15–August 16   Infrequent

Another common name, Pleurisy Root, comes from its use by Native Americans and settlers to treat pleurisy, pneumonia, and other respiratory diseases. It was also used extensively to treat cuts, bruises, sores, and wounds. This plant has also been reported as a source for a permanent red dye.

SPOTTED TOUCH-ME-NOT
Impatiens capensis

Touch-Me-Not Family
Balsaminaceae

The orange flowers spotted with red dangle from a long, delicate, bending stalk growing from the leaf axils. They resemble a windsock with a small curved tail and flaring mouth. The plant has a watery, nearly transparent, 2'- to 5'-tall stem and alternate, pointed ovate, and toothed leaves. (Native)

June 21–September 24   Infrequent

Native Americans reportedly used the plant to make a yellow dye. They also used it as an emetic and as a preventative treatment and cure for poison ivy. The seeds are of some value to wildlife and hummingbirds especially enjoy the blossoms.

TRUMPET CREEPER
Campsis radicans

Bignonia Family
Bignoniaceae

This is a woody, climbing vine without tendrils, which may reach 30' or more in height, depending on its support. It produces clusters of 3"-long, reddish orange, 5-lobed, trumpet-shaped flowers. Leaves are petioled, pinnately compound, with 7 to 11 lanceolate to ovate, sharply toothed leaflets. (Native)

June 26–July 27   Infrequent

Trumpet Creeper can be a serious problem around barns where it climbs the walls, loosening boards and often the roof. Cutting only seems to invigorate the plant. Reports suggest that milk from cows that have eaten this plant may cause skin irritation in certain individuals.

DAYLILY
Hemerocallis fulva

Lily Family
Liliaceae

Flowering stems are 3' to 5' tall, leafless, and have several branches with flowers terminal on the branches. Flowers are orange, erect, unspotted, 4" to 5" long, and have 6 "petals" (really 3 sepals and 3 petals). Each flower lasts only one day. The tall leaves are basal, linear, pointed at the tips, and creased at their centers. (Introduced)

June 13–July 3   Infrequent

The flowers are absolutely delicious when made into fritters. The crisp tubers found early in the year are good in salads or cooked like corn. In the fall they taste terrible. Studies in China indicate that root extracts have antibacterial properties.

MICHIGAN LILY
Lilium michiganense

Lily Family
Liliaceae

The 6 perianth parts of 3 petals and 3 sepals sharply recurve backward, almost to the base of the funnel-shaped flowers. Petals and sepals are orangish to yellowish with dark brown spots inside. Note the absence of a clearly defined basal green zone in the throat, as found in *L. superbum.* The protruding anthers are oblong, and the ribs on the back of petals are flattened. This smooth plant is up to 5' tall with narrow lanceolate leaves in whorls. (Native)

July 7–July 14   Endangered

Although the bulbs of this and most other true lilies are supposedly edible, this rare and regally beautiful plant should be left undisturbed if one is lucky enough to find it.

COMMON MILKWEED
Asclepias syriaca

Milkweed Family
Asclepiadaceae

A plant of old fields and waste places, it is not common in the park. The plant is from 3' to 5' tall and has a single, downy stem. Leaves are short petioled, opposite, oblong, abruptly pointed at the tip, and smooth margined. Flowers are in somewhat drooping, broad, dense umbels in the upper leaf axils. Blossoms are a dull lavender. (Native)

June 20–July 23   Infrequent

Two similar plants are *Asclepias amplexicaulis* with waxy, blunt, clasping leaves, and *A. incarnata,* which has narrow-lanceolate leaves and grows in wet areas.

The fluffy seeds were used as filler in life preservers, the bark as a fiber, and the sap was considered for a rubber substitute. This milkweed has been used to treat warts, ringworm, and asthma and as a contraceptive. Young shoots are eaten in salads or cooked like asparagus and the leaves used as a potherb. The sap is also a good chewing-gum substitute.

DEPTFORD PINK
Dianthus armeria

Pink Family
Caryophyllaceae

A thin, stiff, 8" to 18" plant with few, opposite, needlelike leaves. The flowers are in small clusters among the long, dense, terminal bracts. The 5 pink petals are toothed at their tips, spotted with minute white dots, and about ½" wide. (Introduced)

June 15–July 23   Infrequent

This plant is now widely naturalized from Europe, where the genus was valued in ornamental cultivation. The genus name is from the Greek *Dios,* meaning Jupiter, and *anthos,* meaning flower.

ROUND-LEAVED FIRE PINK
Silene rotundifolia

PINK FAMILY
Caryophyllaceae

Sometimes called Catchfly, this finely hairy, somewhat reclining plant is 1' to 2½' long. Leaves are pointed ovate, with the upper leaves sessile. Flowers are bright red, tubular, and have 5 deeply notched petals. The similar *S. virginica* has much narrower leaves. (Native)

June 13–July 29   Rare

Photographing this plant can be hazardous, since it generally is found on high, narrow, mostly sandstone ledges. This photograph was taken about 40' above the ground on a 6" ledge. The genus name *Silene* is Greek for saliva and refers to the plant's sticky secretions, which aid in holding insects on the plant long enough for pollination.

NODDING THISTLE
Carduus nutans

COMPOSITE FAMILY
Compositae
(Asteraceae)

True to its common name, the large, 1½"- to 2½"-wide, solitary, long-stalked, reddish purple heads are nodding. This 2' to 4' plant has stout, recurving, spiny bracts below the heads. Leaves are lanceolate in outline, very deeply and irregularly cut, and extremely spiny. (Introduced)

June 13–July 23   Infrequent

First reported in Kentucky in 1940, this plant is now found in every county and is listed as one of the state's 10 most serious weeds. The dried flowers were historically used in Europe as a rennet to curdle milk. There has also been some effort to use the down of this plant in papermaking.

SPOTTED KNAPWEED
Centaurea maculosa
(*Centaurea biebersteinii*)

COMPOSITE FAMILY
Compositae
(Asteraceae)

Whitish pink flowers on this occasionally tufted-hairy 2' to 3' plant are in 1"-wide heads. Under a hand lens the individual flowers are seen to be tubular with 5 linear petals. This is a terminally branching plant, and the alternate leaves are entire and cleft almost to the midrib into linear segments. (Introduced)

July 10–September 18   Infrequent

Although not particularly abundant in the park, this plant can be a troublesome weed, especially on the range lands in the northwestern states. European folklore suggests that if a young girl hides one of these flowers under her apron, she will be assured of having the man of her choice.

BLAZING STAR
Liatris squarrosa

COMPOSITE FAMILY
Compositae
(Asteraceae)

Note the thick, pointed, recurved, and spreading bracts and the short flowering stalk. This *Liatris* is from 1' to 2½' tall, with a finely hairy or sometimes smooth stem. Leaves are alternate, linear, and stiff. Flower heads are few, grow from the leaf axils, and have many long, pink, 5-lobed florets. (Native)

July 9–October 5   Locally Frequent

This plant is reported to be helpful for treating snakebite when a root poultice is applied to the bite after the poison has been sucked out. It has been used as an insecticide to protect clothing from moths and, like other *Liatris* species, is a diuretic.

ROSE PINK
Sabatia angularis

GENTIAN FAMILY
Gentianaceae

Flowers are pink, 5-petaled, $1\frac{1}{4}$" wide, and have a red-bordered, yellow, star-shaped center. The plant is 1' to 2' tall, smooth, and has flowering stems branching in pairs from the upper leaf axils. Leaves are opposite, smooth margined, pointed ovate, and have somewhat heart-shaped, almost clasping, sessile bases. (Native)

July 19–September 19   Frequent

Herbalists have recommended this plant as an agent to eliminate fevers. It has also been used in the past by herbalists for the expulsion of intestinal worms.

WOOD SAGE
Teucrium canadense

MINT FAMILY
Labiatae
(Lamiaceae)

Unlike other mints, the stamens stick out through a slit between the 2 upper lips of the reduced hood and curl downward toward the larger, downward-pointed lower flower lip. Blossoms are pinkish, tubular flowers, and are in a dense, terminal, 1' to 3' spike. Leaves are lanceolate, pointed, toothed, and opposite. (Native)

July 2–August 25   Infrequent

In folk medicine, a tea made from the leaves is supposedly effective in promoting urination and sweating. It was also used to treat worms, hemorrhoids, sore throat, and as an antiseptic, though these uses are doubtful.

CROWN VETCH
Coronilla varia

PEA FAMILY
Leguminosae
(Fabaceae)

The pinnate, sessile leaves consist of many small, oblong-ovate, paired leaflets without tendrils. The flowering stalks on this 1'- to 2'-tall branching and creeping plant are longer than the leaves. The dense umbel of pink and white bicolored flowers is cloverlike in appearance. (Introduced)

May 30–August 23   Locally Abundant

An introduced species, Crown Vetch was used in Europe and Asia as a cultivated garden plant. It has found a widely acceptable use in this country as a ground cover along roadside cuts to prevent erosion.

POINTED-LEAF TICK-TREFOIL
Desmodium glutinosum

PEA FAMILY
Leguminosae
(Fabaceae)

This single-stemmed, smooth plant grows up to $3\frac{1}{2}$' tall. The 3-parted leaves are in a whorl from which the flowering stem is produced. The terminal leaflet is broadly oval, abruptly long, and sharply pointed. The 2 lateral leaflets are smaller and more ovate, but also pointed. The pink (bluish when old) flowers are pealike and in a tall raceme. (Native)

June 28–July 29   Frequent

These are also known as Beggarweeds because of the flat, triangular-shaped seed pod segments that stick so tenaciously to clothing. The segments are best removed by shaving clothing with a sharp knife. There are over 50 species of *Desmodium* in the United States.

NAKED-FLOWER TICK-TREFOIL
Desmodium nudiflorum

PEA FAMILY
Leguminosae
(Fabaceae)

A single, slender, leafless flower stem, which is 1' to 2½' long, grows from a whorl of leaves near the base of the plant. The leaves have 3 leaflets, with the terminal leaflet tapering from its center to a pointed tip and base. The lateral leaflets are more lanceolate, but with unequal sides. Flowers are pealike, relatively few, and pink. (Native)

July 12–September 10   Frequent

Native Americans are reported to have chewed the root of this *Desmodium* species to treat various gum diseases and sores in the mouth. A tea made from the roots was also supposedly used externally to relieve cramps.

SWEET PEA
Lathyrus odoratus

PEA FAMILY
Leguminosae
(Fabaceae)

This is the common, flower garden Sweet Pea, an escape that rarely persists in the wild. It is a large, branching, spreading or climbing, vinelike plant with seemingly segmented, wide-winged stems. Leaves are smooth and ovate at the tips of the winged branchlets. Flower clusters are large and showy with ¾"-wide blossoms. The standard and wings are pink, fading to whitish at the base. (Introduced)

June 15–July 10   Infrequent

This plant may be poisonous in large quantities, causing paralysis, convulsions, and skeletal deformities. This foreign species is now a favorite garden plant in this country, producing lush foliage and showy flowers with a very pleasant fragrance.

TRAILING WILD BEAN
Strophostyles helvola

PEA FAMILY
Leguminosae
(Fabaceae)

This plant is similar to *S. umbellata,* but the leaflets on the 3-divided leaves are larger, more pointed ovate, and some have a bulge or shallow lobe. The stalks on the greenish pink, pealike flowers are longer than the leaf petioles, but not longer than the leaves. This trailing plant is slightly hairy and 2' to 8' long. (Native)

July 27–August 23   Infrequent

When found in enough abundance to make gathering them worthwhile, the beans of this species are edible prepared in the ways commercial beans are cooked. The taste, however, may be less than desirable.

GOAT'S-RUE
Tephrosia virginiana

PEA FAMILY
Leguminosae
(Fabaceae)

These typical pea-shaped flowers are bicolored, with a pink keel and a yellowish white standard that is tinged with pink. The 1' to 2' plant is silky hairy. Leaves are pinnately compound with 7 to 14 pairs of very short-petioled, ovate leaflets and a single terminal leaflet. The leaflets have a sharp point on the tips. (Native)

May 30–July 9   Infrequent

This plant contains the chemical rotenone and is poisonous. It was used by Native Americans to kill fish. It was also used to treat worms, tuberculosis, and coughs. Rubbed into scratches, Native Americans thought it would toughen the bodies of ball players. Scientific tests have shown it to have both anticancer and cancercausing properties.

RED CLOVER
Trifolium pratense

PEA FAMILY
Leguminosae
(Fabaceae)

Red Clover is a branching, soft-hairy plant reaching 2' in height. Leaves are long petioled and subtended by stipules. The 3 leaflets are short stemmed, ovate, grow from the same point, and have a prominent, pale, triangular mark in the center. Flower clusters are oval and pinkish purple. (Introduced)

May 30–August 16   Frequent

This is the state flower of Vermont. The flowers can be eaten raw in salads or fried in batter. It has been used to make wine and to repel moths. Medicinally it has been used to treat athlete's foot, asthma, coughs, cuts, and burns. Red Clover is an ideal hay and forage crop and few plants are as valuable to wildlife.

VIRGINIA MEADOW-BEAUTY
Rhexia virginica

MEADOW-BEAUTY FAMILY
Melastomataceae

This 1' to $1\frac{1}{2}$' plant has a square stem. The leaves are pointed ovate, parallel veined, sessile, and have stiff, bristly hair on the toothed margins. Flowers have 4 somewhat less than symmetrical, $1\frac{1}{4}$"-wide, dark pink petals and 8 showy, yellow, drooping anthers. (Native)

June 28–September 14   Rare

A similar plant is *Rhexia mariana,* which does not have the acutely square and winged stem.

In areas where it is more abundant, the sweetish, slightly acidic, or sour taste of the leaves is a pleasant addition to salads. The crisp, chopped tubers are also used in salads. The leaves can be boiled and served as a potherb.

SMOOTH PHLOX
Phlox carolina var. *triflora*
(*Phlox glaberrima* ssp. *triflora*)

PHLOX FAMILY
Polemoniaceae

Leaves on this *Phlox* are opposite, long pointed, narrow lanceolate, and taper at the base to very short petioles on lower leaves, while the upper are sessile. This 1' to 3' plant is mostly hairless and the leaves are single nerved. The 5-petaled, tubular flowers are pink and the lobes may be slightly notched at their tips. (Native)

June 18–July 19   Infrequent

Many plants have had some age-old symbolism ascribed to them. In medieval times, to give a bouquet of phlox meant wishes for sweet dreams or was considered a proposal of love.

FALL PHLOX
Phlox paniculata

PHLOX FAMILY
Polemoniaceae

This can be a very tall plant, often growing from 2' to 5' in height. The stem is usually smooth and has a pyramid-shaped terminal cluster of pink, 5-lobed, tubular flowers. The lobes are rounded, smooth, and shorter than the tube. Leaves are opposite, heavily veined with 3 primary veins, oblong lanceolate and short petioled below, and sessile above. (Native)

July 16–September 13   Frequent

There are about 40 species in this genus whose name, *Phlox,* is the Greek word for flame. Also known as Garden Phlox, this large, showy plant is often cultivated in flower gardens.

WILD ROSE
Rosa carolina

ROSE FAMILY
Rosaceae

This plant is from 1' to 3' tall and the 5 to 7 leaflets are finely toothed. The 5-petaled pink flowers are most often solitary. Note that the thorns are thin and straight. (Native)

May 30–June 30   Frequent

A similar plant is *Rosa setigera,* which has curved thorns and 3 leaflets.

Often holding on the bush through winter, the hips are high in vitamin C and are a good survival food. The hips are used to make tea, juice, wine, jelly, and soup. Children used the hairs of the hips to make an itching powder. Some Native Americans used the skin of the fruit to treat stomach ailments.

SWAMP ROSE
Rosa palustris

ROSE FAMILY
Rosaceae

This wild rose is from 3' to 7' tall and prefers a wet habitat. The leaves have 5 to 9 pointed-ovate leaflets, which are subtended by very narrow stipules. Note that the thorns curve downward. The 5 wavy and slightly notched petals are pale pink. (Native)

June 13–July 6   Frequent

A similar plant is *Rosa multiflora,* which has smaller white flowers.

One recipe for fried rose petals says to dip in whiskey, then in batter, to fry in deep fat, and then dip in sugar. Like *R. carolina* the hips can be used in tea, jelly, soup, syrup, or eaten raw. Three rose hips reportedly have as much vitamin C as an orange.

HAIRY RUELLIA
Ruellia caroliniensis

ACANTHUS FAMILY
Acanthaceae

Very similar to *R. strepens,* this plant is 1' to 3' tall, with opposite, lanceolate leaves. Growing from the leaf axils it has lavender-blue, tubular flowers with 5 flaring lobes. This Ruellia is hairy, has longer tubes, and the flower stems are nearly sessile. (Native)

June 28–September 4   Abundant

A similar plant is *Ruellia humilis,* which is smaller and has sessile leaves.

The paired, tubular flowers fall from the plant at the slightest disturbance and are therefore of no value for bouquets. There are about 200 species of *Ruellia,* most of which are found in tropical America.

SMOOTH RUELLIA
Ruellia strepens

ACANTHUS FAMILY
Acanthaceae

This species of *Ruellia* is hairless, with the exception of some short hair on the sepals. The 1"- to 3"-long, lavender-blue flowers are trumpet shaped with thin tubes flaring widely into 5 spreading lobes. Flowers

grow from the axils of the paired, opposite, lanceolate, untoothed, and distinctly petioled leaves. (Native)

June 12–June 21   Infrequent

Although the genus is named after I. de la Ruellia, an early French herbalist, there is no mention of this plant in the herbal literature cited in the bibliography. Knowledge of medicinal uses has apparently been lost in time.

ANGLE-POD
Gonolobus shortii
(Matelea obliqua)

MILKWEED FAMILY
Asclepiadaceae

This is a twining vine with large, broad, heart-shaped leaves. The flowering stalk grows from the plant stem between the leaf nodes. Individual flowers in the clusters are purple with 5 wavy, linear petals. The broken stem produces a milky sap. (Native)

May 30–July 20   Infrequent

Named for its discoverer, Charles Wilkins Short, an early nineteenth-century botanist, this plant's appearance is unlike our common perception of a milkweed. Though a twining vine, note the typically milky sap of a broken leaf or stem.

TALL BELLFLOWER
Campanula americana
(Campanulastrum americanum)

LOBELIA FAMILY
Campanulaceae

A distinctive characteristic of this 2' to 6' plant is the very long style and the way it curves downward, then upward. Flowers are in a long raceme with the 5 blue, 1"-wide, pointed- petaled flowers growing from the leaf axils. Leaves are longpointed lanceolate, toothed, and the upper are sessile. (Native)

July 16–October 5   Infrequent

Native Americans made a tea from various parts of this plant to treat coughs and several other upper respiratory ailments.

INDIAN TOBACCO
Lobelia inflata

LOBELIA FAMILY
Campanulaceae

Often branching from the upper leaf axils, this plant is 1' to 2½' tall. Flowers are in spikelike racemes with each tubular, pale blue to white blossom growing on a short stem from a leaf axil. Leaves are pointed ovate, sessile, short toothed, and decrease in size from midstem upward. Note the swollen, persistent calyx after flowering. (Native)

July 7–October 4   Abundant

This plant was smoked extensively by Native Americans. Interestingly, the chemical found in the plant, lobeline, is used in some over-the-counter smoking deterrents. Its past use to treat coughs, respiratory ailments, and as an expectorant have been confirmed effective in recent clinical experiments. Lobeline is an ingredient in some cough medicine today.

DAYFLOWER
Commelina communis

SPIDERWORT FAMILY
Commelinaceae

This somewhat reclining, 1'- to 3'-long plant occasionally roots at the nodes. The flowers are borne in a spathelike pair of bracts. There are 2 bright blue, ½"-wide petals above and a much smaller white petal below. Stem leaves are pointed lanceolate, 3" to 5" long, 1" to 1½" wide, and taper into a sheath. (Introduced)

July 7–September 24   Locally Frequent

Supposedly this plant can be eaten as a steamed vegetable and in salads. The boiled roots were reportedly used as a substitute for creamed potatoes. In China, it is used to treat sore throat and tonsillitis. Also, some Native Americans ate the plant in the belief it would increase sexual potency.

ZIGZAG SPIDERWORT
Tradescantia subaspera

SPIDERWORT FAMILY
Commelinaceae

The stem on this species angles or bends slightly at each leaf node. Leaf blades are keeled, long lanceolate, and narrow into a clasping sheath. Leaves are 1" to 2" wide. The petals on the 1"-wide flowers are ovate, blue or occasionally white, and the filaments are conspicuously bearded. The sepals are not inflated. (Native)

May 30–September 6   Locally Frequent

Spiderworts are used by science teachers to study the circulation of protoplasm. They are also useful as a study aid in the detection of pollution, since their cells mutate rapidly in the presence of severe pollution, causing the petals to change color.

CHICORY
Cichorium intybus

COMPOSITE FAMILY
Compositae
(Asteraceae)

The numerous, light blue rays are notched so they are 5-toothed at their tips. The sessile flower heads are about $1\frac{1}{4}$" wide and close before noon. This is an erect, branching plant with a grooved stem. Principal leaves are basal, narrow lanceolate in outline, irregularly coarse toothed or lobed, and narrow into winged petioles. Stem leaves are very small or absent, lanceolate, less lobed, and clasping. (Introduced)

June 22–September 19   Infrequent

Millions of pounds of the root have been use extensively as a substitute for and additive to coffee. In Europe, the young, crisp leaves grown in the dark are highly valued in salads. Long used as a "helpful" herb, recent experiments show the root to be antibacterial. Other results indicate the possibility of its use in treating heart irregularities.

DOWNY WOOD-MINT
Blephilia ciliata

MINT FAMILY
Labiatae
(Lamiaceae)

This hairy, square-stemmed plant is 1' to 2' tall with runners at the base. Leaves on the runners are ovate, petioled, and sparsely shallow toothed. Stem leaves are lanceolate, very short petioled, barely toothed, and are downy hairy, especially below. Pale blue, tubular flowers are in a thick spike and the lower lip is spotted with purple. Bracts subtending the flowers are hairy and fringed. (Native)

May 30–July 12   Frequent

The genus name comes from the Greek *blepharis,* meaning eyelash, and refers to the hairy fringe of the bracts and calyx teeth. Like so many other members of *Labiatae,* this plant makes a pleasant tea.

BERGAMOT
Monarda fistulosa

MINT FAMILY
Labiatae
(Lamiaceae)

Flowers grow from a dense terminal cluster of tiny bracts. The flowers are 2-lipped, 1" tubes, which are lavender or light pink. The filaments protrude above the erect upper lip, while the lower lip curves sharply downward. The plant is 1½' to 2½' tall and has opposite, lanceolate, sharply toothed leaves that are smooth on the upper surface and minutely pubescent below. (Native)

June 15–September 6   Frequent

Bergamot has been widely used by herbalists, Native Americans, and in folk medicine to treat intestinal gas, colds, fever, sore throat, headaches, and bronchial problems. There is also a report of the use of the extracted oil to treat acne.

HAIRY SKULLCAP
Scutellaria elliptica

MINT FAMILY
Labiatae
(Lamiaceae)

As its name implies, this 1' to 2' plant
is hairy, with short curving hairs. It
has only 2 to 5 pairs of petioled, ovate,
and scalloped-margined leaves. Flowers are in terminal racemes of 6 to 20
tubular, hooded blossoms. They are
blue-violet and the lips are unequal.
(Native)

June 12–July 16   Infrequent

Herbalists have widely used a close relative of Hairy Skullcap to treat irritability,
nervous conditions, insomnia, and exhaustion. It was most often used in combination with other herbs.

DOWNY SKULLCAP
Scutellaria incana

MINT FAMILY
Labiatae
(Lamiaceae)

As indicated by the name, this plant is
thickly covered with fine, whitish
hairs. The stem on this 2' to 3' plant
branches above into several racemes of
numerous blue, hooded, lipped, tubular flowers. The leaves are opposite,
lanceolate, pointed, sharply toothed,
and petioled. (Native)

June 30–August 17   Frequent

Like so many other mints, its leaves can
be crushed and used to make a passable
tea. Some Native Americans also used a
poultice made from the leaves to treat
headaches.

HEART-LEAVED SKULLCAP
Scutellaria ovata

MINT FAMILY
Labiatae
(Lamiaceae)

This square-stemmed, 1' to 2' plant has finely hairy stems with tubular, hooded flowers. Flowers are blue with a lighter colored lower lip. Leaves are long petioled, sharply toothed, and heart shaped. Any hair on the leaves is very fine. (Native)

May 30–June 13   Rare

This is the least abundant of our small woodland mints and can be easily over-looked. However, the heart-shaped leaves are distinctive. It can be used to make a reasonable tea, but should be left undisturbed because of its rarity.

PASSION-FLOWER
Passiflora incarnata

PASSION-FLOWER FAMILY
Passifloraceae

It would be difficult to confuse the flowers on this tendril-bearing, long, climbing vine with any other flowers in the park. Flowers are solitary, grow from the leaf axils, have whitish petals with a showy purple fringe above that is as long as the petals. The 5 anthers and 3 styles are conspicuous above. Leaves are petioled, 3-lobed, and finely toothed. (Native)

July 29–August 17   Infrequent

A somewhat similar plant is *Passiflora lutea,* which has much smaller yellow flowers.

Passion-Flower is used herbally as a sedative and pain killer and eaten as a fruit, jelly, and cold drink. The parts are said to be representative of the crucifixion of Christ: the corona is the crown of thorns, the three styles or three bright spots of color are the nails, the five anthers are the five wounds, and the ten parts of the sepals and petals are the ten faithful apostles.

MONKEY-FLOWER
Mimulus alatus

FIGWORT FAMILY
Scrophulariaceae

The stem on this 1' to 3' plant is 4-angled, with wings on the angles. Flowers are pale violet and tubular, with 2 lobes above and 3 spreading lobes below. Note the short flowering stalks in the leaf axils and the petioles on the lanceolate, toothed leaves. Petioles are about the same length as the flower stalks. (Native)

July 29–August 19   Infrequent

The corolla supposedly resembles the face of a monkey, hence the common name. Recognition of this, however, takes an active imagination (or else there are monkeys known to the giver of the name that are unknown to the rest of us). Several varieties of this plant have been developed for gardens.

HORSE-NETTLE
Solanum carolinense

TOMATO FAMILY
Solanaceae

Some references indicate that this plant is up to 4' tall, but the largest observed in the park is 2'. Flowers are short tubular with 5 pointed lobes, are whitish lavender, and the elongated anthers come together at their apex. The plant is branched, with 2"- to 6"-long, ovate, pointed-lobed, petioled, and starry hairy leaves. The plant has thorns on the stem and leaf veins. The fruit is an orange-yellow berry. (Native)

June 13–September 3   Abundant

The berries are eaten by Wood Duck, quail, grouse, turkey, and other birds. It has been used in the past to treat epilepsy, poison ivy, worms, sore throat, and as an ointment to treat mange on dogs. Like other members of this family, it contains toxic alkaloids and has been reportedly fatal to children.

NARROW-LEAVED VERVAIN

Verbena simplex

VERVAIN FAMILY
Verbenaceae

Very small, tubular, lavender flowers with 5 minute lobes are in thin, terminal spikes on this 6" to 18" plant. The spikes often have a green tip because the flowers on the upper part of the spike develop later than the lower flowers. Leaves are narrow lanceolate, toothed, and taper sharply to the plant stem. (Native)

June 12–August 14   Frequent

Closely related species were used by Native Americans and nineteenth-century herbalists to treat difficult menstruation and epilepsy.

FALSE ALOE

Agave virginica
(*Manfreda virginica*)

AMARYLLIS FAMILY
Amaryllidaceae
(Agavaceae)

This tall, 3' to 6' plant has a very slender, solitary stem growing from a basal rosette of fleshy, 6"- to 24"-long, linear-oblong, and pointed leaves, with smooth or very finely toothed margins. Stem leaves are widely separated and scalelike. The flower tubes are in a 1' to 2' spike, and are yellowish green with protruding stamens. (Native)

June 20–September 4   Infrequent

The thick leaves of this and other *Agave* species contain a juice that has laxative properties. Native Americans used the plant to treat diarrhea, worms, and snakebite. It has also been used to treat x-ray burns and in sunburn ointments.

GREEN MILKWEED
Asclepias viridiflora

MILKWEED FAMILY
Asclepiadaceae

True to its name, the flowers on this small, 1' to 2½' milkweed are green. The flowers are in dense, somewhat drooping, terminal umbels and the hoods on the tiny flowers are not horned as in other milkweeds. Leaves are mostly opposite, smooth or slightly rough, hairy, linear oblong, nearly sessile, and entire. (Native)

July 7–August 23   Rare

The genus name comes from Aesculapius, the Greek god of medicine, and indicates the antiquity of the medicinal use of milkweeds. The fluffy seeds of milkweeds are the preferred nest-building material for goldfinches.

ANGLE-POD
Gonolobus gonocarpos
(Matelea gonocarpos)

MILKWEED FAMILY
Asclepiadaceae

This climbing vine is similar to *G. shortii,* but the flowers are smaller and greenish. It has large, broadly ovate, opposite leaves that are pointed at the tip and heart shaped at the base. Note that the flowers are in few-flowered umbels growing from the leaf axils and have 5 linear petals. (Native)

July 12–July 14   Rare

Like *G. shortii,* this is a climbing, twining vine, but its corolla has the distinctive milkweed shape and the broken stem and leaves contain milky sap characteristic of the more common milkweeds.

RAGGED FRINGED ORCHIS
Habenaria lacera
(Platanthera lacera var. *lacera)*

ORCHID FAMILY
Orchidaceae

This is an inconspicuous, but delicately beautiful, orchid growing from 1' to 2' tall. Its leaves are narrow lanceolate, decreasing in size up the stem. The ¾"-long flowers are in a long, loose spike and are greenish white to greenish yellow, with a long downward pointing spur. The distinguishing feature is the 3-segmented lip, with each segment very deeply and narrowly incised to a threadlike appearance. (Native)

June 13–June 18   Rare

The bulbs of all North American orchids are reported to be edible, but surely one would have to be near starvation before destroying such a rare and delicately beautiful plant as the Ragged Fringed Orchis.

SMALL GREEN WOOD ORCHIS
Habenaria clavellata
(Platanthera clavellata)

ORCHID FAMILY
Orchidaceae

This little, smooth-stemmed orchid is from 8" to 16" tall and has mostly a single, large, narrow-oblong or spatulate lower leaf, and several very small, bractlike, upper leaves. The flowers are greenish to yellowish white. Note the only slightly lobed lip and the long, curved spur with a slightly swollen tip. (Native)

July 29   Rare

The species name refers to the swollen tip or clublike appearance of the spur. Although the bulbs of all our orchids are reportedly edible, starvation should be the only excuse for digging the bulbs of these rare and beautiful plants.

CRESTED CORAL-ROOT ORCHID
Hexalectris spicata

ORCHID FAMILY
Orchidaceae

There is no green on this, the showiest of our saprophytic orchids. The 6" to 24" stem is yellow-brown with scalelike leaves. The 8 to 12 flowers are 1" long and in a raceme on short, fleshy stems. The lower lip is streaked with purple and is somewhat fringed at its tip. Other parts are yellowish brown, free, somewhat recurved, and there is no spur. (Native)

July 29   Endangered

This is not a true coral-root and is either exceptionally rare or extremely difficult to find in the park. It is nearly impossible to transplant. Because of the rarity of this small, colorful, leafless orchid, it should be left undisturbed.

CRANEFLY ORCHID
Tipularia discolor

ORCHID FAMILY
Orchidaceae

Flowers are in a raceme on a leafless, purplish brown, 8" to 14" stem. The flowers are purplish brown with a very long, lighter colored spur. The single, 2" to 3" leaf, not present at flowering time, is deeply pleated and is dark green above and maroon beneath. Because their color resembles the forest floor, the flowers are quite difficult to find. (Native)

July 29–August 29   Infrequent

This orchid produces a single leaf in the fall that persists through the winter and spring, but is gone by the time the flower stalk appears. The species name, *T. discolor,* is in reference to the two different colors of the leaf surfaces.

PINESAP
Monotropa hypopithys

WINTERGREEN FAMILY
Pyrolaceae
(Monotropaceae)

There are no green parts on this plant. Its flowers are on a scaly, 4"- to 10"-tall stem, whose color is similar to the flower. Several flowers, nodding at first, then erect, are about ¾" long and are from yellow to reddish in color. This plant is similar to *M. uniflora,* having no chlorophyll and being saprophytic. (Native)

July 2–September 26   Rare

This plant is usually found in coniferous woods. Its roots are covered with a fungus, which, it is theorized, aids the plants in absorbing their food from the organic matter in the soil.

WHITE WILD LICORICE
Galium circaezans

MADDER FAMILY
Rubiaceae

This species of *Galium* has leaves in whorls of 4. Leaves are ovate to ovate lanceolate, 3-veined, and may be very finely hairy on both surfaces. The plant is from 1' to 2' tall with few-flowered clusters of greenish white, 4-petaled, minute flowers. (Native)

June 12–July 23   Frequent

Another common family name, the Bedstraw Family, refers to its past use as a mattress fiber. This species does have a licorice flavor, as implied by the common name.

FALL FLOWERS

August 1–October 22

ARROWHEAD
Sagittaria latifolia

WATER-PLANTAIN FAMILY
Alismataceae

The long-petioled leaves are basal, and although individual leaves vary greatly in size
and shape, they are mostly broadly arrow
shaped with long basal lobes. The 3-petaled,
1"-wide, white flowers, with clusters of yellow stamens, are in whorls of 3 on a tall,
fleshy stem. (Native)

August 1–August 19   Infrequent

The tubers of this plant were a nutritious staple
in the diet of most Native Americans. They can be baked, boiled, roasted,
french fried, creamed, scalloped, or prepared in any way potatoes are prepared.
Its seed and tubers are favorite foods for geese, muskrats, and beavers. Fever, indigestion, and rheumatism are a few of the maladies Native Americans treated
with this plant.

COMMON BURDOCK
Arctium minus

COMPOSITE FAMILY
Compositae
(Asteraceae)

Tiny, lavender, tubular florets, with 5
pointed lobes, sit atop a more conspicuous "burr" on this bushy, 2' to
$3\frac{1}{2}$' plant. The hooked bracts form a
$\frac{5}{8}$"-wide burr under the flower heads.
Leaves are broadly ovate, hollow petioled, entire, and the lower have somewhat heart-shaped bases. (Introduced)

August 16–September 20   Infrequent

Once used as a love potion and to improve memory, Burdock is now probably
best known for its tenacious burrs. It has been used to treat venereal disease,
scurvy, rheumatism, tonsillitis, sores, boils, burns, and colds. The roots make a
good potherb and the pith of the flowering stems can be simmered in sugar to
make candy.

WHITE WOOD ASTER
Aster divaricatus

COMPOSITE FAMILY
Compositae
(Asteraceae)

The 1"-wide heads, with usually 6 to 9 white rays, are in a flat-topped cluster of freely branching, flowering stems. The plant is from 1½' to 2½' tall, is smooth, and bends slightly at the leaf axils. Lower leaves are pointed, heart shaped, coarsely toothed, and long peti-oled. Upper leaves are more lanceolate, sharply toothed, and have shorter petioles. Note that the disk turns brown with age. (Native)

August 29–October 7   Rare

The primary historical—and current—use for many of the species of *Asters* may well be to test the fortitude and mental stability of those who are so foolish as to choose to sort and identify them with any degree of certainty.

CALICO ASTER
Aster lateriflorus

COMPOSITE FAMILY
Compositae
(Asteraceae)

This plant is another quite variable *Aster*, with numer-ous ½"-wide heads and 10 to 20 white rays. The plant is widely branching, nearly smooth, and may be from 1' to 4' tall. Leaves are lan-ceolate to narrow lanceolate above, toothed to nearly entire at the top, and very short petioled to mostly sessile. Note that the disk turns from yellow to purple with age. (Native)

September 24–October 22   Frequent

Some Native Americans used the entire plant as an incense in their sweat baths. The flowers alone used in the sweat baths were thought to cure one who had be-come mentally deranged.

CORNEL-LEAF ASTER
Aster infirmus

COMPOSITE FAMILY
Compositae
(Asteraceae)

This *Aster* is sparingly branched with few, 1"-wide heads forming a wide, open, flat-topped cluster. There are from 5 to 10 creamy white rays on each head. The leaves are oblong lanceolate, wider above the middle, mostly sessile, entire, and hairy on the margins and veins underneath. This plant is from 1' to 2½' tall. (Native)

August 23–September 24   Rare

In ancient Greek legends, asters were sacred to the multitudes of gods and goddesses. Wreaths made from the flowers were used to decorate places of worship on special occasions.

ONTARIO ASTER
Aster ontarionis

COMPOSITE FAMILY
Compositae
(Asteraceae)

The stem on this 1½' to 4' *Aster* is somewhat wooly-hairy at the base. It is a compact, branching plant with the small, white flower heads in a panicle. Flower heads have 15 to 26 rays. Note the solitary branchlets or heads in the middle leaf axils. Lower leaves are sparingly sharp toothed, tapering gradually at both ends, densely short-hairy, and sessile. Upper and branch leaves become extremely small. (Native)

September 23–October 7   Infrequent

No common name for this *Aster* could be found in any of the references listed in the bibliography. The name Ontario Aster was invented for this account. According to Greek legend, asters were crated out of star dust.

FROST-WEED ASTER

Aster pilosus

COMPOSITE FAMILY
Compositae
(Asteraceae)

Stems on this species of *Aster* are somewhat woody, finely hairy, and many branched. The plant is from 2' to 5' tall and almost bushy. Heads are numerous with many linear white rays. Disk florets turn reddish brown with age. Upper branch leaves are almost needlelike and lower leaves are more linear to linear lanceolate. (Native)

September 14–October 22   Abundant

According to Greek legends, asters were formed of star dust and this is indicated in the genus name. It is also the cause of an old English name, Star-Wort. This *Aster* is of no value for forage and may crowd out other valuable plants.

SMALL WHITE ASTER

Aster vimineus
(*Aster lateriflorus* var. *lateriflorus*)

COMPOSITE FAMILY
Compositae
(Asteraceae)

Stems on this widely branching, 2' to 4' *Aster* are smooth and often purplish. Flower heads are small, numerous, and have 15 to 30 rays. Leaves are linear lanceolate, sessile, and widely toothed below to entire above. Note the small reduced leaves in the primary leaf axils. (Native)

September 15–October 7   Infrequent

There are at least 28 (maybe more) species of *Asters* in Kentucky. Of the 250 (maybe more) known species of *Asters,* nearly half (maybe more) are found in the United States. Botanists have difficulty with precise classification of *Asters* largely because of the plants' ability to hybridize.

PALE INDIAN PLANTAIN
Cacalia atriplicifolia
(Arnoglossum atriplicifolium)

Composite Family
Compositae
(Asteraceae)

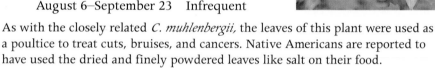

This plant is very similar to *C. muhlenbergii,* but the stem has a whitish film and is not grooved or angled. The roundish, unevenly lobed, toothed, and petioled leaves are more sharply toothed and somewhat whitish beneath. This plant is 3' to 6' tall. Flower heads are in wide, flat-topped clusters and are greenish white. (Native)

August 6–September 23   Infrequent

As with the closely related *C. muhlenbergii,* the leaves of this plant were used as a poultice to treat cuts, bruises, and cancers. Native Americans are reported to have used the dried and finely powdered leaves like salt on their food.

PILEWORT
Erechtites hieracifolia

Composite Family
Compositae
(Asteraceae)

Note the grooved, mostly smooth, succulent stem on this terminally branching, 1' to 8' plant. Leaves are variable, but middle stem leaves are generally lanceolate, short petioled, and coarsely toothed, with upper leaves cut and sessile. Flower heads are rayless and enclosed within a tube of green bracts that have a noticeably swollen base. (Native)

September 3–October 7   Frequent

This plant is reported to be good as a cooked green. However, the rank, obnoxious odor of the plant makes wide use as a green unlikely. It is especially abundant after fires, thus another of its common names, Fireweed. Native Americans used it widely to treat ailments of mucous tissue of the lungs and as an internal astringent.

HORSEWEED

Erigeron canadensis
(*Conyza canadensis*)

COMPOSITE FAMILY
Compositae
(Asteraceae)

This coarse, somewhat hairy plant is from 2' to 8' tall, with a very large dome of branching, flowering stems. The flower heads are very numerous, greenish white, and are only $\frac{1}{8}$" to $\frac{1}{4}$" high. The lower leaves are finely hairy, spatulate, tapering into petioles, and widely toothed. Numerous upper leaves are linear, few toothed to entire, and become sessile. (Native)

August 15–October 2   Frequent

Handling this plant, especially when it is dry, may cause skin, eye, and throat irritations. It was used externally by Native Americans as an astringent to stop minor bleeding. Long thought to repel fleas, the plant has been recently shown to be an effective insecticide.

HYSSOP-LEAVED THOROUGHWORT
Eupatorium hyssopifolium

COMPOSITE FAMILY
Compositae
(Asteraceae)

This 2' to 4' plant is rough-hairy and densely branched. The numerous heads have about 5 white disk florets. The leaves are opposite or in whorls of 4, strictly linear or grasslike, with tiny, petioled leaves in the axils. (Native)

August 23–October 7   Infrequent

A similar plant is *Eupatorium hyssopifolium* var. *laciniatum,* which has linear-lanceolate leaves.

Historically, herbalists have recounted the merits of this plant as an antidote to the poisonous bites of reptiles and the venomous stings of insects.

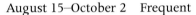

WHITE SNAKEROOT
Eupatorium rugosum
(*Ageratina altissima* var. *altissima*)

Composite Family
Compositae
(Asteraceae)

The heads have 15 to 30 tiny, white, tubular disk flowers and are arranged in a flattopped cyme. The plant is smooth and from 1' to 5' tall. Its leaves are toothed, opposite, petioled, and ovate, tapering to a point at the apex. The base of the leaves can be rounded, flat, heart shaped, or in many plants, tapering abruptly to the petiole. (Native)

August 10–October 22   Abundant

The leaves and stems contain a poisonous alcohol. Cattle that eat the plant produce poisonous milk. People who drink the milk may develop milk sickness, which can be fatal. Native Americans used a root tea of the plant to treat diarrhea, painful urination, fevers, and kidney stones.

LATE-FLOWERING THOROUGHWORT
Eupatorium serotinum

Composite Family
Compositae
(Asteraceae)

This 3' to 6' plant has a finely hairy stem, with leaves opposite below and alternate above. Heads of 7 to 15 greenish white, disk florets are in flat-topped clusters. Leaves are pointed lanceolate, long petioled, sharply toothed, 3" to 6" long, and have 3 primary veins. (Native)

August 23–October 2   Frequent

The genus name is dedicated to Mithridate Eupator, 132-63 B.C., ancient king of Ponthus (in an area that is now Turkey), who defeated the armies of Rome on several occasions. Mithridate is said to have used the genus medicinally.

SWEET EVERLASTING
Gnaphalium obtusifolium

COMPOSITE FAMILY
Compositae
(Asteraceae)

Note that the stem and underside of the leaves are cottony white on this 1' to 3' cobwebby plant. The leaves are alternate, almost linear, sessile, and downy hairy above, and have sparse, shallow, wavy teeth with margins slightly turned down. Clusters of flower heads, with thin, scalelike white bracts, are on terminal branches. (Native)

September 3–October 22   Frequent

A similar plant is *Gnaphalium purpureum,* which is smaller and has a spikelike inflorescence.

Folk medicine and Native Americans used this plant to treat worms, various types of minor bleeding, colds, diarrhea, stomach cramps, rheumatism, and as a sedative. It was also thought to be an aphrodisiac.

WHITE WINGSTEM
Verbesina virginica

COMPOSITE FAMILY
Compositae
(Asteraceae)

The stem on this 2' to 6' plant is winged. Leaves are alternate, broad lanceolate to lanceolate, with those below having somewhat winged petioles and those above becoming sessile. The plant branches at the top with flower heads terminal. Note the 3 to 5 white, ovate rays. (Native)

August 15–October 2   Infrequent

The common name for this lowland plant is derived from the wide wings running down the stem. Another common name for the plant is Crown-Beard. Apparently, no medicinal or food values have been attributed to this plant.

SMALL WHITE MORNING-GLORY
Ipomoea lacunosa

MORNING-GLORY FAMILY
Convolvulaceae

From only ½" to 1" wide, the small size of the white, 5-lobed, bell-like, tubular flowers is distinctive on this morning-glory. This hairy, twining plant is from 2' to 10' long. Flowering stems grow from the leaf axils and the long-petioled leaves are either heart shaped or 3-angular lobed. (Native)

August 23–September 14   Infrequent

The flowers are the smallest of any of our morning-glories. The genus name is from the Greek, *ips,* meaning worm, and is in reference to the twining habit of plants in the Morning-Glory Family.

STRIPED GENTIAN
Gentiana villosa

GENTIAN FAMILY
Gentianaceae

The flowers are in a dense, mostly terminal, sessile cluster and are about 1½" long, greenish white, purplish striped inside, and the lobes only partially open. The plant is smooth and from 6" to 24" tall. Leaves are smooth, opposite, entire, sessile, and ovate below, to narrow lanceolate near the top. (Native)

October 2–October 22   Infrequent

Herbalists of the past specified the use of gentian to treat the "bites of mad dogs," snakebite, rheumatism, and gout. More recently, herbal medicine has prescribed a tea from the plant as an appetite stimulant, which has been recently verified by scientific research.

BUGLEWEED
Lycopus virginicus

Mint Family
Labiatae
(Lamiaceae)

One may need a hand lens to see the form of the tiny, tubular, stalkless flowers clustered in the leaf axils on this 6" to 24" plant. Leaves are sharply toothed, pointed ovate, opposite, sessile above, and tapering to a very short petiole below. This is a smooth, odorless plant. (Native)

August 6–September 23   Frequent

The small, crisp tubers are said to be good raw or boiled. Several Native American tribes claimed Bugleweed was a mildly narcotic sedative. The Cherokee believed that the root given to children to chew, or rubbed on their lips, would give them the gift of eloquence.

HOG PEANUT
Amphicarpa bracteata
(*Amphicarpaea bracteata*)

Pea Family
Leguminosae
(Fabaceae)

This twining vine has a very slender, hairy stem. The leaves are long petioled and 3-divided. The leaflets are ovate and entire, with the terminal leaflet slightly broader and larger than the lateral. Flowers are pealike, usually white, and are in small, dangling clusters growing from the leaf axils. (Native)

August 17–September 14   Frequent

This plant has two kinds of seed pods, one above ground on the plant and one subterranean. Mice, voles, and other rodents relish the beans and store them in large quantities. Native Americans regularly ate the beans and collected them by raiding the stores of rodents. Though high in protein, the taste is perhaps an acquired one.

SERICEA LESPEDEZA
Lespedeza cuneata

PEA FAMILY
Leguminosae
(Fabaceae)

This erect, compact, leafy plant is from 2' to 4' tall. The leaves are linear, 1" to 1½" long, V-shaped with a sharp point on the tip, entire, and sessile. The tiny, white, pealike flowers are scattered up the stem in the leaf axils and have a purple spot on the standard. (Introduced)

August 23–September 30   Frequent

This often-cultivated *Lespedeza* was introduced and naturalized from Asia. It is used as a ground cover and provides considerable cover and protection for wildlife.

HAIRY BUSH-CLOVER
Lespedeza hirta

PEA FAMILY
Leguminosae
(Fabaceae)

This 2'- to 4'-tall plant has a rather stout and mostly erect stem and is very densely finely hairy. The pealike flowers are on branching, whitish, flowering stalks that are longer than the leaves and have purple at the base of the standard. The 3-divided leaves have fine hair even on the petioles of the broadly ovate to roundish leaflets. (Native)

September 4–September 14   Infrequent

A similar plant is *Lespedeza capitata,* which has more dense clusters of flowers and has narrow-lanceolate leaflets.

Though common, few of our native *Lespedeza* species are truly abundant. Several contain biologically active compounds and are being studied for potential medical uses.

SLENDER-STALKED GAURA
Gaura filipes

EVENING-PRIMROSE FAMILY
Onagraceae

This 1½' to 3½' plant is somewhat unusual with its very slender corolla tube below the reflexed calyx lobes and 4 spreading, somewhat single-sided, pinkish white petals. Note the cross-shaped stigma and the drooping stamens. Leaves are lanceolate, widely toothed, and nearly sessile. Flowers are in branched terminal spikes. (Native)

August 10–September 30   Infrequent

A hand lens is necessary to really appreciate the intricate beauty of this flower. Perhaps the most important fact about this plant and its need for preservation is that it is the single host for a very rare species of moth.

NODDING LADIES'-TRESSES
Spiranthes cernua

ORCHID FAMILY
Orchidaceae

Flowers are white, nodding, and arranged in a multiple (usually double) spiral around the stem. The stem is from 6" to 24" tall and microscopically hairy. The side petals, which are really sepals, are free and the lip is very finely scalloped on its edge. Leaves are mostly basal, up to 8" long, narrowing at the base, and broadest toward the apex. Stem leaves are very small and sheathing. (Native)

September 10–October 22   Infrequent

One account says this plant was used as an aphrodisiac by Native Americans. Its common name refers to the resemblance of the flower arrangement to the long, twisted curls once so fashionable for women's hair.

SLENDER LADIES'-TRESSES
Spiranthes gracilis
(*Spiranthes lacera* var. *gracilis*)

ORCHID FAMILY
Orchidaceae

The small, white, orchid flowers are in a single, distinct spiral on this slim, 8" to 20" plant. Flowers are about $\frac{1}{4}$" long with a smooth lip and free lateral sepals. Note the green spot on the base of the lip. Leaves are basal, ovate, and short petioled, but are usually absent at flowering time, leaving only a few scalelike leaves on the stalk. (Native)

August 25–October 5   Rare

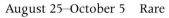

The genus name is from the Greek, *speira,* a coil or spiral, and *anthos,* a flower, and obviously refers to the way the small, orchid flowers spiral around the flowering stalk.

SMALL-FLOWERED LADIES'-TRESSES
Spiranthes ovalis

ORCHID FAMILY
Orchidaceae

This delicate little Ladies'-Tresses has a double spiral and is 4" to 15" tall. It may be minutely fine-hairy above. Leaves are mostly basal, with 1 or 2 stem leaves, and are linear to linear lanceolate, tapering into long, sheathing petioles. Flowers are white with lateral sepals free and the lower lip is very slightly fringed. (Native)

September 23–October 5   Rare

The common name Ladies'-Tresses refers to the similarity of the tight spirals of the flowers to the long, coiled hair fashions of the past. Native Americans used *Spiranthes* as a wash to strengthen their babies.

LADIES'-TRESSES
Spiranthes tuberosa

ORCHID FAMILY
Orchidaceae

This little, white orchid has a variable degree of twist in its single spiral, occasionally being almost single sided. Its basal, ovate leaves are generally gone by flowering time, leaving only a few lower, scalelike stem leaves. The very slender stem is smooth and the tip of the lower lip is crisped. Note that there is no green in the throat, as in *S. gracilis*. (Native)

August 6–September 20   Infrequent

Native Americans reportedly believed that *Spiranthes* was effective as an aphrodisiac. Native Americans regularly used these plants medicinally as a diuretic.

NODDING POGONIA
Triphora trianthophora

ORCHID FAMILY
Orchidaceae

This dainty little orchid usually has 3 pale pink to white, ⅝"-long flowers, with a somewhat crisped and green-striped lower lip. The flowers are nodding from the upper leaf axils. The plant is from 3" to 10" tall and has small, alternate, roundish leaves that form a sheath around the stalk at their base. (Native)

August 25   Rare

These plants won't be found in the same place each year because they die after flowering but produce new tubers that lie dormant for a variable number of years. Perhaps one reason for its rareness is the fondness rodents have for the tubers.

WHORLED MILKWORT
Polygala verticillata

MILKWORT FAMILY
Polygalaceae

This very slender, somewhat weak plant is 6" to 12" tall, with a smooth, branching stem. Note the linear, sessile, entire leaves in whorls of 3 to 6 with a minute, sharp tip. The tiny, greenish white flowers are in conelike spikes on long, slim flowering stalks. (Native)

August 1–September 14   Infrequent

Several species of this genus were used medicinally by both Native Americans and early settlers. One species was used widely to treat coughs and other bronchial ailments. Another was used to treat earaches.

SMARTWEED
Polygonum spp.

BUCKWHEAT FAMILY
Polygonaceae

One must resort to technical manuals to be sure of species identification with the Smartweeds. The genus, however, is not so difficult to identify. At the leaf joints there is a sheath-enclosed swelling. The tiny flowers consist of only sepals, are white to pink, and are in dense spikes on a long, flowering stem that is terminal or branching from the upper leaf axils. Leaves are alternate, and most in our area are linear lanceolate. This plant is found mostly in wet areas. (Native)

August 15–October 2   Abundant

Most members of this genus have an acrid-peppery taste and some of the milder species make an excellent seasoning in camp cooking. Some are like cayenne pepper. Native Americans used the plant to treat headaches, as a stimulant, and an antiseptic.

VIRGIN'S-BOWER
Clematis virginiana

BUTTERCUP FAMILY
Ranunculaceae

This is a climbing vine without tendrils whose height depends on the supporting vegetation. Leaves are petioled and divided into 3 ovate, lobed, or few sharp-toothed leaflets. The ⅝"-wide flowers are creamy white, 4-petaled (really sepaled), have bushy stamens, and are in spreading clusters growing from the leaf axils. (Native)

August 16–August 25   Infrequent

Weak preparations of this plant were used by Native Americans and early settlers to treat "the itch" and various skin irritations. The juice of this plant, as confirmed by recent scientific studies, may cause a serious dermatitis. Like other members of the Buttercup Family, the plants should be considered toxic.

TURTLEHEAD
Chelone glabra

FIGWORT FAMILY
Scrophulariaceae

Flowers are pale pink to whitish, about 1" long, tubular, 2-lipped with the upper lip forming a hood over the lower lip, and are arranged in a tight, mostly terminal cluster. The smooth plant is 1' to 3' tall. Leaves are opposite, pointed, narrow lanceolate, toothed, and from 1½" to 5" long. (Native)

September 23–October 6   Rare

Turtlehead had two primary uses by Native Americans and in folk medicine: to treat ailments of the liver and gallbladder and as a laxative, purgative, and worm medicine. It was also reported to have been used to prevent pregnancy.

CULVER'S-ROOT
Veronicastrum virginicum

FIGWORT FAMILY
Scrophulariaceae

Terminal on this 2' to 6' plant are several long, dense, spikelike racemes of $\frac{1}{4}$"-long, tubular flowers with 2 protruding stamens. The leaves are lanceolate, toothed, in whorls of from 3 to 7, and decrease in size as they ascend the stem. (Native)

August 3–August 14   Endangered

Native Americans used the dried root of Culver's-Root to purify themselves in their spiritual ceremonies. They drank a tea from the dried root to induce vomiting, to cause sweating, and as a powerful laxative. Only the dried root was used because of the dangerously violent reactions to the fresh plant.

JIMSONWEED
Datura stramonium

TOMATO FAMILY
Solanaceae

The 3"- to 4"-long, white flowers are trumpet shaped with pleated sides, and are tinged with purple. The 5 flaring lobes are pointed and somewhat swirling in appearance. The plant is smooth, 1' to 5' tall, and the stem is often purplish. Leaves are long petioled, irregularly lobed, and coarsely toothed. (Introduced)

August 17–September 6   Infrequent

Jimsonweed can be violently poisonous. Native Americans sometimes used measured doses of the hallucinogenic seeds to aid in producing visions. It contains the alkaloid atropine, which is used in modern medicine to treat eye, skin, rectal, stomach, and intestinal disorders.

WINGSTEM
Actinomeris alternifolia
(*Verbesina alternifolia*)

COMPOSITE FAMILY
Compositae
(Asteraceae)

The yellow flower heads on this 3' to 9' plant are rather ragged looking, with numerous heads on terminal branching stems. The 2 to 8 somewhat reflexed rays are often of unequal length, and the disk flowers are loosely arranged. Leaves are rough, pointed lanceolate, toothed, and the short petioles spread into wings on the stem of the plant. (Native)

August 13–October 7   Abundant

The genus name is from the Greek words *actis,* meaning ray, and *meris,* meaning part, and alludes to the irregular number and length of the rays. This tall plant is numerous and, despite the few rays, often blankets river terraces in yellow in the early fall.

TICKSEED SUNFLOWER
Bidens aristosa

COMPOSITE FAMILY
Compositae
(Asteraceae)

This much-branched, dark-stemmed plant is from 1' to 3' tall. The flower heads are about 1¾" wide, numerous, and have from 6 to 9 bright yellow rays. Note that the inner and outer bracts are about the same length. Upper leaves are 3-divided and lower leaves are 5- to 7-divided. Leaflets are lanceolate, variously lobed, and toothed. (Native)

September 4–September 24   Infrequent

Bidens has been employed for centuries by folk medicine practitioners to treat everything from liver complaints, colds, headaches, coughs, and heart palpitations to skin irritations, nervous conditions, and insomnia.

STICKTIGHT
Bidens frondosa

Composite Family
Compositae
(Asteraceae)

Stems on this 1' to 3' plant are smooth, branching, and sometimes purplish. The disk flowers
on the ½"- to ¾"-wide heads are orange and
the rays are either very small or absent. Note
the long, leafy bracts subtending the heads.
Leaves are long petioled and divided into 3 to 5
lanceolate and toothed segments. (Native)

September 3–October 2   Frequent

A similar sticktight is *Bidens comosa,* which has
undivided, lanceolate, wing-margined leaves.

People who spend time in the fields and woods during the fall will recognize the
fruits that stick by barbed awns to clothes, and few plants have a common name
so appropriate. The stiff-awned fruits may cause serious irritation to animals if
they work their way to the skin in numbers.

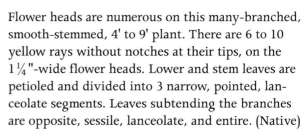

TALL COREOPSIS
Coreopsis tripteris

Composite Family
Compositae
(Asteraceae)

Flower heads are numerous on this many-branched,
smooth-stemmed, 4' to 9' plant. There are 6 to 10
yellow rays without notches at their tips, on the
1¼"-wide flower heads. Lower and stem leaves are
petioled and divided into 3 narrow, pointed, lanceolate segments. Leaves subtending the branches
are opposite, sessile, lanceolate, and entire. (Native)

August 3–September 30   Infrequent

The genus name comes from the Greek *coris,* meaning
bug, and *opsis,* meaning appearance, and refers to the achene, which has a fancied resemblance to a bug. The second word in the scientific name, *tripteris,* refers to the 3-parted leaves. This is a mostly barren-area plant and is indeed tall,
reaching up to 9' in height.

AUTUMN SNEEZEWEED
Helenium autumnale

COMPOSITE FAMILY
Compositae
(Asteraceae)

This 2' to 3' plant is similar to *H. nudiflorum,* but has a yellow globular disk and lacks the winged-petioled lower leaves of *H. nudiflorum.* This smooth, wing-stemmed plant branches above and has numerous heads. There are 10 to 18 wedge-shaped, 3-toothed, drooping, yellow rays. Leaves are lanceolate, toothed, and sessile. (Native)

September 19–October 6   Rare

Livestock grazing on the mature flower heads may be poisoned. Symptoms of poisoning include labored breathing and staggering. Death is normally preceded by convulsions. Herbal medicinal uses include treatment for worms and fever. Native Americans used powdered disk florets as a snuff to treat headaches. Scientific tests have indicated significant antitumor properties.

EGGERT'S SUNFLOWER
Helianthus eggertii

COMPOSITE FAMILY
Compositae
(Asteraceae)

This sunflower is 2' to 4' tall with a smooth, bluish, waxy stem. The leaves are lanceolate, opposite, nearly sessile, entire to very lightly toothed, and reduced in size toward the summit. The leaves are whitish and waxy beneath. The flower heads are about $2\frac{1}{2}$" wide with approximately 10 yellow rays. (Native)

July 29–September 26   Endangered

This plant is currently under review for endangered status by the United States Fish and Wildlife Service. It is known from only 16 counties in three states and most of the Kentucky locations are in or near the park. This plant should be zealously protected.

SMALL WOOD SUNFLOWER
Helianthus microcephalus

COMPOSITE FAMILY
Compositae
(Asteraceae)

Flower heads on this terminally branching, 3' to 6' plant
are only about 1¼" wide and
have from 5 to 10 yellow rays
with a yellow disk. The stem
is smooth and the leaves are rough above and pale downy below. Leaves are
opposite, petioled, sharply toothed, and lanceolate below to pointed and
narrow lanceolate above. (Native)

August 11–September 30   Frequent

Sunflowers are the flower emblem of Peru. The Aztecs of Mexico saw the sunflower as the emblem of the sun and their reverence for the flower is manifested
in their art and architectural decorations. One tribe of Native Americans prescribed the application of wild sunflower for the treatment of spider bites.

HAIRY SUNFLOWER
Helianthus mollis

COMPOSITE FAMILY
Compositae
(Asteraceae)

The 2' to 3½' stem is densely whitish-hairy and
may be somewhat rough on this generally
unbranching plant. Flower heads are terminal,
usually solitary, 2½" wide, and have 15 to 25
yellow rays. Leaves are short, opposite, toothed,
and pointed ovate with a somewhat clasping,
heart-shaped base. The leaves are rough-hairy
above and whitish-downy below. (Native)

August 1–August 25   Rare

The leaves of a closely related species have been
used to treat malaria. Some Native Americans reportedly used the leaves as a substitute for tobacco.

WESTERN SUNFLOWER
Helianthus occidentalis

COMPOSITE FAMILY
Compositae
(Asteraceae)

Leaves on this 1' to 3' sunflower are mostly basal, with perhaps 1 or 2 pairs of stem leaves. Basal leaves are lanceolate, have barely noticeable teeth, are finely hairy, and taper into very long, hairy petioles. Stem leaves are much smaller and short petioled. Flower heads have 12 to 15 yellow rays and are about 2" wide. (Native)

August 16–September 18   Infrequent

Some Native Americans are reported to have thoroughly mashed the roots of this plant and used the pulpy remains in a poultice to draw blisters. Sunflower heads turn with the movement of the sun and thus remain facing the sun throughout the day.

JERUSALEM ARTICHOKE
Helianthus tuberosus

COMPOSITE FAMILY
Compositae
(Asteraceae)

This big, hairy-stemmed sunflower is from 5' to 10' tall, branching above with numerous 2"- to 3"-wide, yellow flowers. The flower heads have 12 to 20 rays. Leaves are 3-veined, stiff, very rough above, finely hairy beneath, and sharply toothed. Lower leaves may be 4" to 8" long, opposite, broadly lanceolate, tapering into winged petioles. Upper leaves are alternate, lanceolate, and short petioled. (Native)

August 19–September 24   Rare

This sunflower was cultivated by Native Americans, who introduced it to the settlers. The tubers may be prepared as potatoes, but are lower in starch. Available in specialty stores today, the plant has been cultivated more in Europe than in North America.

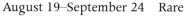

HAIRY HAWKWEED
Hieracium gronovii

Composite Family
Compositae
(Asteraceae)

This 1' to 3' plant is very hairy, especially below. The solitary stem is slender and has a panicle of small heads with yellow rays. Basal leaves are hairy, smooth margined, and pointed spatulate, tapering into petioles. Lower stem leaves are hairy, ovate, sessile, and entire. There are no middle or upper stem leaves. (Native)

August 10–September 24   Frequent

We have three or possibly four of the approximately 50 North American species of Hawkweed in the park. The basal leaves are readily eaten by both Wild Turkey and White-Tailed Deer.

ROUGH HAWKWEED
Hieracium scabrum

Composite Family
Compositae
(Asteraceae)

The yellow, dandelion-like, $\frac{1}{2}$"-wide flower heads are in a short, spreading panicle on this rough, hairy, 1' to 3' plant. Leaves are ovate, short petioled to mostly sessile, entire, hairy, and become smaller upward to the flowering stalks. Note the absence of margined and long petioled basal leaves. (Native)

September 23–October 2   Infrequent

Folk and herbal medicine suggest that the juice of the hawkweeds mixed in wine helps digestion and dispels gas. It was also mixed with honey to treat coughs, asthma, and upper respiratory ailments.

ORANGE CONEFLOWER
Rudbeckia fulgida

COMPOSITE FAMILY
Compositae
(Asteraceae)

This 1' to 3' plant has a hairy stem and is usually solitary or very sparingly branched. Flower heads are 1¼" wide with 8 to 15 notched yellow rays, which have darker, often orangish, bases. Leaves are widely shallow toothed, lightly hairy, with the basal and lower being 3-veined, ovate, and tapering into long, margined petioles. Upper leaves become lanceolate and sessile. (Native)

August 3–September 30   Infrequent

This *Rudbeckia* was used by Native Americans to treat inflamed eyes, which probably originated from the resemblance of the flower head to the eye. It was also used as a wash for snakebite.

THIN-LEAVED CONEFLOWER
Rudbeckia triloba

COMPOSITE FAMILY
Compositae
(Asteraceae)

Lower leaves on this branched, hairy-stemmed, 1' to 4' plant are rough on both surfaces, 3-lobed, tapering into petioles, and the lobes are lanceolate and toothed. Upper leaves are alternate, solitary, broadly lanceolate, toothed, and decrease in size at the top. Flower heads are numerous, 1½" to 2" wide, with 8 to 12 slightly notched, yellow rays and a dark purple center. (Native)

August 3–October 2   Frequent

In a robust individual, Thin-Leaved Coneflower could be mistaken for Black-Eyed Susan. The 3-part basal leaves are distinctive. Like other *Rudbeckia,* it may have antibiotic properties that would verify past medicinal uses.

WOODLAND CONEFLOWER
Rudbeckia umbrosa
(Rudbeckia fulgida var. *umbrosa*)

<small>COMPOSITE FAMILY</small>
Compositae
(Asteraceae)

This plant has a 1½' to 3½', short-hairy, mostly single but occasionally branched, stem. There are 8 to 12 orange-yellow rays and the dark purple disk is somewhat depressed. Basal leaves are oval, widely toothed, finely hairy, long petioled, and some may have slightly heart-shaped bases. Upper leaves become ovate, alternate, and nearly sessile. (Native)

August 1–October 7   Infrequent

Of the approximately 30 species of *Rudbeckia* native to North America, this is one of the few that thrive in a moist woodland habitat. The genus *Rudbeckia* is named after the seventeenth-century father and son botanists, the Rudbecks of Sweden.

PRAIRIE-DOCK
**Silphium terebinthinaceum
var. *pinnatifidum***
(Silphium pinnatifidum)

<small>COMPOSITE FAMILY</small>
Compositae
(Asteraceae)

This is a very tall, 4' to 9' plant with a nearly leafless, smooth stem. Leaves are basal, 10" to 14" long, mostly deeply lobed, and rough. The large flower heads are in a terminal panicle and have 12 to 20 notched, yellow rays. (Native)

August 23   Rare

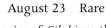

Like several species of *Silphium,* the Prairie-Dock produces a hardened sap that makes a pleasant chewing gum. Native Americans used a leaf tea to treat coughs and lung ailments.

TALL GOLDENROD
Solidago altissima
(Solidago canadensis var. *scabra)*

COMPOSITE FAMILY
Compositae
(Asteraceae)

The stem on this 2' to 7' plant is somewhat rough
and grayish-downy, especially above. The
crowded, 3-veined leaves are narrow lanceolate.
Those below are sharply toothed and short petioled, and those above are sessile with fewer teeth,
becoming almost entire at the top. Leaves are
rough above and finely hairy beneath. Flower
heads on the large, plume-shaped arrangement
have 9 to 15 yellow rays. (Native)

September 6–October 6   Frequent

Native Americans used the dried flowers in a wet
poultice to treat sores. Mixed with other plants,
goldenrod was also used similarly to treat snakebite.

SHARP-LEAVED GOLDENROD
Solidago arguta

COMPOSITE FAMILY
Compositae
(Asteraceae)

The stem is from 2' to 5' tall, mostly smooth,
and often reddish brown in color. The lower
leaves are from 3" to 12" long, ovate tapering to
margined petioles, sharply double toothed, and
acute. Upper leaves are broad lanceolate, shal-
lowly sharp toothed, and sessile. Heads are
single-sided with 5 to 8 yellow rays. (Native)

August 7–September 30   Rare

According to the ancient practice of assigning a
meaning or symbolism to each flower, the senti-
ment and symbolism of giving goldenrod is a
wish of good fortune for the recipient.

BLUE-STEMMED GOLDENROD
Solidago caesia

COMPOSITE FAMILY
Compositae
(Asteraceae)

The stem on this 1' to 3' plant is arching, slender, often with a bluish film, and bends slightly at the leaf axils. Leaves are alternate, sessile, sharply toothed, and narrow lanceolate. The flower heads are in small clusters in the leaf axils, becoming more numerous toward the summit. The individual flower heads have 3 to 5 yellow rays. (Native)

August 16–October 7   Frequent

Goldenrod is the state flower of Nebraska, North Carolina, Alabama, and Kentucky. Like most of the other states, Kentucky is not very specific about which of the many species is the state flower.

ERECT GOLDENROD
Solidago erecta
(*Solidago speciosa* var. *erecta*)

COMPOSITE FAMILY
Compositae
(Asteraceae)

This is a strictly erect species, with 6 to 9 yellow rays. The flower heads are in shortstalked clusters in a spike-like arrangement. Lower leaves are toothed, pointed spatulate, and taper into long, winged petioles. Middle and upper leaves are small, alternate, lanceolate, sessile, and entire. This 1' to 3' plant is similar to *S. hispida,* but is not hairy except for some very fine hair above. (Native)

August 23–October 7   Frequent

Two similar plants are *Solidago bicolor,* with whitish flowers, and *S. speciosa,* which is larger and short branched.

At about the time of the American Revolution, a widely used tea was made from goldenrod. Because of the possible presence of a poisonous fungus that often grows on the plants, such a tea is not recommended. Goldenrods are almost exclusively New World plants.

BROAD-LEAVED GOLDENROD
Solidago flexicaulis

COMPOSITE FAMILY
Compositae
(Asteraceae)

The smooth, 1' to 3' stem bends or angles at the leaf axils. Flower heads are in small clusters on short stalks from the upper leaf axils and there are 3 to 4 rays. Leaves are very sharply toothed, pointed and broadly ovate, tapering to short, somewhat winged petioles. Uppermost leaves become lanceolate. (Native)

August 25–October 7   Infrequent

At least one of the northern tribes of Native Americans reportedly used this plant medicinally. The dried root was chewed to aid in the treatment of sore throats.

LATE GOLDENROD
Solidago gigantea

COMPOSITE FAMILY
Compositae
(Asteraceae)

The plumelike arrangement of the flowering heads is terminal on this 3'- to 7'-tall, smooth, sometimes purplish stem, which often has a whitish film. The leaves have 3 primary veins, are lanceolate, sharply toothed, sessile, and may have some fine hair on veins beneath. The yellow flower heads have from 7 to 15 rays. (Native)

August 1–September 24   Frequent

Goldenrods are pollinated by bees and other insects and are not dependent on airborne pollen. Yet, goldenrods have been cursed for centuries by those who suffer from hay fever. The goldenrods have gotten this bum rap by being conspicuous and in flower at the same time as the probable culprits, the ragweeds.

LANCE-LEAVED GOLDENROD
Solidago graminifolia
(Euthamia graminifolia)

COMPOSITE FAMILY
Compositae
(Asteraceae)

Note that the heads on this 2' to 4' plant are in a flat-topped arrangement terminal on numerous branches. There are from 12 to 20 yellow rays on the flower heads. Leaves are numerous, linear, pointed at both ends, and have 3 to 5 parallel veins. (Native)

August 1–September 30   Locally Frequent

The Chippewa are reported to have boiled the roots of this goldenrod to extract the active ingredients needed to treat a patient for chest pain. Other Native Americans also used goldenrod in steam baths to ease pain.

HAIRY GOLDENROD
Solidago hispida

COMPOSITE FAMILY
Compositae
(Asteraceae)

This 1' to 3' plant is very similar to *S. erecta,* but is densely covered with short hair. There are 7 to 14 yellow rays on heads in clusters at the upper leaf axils and at the summit in a spikelike arrangement. Lower leaves are pointed spatulate and toothed, tapering into long, winged petioles. Upper leaves become lanceolate, sessile, and entire. (Native)

August 25–October 7   Rare

Goldenrods flower in late summer and early fall when few other plants bloom, making them desirable garden plants. They require little attentive cultivation and are mostly disease and insect resistant, with the main exception being aphids.

GREY GOLDENROD
Solidago nemoralis

COMPOSITE FAMILY
Compositae
(Asteraceae)

Growing from 6" to 24" tall, this plant has a mostly narrow plume, with heads on the upper side. The stem is densely covered with very fine, gray hair. Lower leaves are pointed spatulate, toothed, and taper gradually to the stalk. Upper leaves are lanceolate, becoming entire and sessile, and have a pair of tiny leaflets in the axils. Note the 5 to 9 yellow rays. (Native)

August 13–October 7   Frequent

Herbalists have recommended this goldenrod as an agent for expelling intestinal gas. Clinical tests indicate that its use as a carminative is probably valid.

SWEET GOLDENROD
Solidago odora

COMPOSITE FAMILY
Compositae
(Asteraceae)

Flower heads are single sided in a loose, few-branched, plumelike cluster and the flower heads have 3 to 5 yellow rays. Leaves on this 2' to 4' goldenrod are very narrow lanceolate, sessile, entire, and from 2" to 4" long. Note that the leaves have tiny, transparent dots. (Native)

September 10–October 7   Infrequent

Sweet Goldenrod can be identified by the sweet odor of its crushed leaves. Its dried leaves have been widely recommended for use in making a delicious tea. In the early 1800s, the dried leaves were exported to China for tea. The Cherokee used the plant to treat fevers.

ROUGH-STEMMED GOLDENROD
Solidago rugosa

COMPOSITE FAMILY
Compositae
(Asteraceae)

This 2' to 6' goldenrod has a usually rough-hairy stem and several spreading and arching flowering stems. Flower heads have from 6 to 10 rays. Lowest leaves are pointed spatulate, ragged toothed, somewhat fine-hairy, and taper into winged petioles. Upper leaves becoming lanceolate, toothed, less hairy, and short petioled to nearly sessile. Note that the leaves have a wrinkled appearance. (Native)

September 13   Infrequent

Goldenrods are widely known to produce a yellow dye of reliable fastness. Its use, however, has been mostly restricted to home and craft dyers and ignored by professionals for some unexplained reason.

FALSE GOLDENROD
Solidago sphacelata

COMPOSITE FAMILY
Compositae
(Asteraceae)

There are only a few flowering stems on this 2' to 4' goldenrod. The basal leaves, which are more numerous than the flowering stems, are long petioled, sharply toothed, and broadly ovate or heart shaped. Leaves become progressively smaller up the stem until the uppermost are sessile. The yellow flower heads have about 5 rays. (Native)

August 25–September 23   Infrequent

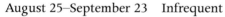

Goldenrods contain latex in their leaves. A few species contain enough to have warranted research in the past to develop hybrids for use in rubber production. Goldenrods were once exported to England, where they were thought to have the power to heal wounds.

ELM-LEAVED GOLDENROD
Solidago ulmifolia

<small>COMPOSITE FAMILY</small>
Compositae
(Asteraceae)

The few flowering branches are finely hairy, leafy, and spreading, with 3- to 5-rayed, yellow flower heads on the upper side only. The stem on this 1½' to 3' plant is smooth below and very finely hairy above. Lower leaves are pointed spatulate to widely lanceolate, nearly smooth on the surface, sharply toothed, and taper into winged petioles. Upper leaves are nearly sessile, lanceolate, and toothed to nearly smooth margined at the top. (Native)

August 3–September 23   Frequent

Given their enormous abundance, the goldenrods have relatively little food value for most wildlife, though they provide a small amount of food for several birds, rabbits, mice, and even deer. Herbalists have recommended a leaf tea of goldenrod to treat fevers.

COPPERY ST. JOHN'S-WORT
Hypericum denticulatum

<small>ST. JOHN'S-WORT FAMILY</small>
Guttiferae

This 8" to 20" species has a smooth, slender, 4-angled stem. The leaves are about ¾" long, ovate, sessile, entire, and somewhat erect. The scattered flowers are on terminally branching stems, are coppery yellow, and the pinwheel-like petals are about ⅖" long. (Native)

August 1–August 19   Infrequent

Two smaller St. John's-Worts are *Hypericum mutilum,* which has ½"-wide flowers and 5-veined ovate leaves, and *H. drummondii,* which has short, rigid, linear leaves.

Recent studies indicate that this genus contains compounds that have antiretroviral effects. They are also being researched as a treatment for AIDS.

HORSE-BALM
Collinsonia canadensis

MINT FAMILY
Labiatae
(Lamiaceae)

A hand lens is needed to really appreciate the beauty of these ½"-long, yellow, tubular flowers with their delicately fringed lower lip and 2 protruding stamens. The flowers are in a 6" to 12" terminal panicle on this 2' to 3' plant. Leaves are opposite, pointed, broadly ovate, toothed, and long petioled, except for the very uppermost, which are much smaller and sessile. (Native)

August 25–October 7   Infrequent

Horse-Balm has a strong lemon smell. It was used by mountain settlers and Native Americans in teas to treat headaches and constipation, and in poultices to treat cuts, burns, bruises, and more serious wounds.

PARTRIDGE-PEA
Cassia fasciculata
(*Chamaecrista fasciculata*)

PEA FAMILY
Leguminosae
(Fabaceae)

This low, widely branching plant is 1' to 2½' tall with alternate, pinnately compound leaves. The 10 to 15 pairs of leaflets are linear and pointed at both ends. Flowers are in 2- to 4-flowered clusters in the leaf axils, have 5 yellow petals with red spots at the bases and drooping stamens. Note that there are 4 yellow anthers and 6 purple anthers. (Native)

August 3–September 20   Abundant

The pitted seeds are a valuable food source for Bobwhite Quail and the plant is eaten to a limited extent by deer. Interestingly, the bright yellow flowers do not contain nectar. It is the glands below the first pair of leaflets that contain the nectar attractive to pollinating insects.

WILD SENNA
Cassia marilandica
(*Senna marilandica*)

PEA FAMILY
Leguminosae
(Fabaceae)

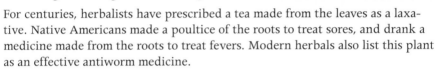

Note the unequal length of the stamens and how the lower ones curve downward, then back up. Clusters of 5-petaled flowers grow from the upper leaf axils on this heavy, sparingly branched, 3' to 5' plant. The leaves are pinnately compound with 6 to 10 pairs of pointed-oblong to lanceolate leaflets with tiny, spinelike tips. (Native)

August 6–August 19   Infrequent

For centuries, herbalists have prescribed a tea made from the leaves as a laxative. Native Americans made a poultice of the roots to treat sores, and drank a medicine made from the roots to treat fevers. Modern herbals also list this plant as an effective antiworm medicine.

EVENING-PRIMROSE
Oenothera biennis

EVENING-PRIMROSE FAMILY
Onagraceae

Flowers open at dusk on this mostly hairy, 2' to 5' plant. If not pollinated during the night, they will stay open for several hours the next day. The flower is about 1" wide and has 4 broad, yellow petals, 4 deeply reflexed sepals, and a cross-shaped stigma. The leaves are nearly sessile, alternate, lanceolate, wavy edged, toothed, and 1" to 5" long. (Native)

August 3–September 23   Frequent

The night-blooming flowers are pollinated by night-flying insects such as moths. The roots and flowers are widely eaten by humans, and the plant and its seeds are eaten by deer, birds, and small rodents. Claims for its medicinal benefits include the prevention of acne, alcoholism, and obesity.

MULLEIN FOXGLOVE
Seymeria macrophylla
(Dasistoma macrophylla)

FIGWORT FAMILY
Scrophulariaceae

This slightly hairy, many-branched plant is from 3' to 5' tall. The lower leaves are large, deeply cut, and the segments are irregularly lobed or toothed. Upper leaves are oblong lanceolate, becoming much smaller at the summit, short petioled, and entire. The short, ¾"-long, yellow, tubular flowers have 5 spreading lobes, hairy throats, and are in the leaf axils. (Native)

August 1   Rare

Like some other members of this family, the Mullein Foxglove turns black when dried, which makes herbarium specimens aesthetically unappealing but still usable. The common name may have been derived from the superstition that the "little people," or fairies, gave these blossoms to foxes to wear as gloves, which kept them from being caught when raiding chicken houses.

CARDINAL FLOWER
Lobelia cardinalis

LOBELIA FAMILY
Campanulaceae

Words cannot convey the brilliance of the scarlet red flowers on this unbranched, 2' to 4' plant. The tight raceme of flowers is 6" to 12" long and the blossoms are tubular, 1½" long, with a 3-lobed lower and 2-lobed upper lip. The tall, nodding tube of stamens project up and over the flower through a cleft in the tube. Leaves are alternate, toothed, and lanceolate, tapering at both ends. (Native)

August 10–October 6   Infrequent

The root of the Cardinal Flower was an ingredient in several Native American love potions. They also used the root to treat intestinal worms. A leaf tea was used to treat colds, headaches, fevers, and rheumatism. Taken in quantity, the several alkaloids in the plant may prove toxic.

TALL THISTLE
Cirsium altissimum

Cᴏᴍᴘᴏsɪᴛᴇ Fᴀᴍɪʟʏ
Compositae
(Asteraceae)

This 3' to 10' plant does not have the deeply incised, sharp leaf lobes characteristic of our other thistles. The upper leaves are more linear with fewer spine-tipped teeth than the lower ones. Leaves are sessile and whitish short-hairy beneath. Flower heads are about 2" wide and pinkish purple. Outer bracts have short spines on their tips. (Native)

August 14–October 22   Infrequent

A similar plant is *Cirsium carolinianum,* which has less than 20, narrow-lanceolate, remotely lobed leaves.

The young stems are said to be excellent when peeled and eaten either raw or cooked. They are also recommended when prepared as you would sweet cucumber pickles. Raw roots are a reasonable survival food.

FIELD THISTLE
Cirsium discolor

Cᴏᴍᴘᴏsɪᴛᴇ Fᴀᴍɪʟʏ
Compositae
(Asteraceae)

The stem on this 3' to 7' plant has no wings. Note how the very uppermost leaves form a rosette under the 1 $\frac{1}{2}$"- to 2"-wide, pink flower heads. Leaves are cut almost to the midrib and the narrow segments are bristle tipped. Also note that leaves are white-woolly beneath. Bracts are tipped with colorless bristles. (Native)

August 14–September 23   Infrequent

This thistle contains a substance that in very small amounts will cause milk to curdle. It has been used in the past in cheesemaking. With the spines removed, or the stems peeled, it is an excellent potherb when boiled in salted water.

BULL THISTLE
Cirsium vulgare

COMPOSITE FAMILY
Compositae
(Asteraceae)

Growing from 3' to 5' tall, this thistle has mostly 1 to 3 heads of reddish purple flowers. Note the stiff, yellowish tipped spines on the bracts. Leaves are deeply cut, with irregular, sharp, spine-tipped teeth and are whitish woolly beneath. Bases of the leaves continue into spine-tipped wings on the stem. (Introduced)

August 16–September 6   Infrequent

Thistle (though not this particular species) is the national emblem of Scotland. The seeds of this much-maligned plant are perhaps the favorite food of the American Goldfinch. The roots are said to be good when boiled, sliced, and stir fried. It is used widely in China to treat internal bleeding and inflammation.

BLAZING STAR
Liatris aspera

COMPOSITE FAMILY
Compositae
(Asteraceae)

The numerous, alternate leaves on this 1' to 2½' plant are nearly linear, entire, and smooth. The several, almost sessile, flower heads are in a spike and there are from 25 to 40 tiny, pink, tubular florets in each head. Note the rough, spreading, rounded bracts with their somewhat crisped and purplish colored edges. (Native)

August 15–September 23   Infrequent

A similar plant is *Liatris spicata,* which has sessile heads with more pointed bracts.

Now widely used as a garden plant, *Liatris* has been used as an additive to tobacco for flavoring. Folk remedies include Blazing Star for treatment of kidney and bladder problems, as well as sore throat.

THREE-SEEDED MERCURY
Acalypha virginica

SPURGE FAMILY
Euphorbiaceae

Note the pairs of small, reddish, and deeply lobed bracts in the leaf axils, which may be mistaken for petals at first glance. The flowers, which have no petals, are inconspicuous and somewhat enclosed in the bracts. The plant is 6" to 20" tall and the stem may become reddish with age. Leaves are alternate, toothed, petioled, and pointed ovate. (Native)

August 15–October 6   Frequent

A similar plant is *Acalypha rhomboidea,* which has rhombic-ovate leaves with much longer petioles.

The genus name is from the Greek, *acalephe,* meaning nettle, which the plant somewhat resembles. Tiny pistillate and staminate flowers are on the same spike on this plant mostly of roadsides and waste places.

SPEARMINT
Mentha spicata

MINT FAMILY
Labiatae
(Lamiaceae)

Flowers on this 1' to 1½' plant are often in dense whorls on paired spikes growing from the leaf axils. In addition, there is a single, larger, terminal spike. The individual flowers are pale pink, tubular, have 4 corolla lobes, and the style protrudes past the corolla. Leaves are lanceolate, toothed, opposite, sessile above, and very short petioled below. (Introduced)

August 17   Rare

Besides its well-known use in chewing gum, Spearmint is widely used as a flavoring in sauces, drinks, and dressings. Less known is its past use by Native Americans to treat stomach gas and as a worm medicine.

JAPANESE MINT
Mosla dianthera

MINT FAMILY
Labiatae
(Lamiaceae)

This is a small, inconspicuous mint with tiny, pinkish, tubular flowers, with the upper lip notched and the lower lip 3-lobed. It is an erect plant 6" to 20" tall. Leaves are lanceolate, petioled and toothed. (Introduced)

September 14–October 5   Infrequent

First found in this country in McCreary County, Kentucky, it was thought to be a plant previously unknown to science. Upon presentation as a new species, it was determined to be a common and abundant plant in Asia, from where it was introduced. The species name refers to the two anthers. The common name is my invention.

FALSE DRAGONHEAD
Physostegia virginiana

MINT FAMILY
Labiatae
(Lamiaceae)

As others in the Mint Family, this 1' to 3' plant has a square stem. The flowers are about 1" long, pinkish or pale purple, tubular, with a spotted, 3-lobed lower lip. They appear in tall, dense spikes. Leaves are lanceolate to narrow lanceolate above, toothed, and sessile. (Native)

September 4–October 7   Rare

The common name comes from a fancied resemblance of the flower to the head of a dragon with its mouth open. Another common name, Obedient Plant, came from the belief that if the position of the flowers is changed they will remain in the new position.

GROUNDNUT
Apios americana

PEA FAMILY
Leguminosae
(Fabaceae)

This slender, climbing vine has short-stalked, compact clusters of $\frac{1}{2}$"-wide, maroon, pealike flowers growing from the leaf axils. The leaves are alternate, long petioled, and divided into 5 to 7 broadly lanceolate leaflets. (Native)

August 15–August 25   Infrequent

The seeds are edible when prepared as peas. The high-protein tubers are a great potato substitute, and can be cooked in any of the ways potatoes are prepared. It is said that the pilgrims at Plymouth may have perished in their first winter had they not been introduced to this plant by friendly Native Americans.

HOARY TICK-TREFOIL
Desmodium canescens

PEA FAMILY
Leguminosae
(Fabaceae)

Very sticky-hairy to the touch, this plant is hairy all over. It is many branched and from 3' to 5' tall. Its leaves are on long petioles, are 3-divided, and the leaflets are ovate, and entire. The terminal leaflet is larger than the lateral. The pealike flowers are in terminal branched racemes, are about $\frac{1}{4}$" long, and may lose their color rather quickly. Note the hairy, pointed-ovate stipules. (Native)

August 25–September 26   Frequent

A similar species is *Desmodium perplexum,* which is more branched, has smaller leaves, and is less hairy.

A useful aid in identifying this plant is to grip the terminal branches and let them move through your hands, noting how very sticky the plant feels. Though in great abundance in the eastern United States, there are few records of Native Americans making use of this genus of plants.

SMALL-LEAVED TICK-TREFOIL
Desmodium ciliare

PEA FAMILY
Leguminosae
(Fabaceae)

This finely hairy, somewhat bushy, 1' to 3' plant could be confused with a Bush-Clover because of the appearance of the small, ovate leaflets. The leaves have finely hairy petioles, are 3-divided, and the leaflets are less than 1" long. The pink, pealike flowers are only $\frac{1}{4}$" long and in terminal racemes. (Native)

August 10–September 14   Infrequent

The genus name is derived from the Greek *desmos,* meaning chain. This refers, of course, to the way the jointed, triangular-shaped seed pods are connected in a series.

LARGE-BRACTED TICK-TREFOIL
Desmodium cuspidatum

PEA FAMILY
Leguminosae
(Fabaceae)

This is a mostly smooth Tick-Trefoil, from 2' to 6' tall, with its leaves occurring alternately over most of the stem. Leaves are petioled and 3-divided, and the leaflets have rounded bases and are pointed ovate, with the terminal leaflet slightly larger. The pealike flowers are about $\frac{1}{2}$" long, purple, and in loose racemes. (Native)

August 25–September 13   Infrequent

This genus is found in such diverse locations as Africa, Australia, and South America, with 50 or more species in North America alone. It is interesting that the plants are absent from the western United States.

PANICLED TICK-TREFOIL
Desmodium paniculatum

PEA FAMILY
Leguminosae
(Fabaceae)

Note that the leaves are long petioled and the 3 leaflets are narrow lanceolate. The plant is from 2' to 3' tall and is smooth, or very finely hairy above. Flowers are pealike, about ⅓" long, pink, and on short branchlets toward the summit of the primary branch. (Native)

August 29–September 14   Frequent

Although there are numerous species of *Desmodium* in the eastern United States and the plants are abundant, wildlife make little use of them. However, the Bobwhite Quail regularly eats the seeds and there is some minor use by the White-Footed Mouse, Wild Turkey, and White-Tailed Deer.

ROUND-LEAF TICK-TREFOIL
Desmodium rotundifolium

PEA FAMILY
Leguminosae
(Fabaceae)

It is sometimes called Prostrate Tick-Trefoil because of the trailing habit of the slim, hairy, 2' to 6' stems. The leaves are 3-divided, petioled, and the leaflets are entire and almost completely round, subtended by small stipules. The pink, pealike flowers are few. (Native)

August 11–September 16   Frequent

This is mostly a plant of dry woods and grows flat on the ground. If the "Beggar-Lice" burrs stick to the coats of passing animals as tenaciously as they do to one's socks, it is easy to understand how this genus has become so widely distributed and abundant.

BUSH-CLOVER
Lespedeza intermedia

PEA FAMILY
Leguminosae
(Fabaceae)

The stem on this little-branched, 1' to 3' Bush-Clover is erect and nearly smooth. The leaves are short petioled and 3-divided, and the leaflets are ovate, entire, dark green above, and very finely hairy beneath. The violet, pealike flowers are in small clusters in the leaf axils, becoming crowded
toward the summit. (Native)

August 25–September 13   Infrequent

Like the tick-trefoils, our bush-clovers, of which there are about 15 species, are confined to the eastern United States. The apparent hybridization of species adds to the difficulty of identifying the members of this genus.

TRAILING BUSH-CLOVER
Lespedeza procumbens

PEA FAMILY
Leguminosae
(Fabaceae)

As the name implies, this is a mostly trailing plant. It is from 1' to $2\frac{1}{2}$' long, with a soft, hairy stem. The alternate, petioled leaves are 3-divided into $\frac{1}{2}$"- to $\frac{3}{4}$"-long, ovate leaflets. Note that the petioles are shorter than the leaves. The pink, pealike flowers are on tall flowering stems in the leaf axils. (Native)

September 6–September 16   Frequent

The bush-clovers are an important food source for the Bobwhite Quail and are widely, but lightly, browsed by White-Tailed Deer. The Wild Turkey, Mourning Dove, Junco, and a few song birds make minor use of the seeds.

SLENDER BUSH-CLOVER
Lespedeza virginica

PEA FAMILY
Leguminosae
(Fabaceae)

This bush-clover can be distinguished by its crowded, almost linear leaflets. It is a mostly erect plant, up to 3' tall. Like other bush-clovers, the petioled leaves are 3-divided. Flowers are pinkish purple, $\frac{1}{4}$" long, pealike, and crowded in the upper leaf axils. (Native)

August 29–September 18   Frequent

This is a plant of open woods and barrens. The genus is a misspelling of the name Vincente Manuel de Cespedes, who was the Spanish governor of East Florida during the explorations of the botanist Michaux in the late eighteenth century.

WILD BEAN
Phaseolus polystachios

PEA FAMILY
Leguminosae
(Fabaceae)

This twining plant is from 4' to 15' long. The leaves are 3-divided and the leaflets are ovate and entire. The lateral leaflets are distinctly unequal-sided, and the terminal leaflet is somewhat broader. Flowers are in long racemes from the leaf axils. The keel is somewhat coiled on the $\frac{1}{2}$"-long, dark pink, pealike flowers. (Native)

August 14–August 29   Rare

This wild bean has become very uncommon in our area. It has in the past, however, been used and cooked in the same way as our cultivated dried beans. The beans are difficult to gather because the pods coil and expel them as soon as they are ripe.

PINK WILD BEAN
Strophostyles umbellata

PEA FAMILY
Leguminosae
(Fabaceae)

This is a mostly trailing vine with a lightly hairy stem that may reach 4' or longer. The ½"-wide, pink, pealike flowers are on tall, flowering stalks growing from the leaf axils, and turn yellowish with age. Flowering stalks may be 4" to 8" long and are taller than the long-petioled, 3-part leaves. Leaflets are ovate, broad at their base, and smooth margined. (Native)

August 7–September 6   Infrequent

This wild bean has a close relationship to some of the cultivated beans we are familiar with. Where found in sufficient quantity, they are a significant food source for game birds, especially the Bobwhite Quail.

FIELD MILKWORT
Polygala sanguinea

MILKWORT FAMILY
Polygalaceae

Note the oblong heads of rose-colored flowers on this slender, branching, 6" to 15" plant, with its somewhat angled stem. Stem leaves are about 1" long, pointed linear to linear lanceolate, entire, and alternate. (Native)

October 5   Infrequent

A somewhat similar plant is *Polygala incarnata,* which is taller, nearly leafless, and has no white in the flower head.

From the large number of common names given this little plant, it has obviously attracted much attention in the past. It possibly shares the numerous medicinal qualities Native Americans found in other *Polygala* species such as *P. alba, P. paucifolia, P. polygama,* and *P. senega.*

SLENDER GERARDIA
Gerardia tenuifolia
(*Agalinis tenuifolia* var. *tenuifolia*)

FIGWORT FAMILY
Scrophulariaceae

The tube on this lavender gerardia is only about ½" long. Note the spotted throat below the 5 spreading lobes. This smooth, many-branched plant has very thin stems. Leaves are opposite, about 1" long, pointed, and linear. Note the very short teeth on the calyx. (Native)

September 4–October 22   Locally Frequent

This plant is a member of the *Scrophulariaceae,* the Foxglove or Figwort Family, which includes about 75 genera and 3000 species worldwide. The family name is from scrofula, a disease of the lymph nodes, which a species of this family was supposed to cure.

DOWNY LOBELIA
Lobelia puberula

LOBELIA FAMILY
Campanulaceae

As indicated by the name, this 1' to 3' plant is finely hairy all over, including the leaves. Flowers are in a mostly one-sided spike, are bright blue, tubular with 5 spreading lobes, and about ¾" long. Leaves are alternate, toothed, ovate and sessile above to short petioled below. (Native)

August 15–October 4   Frequent

The several species of *Lobelia* were some of the Native Americans' most valued medicinal plants. They were used to treat colds, coughs, headaches, diarrhea, fevers, worms, and sores, and to induce sweating and urination. Few, if any, of these uses have been validated scientifically.

GREAT LOBELIA
Lobelia siphilitica

LOBELIA FAMILY
Campanulaceae

Flowers are blue, 1" long, tubular, 5-lobed, and the somewhat inflated tube is striped with white. The calyx lobes are conspicuous and hairy in the dense spike on this 1' to 3' plant. Leaves are numerous, alternate, sessile, long lanceolate, and shallow toothed below to nearly entire above. (Native)

September 10–October 6   Infrequent

Several Native American tribes used this plant as a love medicine with the roots finely chopped and put in the food of a feuding couple without their knowledge. It was also widely used to treat syphilis, from which the second word of the species name was derived.

VIRGINIA DAYFLOWER
Commelina virginica

SPIDERWORT FAMILY
Commelinaceae

Although similar to *C. communis,* this 1½' to 2½' plant is more erect, has broader leaves, and 3 blue petals with the lower petal only slightly smaller. Leaves are linear lanceolate, from 3" to 5" long, and ½" to 1" wide. The 1"-wide flowers are in sheathlike bracts. (Native)

August 10–September 10   Infrequent

In the past this plant was believed to increase sexual potency and was fed to stud animals. The young leaves are reported to make a good potherb. The boiled roots served with white sauce are said to make an acceptable substitute for creamed potatoes.

HEART-LEAVED ASTER
Aster cordifolius

COMPOSITE FAMILY
Compositae
(Asteraceae)

This mostly smooth, 1' to 3½' *Aster* has numerous
⅝"-wide, light blue flower heads with 10 to 20 rays
on the heads. Heads are arranged in a dense panicle. The middle to lower leaves have long, thin petioles, are heart shaped and sharply toothed. Upper
leaves become smaller, lanceolate, short petioled to
sessile, and less toothed to entire at the top. (Native)

September 20–October 22   Frequent

According to Rafinesque, a botanist in the early
1800s, this aster was an excellent sedative. In many
cases it provided a more calming effect than even
Valerian, which was much in use at the time for nervous disorders.

SMOOTH ASTER
Aster laevis

COMPOSITE FAMILY
Compositae
(Asteraceae)

This sparingly branched, 1' to 3' *Aster* has
a smooth, somewhat whitish filmed stem.
Lower leaves are lanceolate, tapering into
long, winged petioles and may be sparingly toothed. Stem and upper leaves are
toothless, pointed lanceolate, with
rounded, clasping bases. Flower heads are
violet-blue and have 15 to 30 rays. (Native)

September 19–October 5   Frequent

Native Americans used this plant to furnish
smoke in their sweat baths. The smoke of the
plant was also blown into the nostrils to revive a person who was ill or uncon-
scious in the belief that it would revive the patient.

STIFF-LEAF ASTER

Aster linariifolius
(Ionactis linariifolius)

COMPOSITE FAMILY
Compositae
(Asteraceae)

Several of the stiff, 1'- to 2'-tall stems grow from the same base. Note the crowded, stiff, strictly linear, entire, and rough-margined leaves. The plant has erect terminal branches with numerous short, needlelike leaves and a solitary flower head with from 10 to 15 lavender rays. (Native)

September 19–October 4   Rare

Native Americans used several species of *Aster* finely ground and smoked in a pipe. They believed the smell would attract deer close enough to kill with an arrow. The smell was supposed to mimic the spoor scent of the animal.

LOWRIE'S ASTER

Aster lowrieanus
(*Aster cordifolius* var. *laevigatus*)

COMPOSITE FAMILY
Compositae
(Asteraceae)

This 1' to 3' *Aster* is similar to *A. cordifolius,* except that the stem leaves are somewhat less toothed, are smooth and greasy feeling, and the petioles are distinctly winged. Basal leaves are slender petioled and heart shaped. The uppermost leaves are small, lanceolate, entire, and sessile. The light blue, 1"-wide flower heads are in a loose panicle. (Native)

September 23   Frequent

Insects apparently find the foliage of many asters irresistible. By the time many asters flower, the leaves necessary for identification have been mostly eaten.

LARGE-LEAVED ASTER
Aster macrophyllus

COMPOSITE FAMILY
Compositae
(Asteraceae)

Flowering stems may be few within extensive colonies of this species, which have very large 4"- to 6"-wide, pointed, heart-shaped, rough, and sharp-toothed basal leaves. Flowering stems are from $1\frac{1}{2}$' to $2\frac{1}{2}$' tall with small, alternate, toothed, and ovate leaves that are sessile above and short petioled below. Flower heads have about 16 lavender rays. Note that the disk becomes reddish with age. (Native)

August 17–September 23 Infrequent

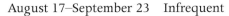

Several authors recommend the leaves of this *Aster* as a cooked green comparable to dandelion or spinach. They quickly become very tough, however, and only the newly sprouted leaves should be gathered. Native Americans bathed their heads with a tea made from this plant to soothe headaches.

NEW ENGLAND ASTER
Aster novae-angliae

COMPOSITE FAMILY
Compositae
(Asteraceae)

This large, showy, branching *Aster* is from 2' to 6' tall, with $1\frac{1}{2}$"- to 2"-wide, dark violet flower heads and a stout, hairy stem. The flowers have 40 to 50 very narrow rays. The numerous leaves are from 2" to 5" long, entire, and long lanceolate with heart-shaped clasping bases. (Native)

September 20–October 3 Rare

This species is the largest, most showy, and perhaps our most beautiful *Aster*. It is often a prized component of flower gardens, providing bright fall color. Dense stands furnish good cover for small game animals. Native Americans are reported to have used this aster to treat poison ivy and diarrhea.

LATE PURPLE ASTER
Aster patens

COMPOSITE FAMILY
Compositae
(Asteraceae)

Flowering stems branch from the upper leaf axils on this hairy, 1' to 3' plant. The alternate, toothless leaves are pointed oblong with heart-shaped bases that nearly circle the stem. Flower heads are blue-violet, about 1" wide, and have from 20 to 30 rays. Heads are mostly solitary on the tips of branches. (Native)

September 4–October 7   Abundant

The Shakers reportedly used asters to clear their complexions. The ancient Greeks thought that asters repelled snakes and also used them in treatment of snakebites. The genus name is the Greek, *aster,* meaning star.

CROOKED-STEMMED ASTER
Aster prenanthoides

COMPOSITE FAMILY
Compositae
(Asteraceae)

The flower heads with 20 to 30 pale blue rays are 1" wide and on a 1'- to 2½'-tall, smooth stem. Note that the stem angles somewhat at the leaf axils. The leaves are toothed on the upper half, pointed lanceolate, and taper from the middle into a wide, winged, entire petiole. The base of the winged petiole expands into lobes that clasp the stem. (Native)

September 20   Infrequent

Considering that there are about 125 species of *Asters* in the United States, it is surprising that they are hardly used by wildlife. Birds and animals making at least some minor use of these plants include Ruffed Grouse, Wild Turkey, Tree Sparrow, Cottontail Rabbit, Chipmunk, White-Footed Mouse, and White-Tailed Deer.

ARROW-LEAVED ASTER
Aster sagittifolius
(*Aster cordifolius* var. *sagittifolius*)

Composite Family
Compositae
(Asteraceae)

The ¾"-wide flower heads on this mostly smooth, 2' to 4' *Aster* are in a branching terminal panicle, with 10 to 15 lavender-blue rays. Lower leaves are toothed and heart shaped with even, narrow margins on the petioles. Upper leaves become lanceolate, sessile, and nearly entire. Bracts are smooth. Hairs behind the bracts are white. (Native)

September 4–October 6   Infrequent

There are approximately 28 species of *Aster* in Kentucky. Of this number, 19 have mostly blue or lavender ray flowers and the rest have white ray flowers. However, many of the blue-flowered plants may produce white or whitish ray flowers and the flowers may fade with age.

SILKY ASTER
Aster sericeus

Composite Family
Compositae
(Asteraceae)

There are 15 to 25 violet-blue rays on each of the 1½"-wide flower heads, which are mostly solitary on leafy, branching stems on this 1' to 2' plant. Basal leaves are entire and spatulate and taper into long, winged petioles. Stem and upper leaves are oblong lanceolate, entire, and sessile or somewhat clasping. Note the very thick, short, silvery white hair on both surfaces of the leaves. (Native)

September 3–October 22   Endangered

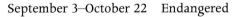

This is perhaps the least common, but one of the most beautiful, *Asters* in the park. It is restricted to limestone barrens or to road cuts in limestone that expose steep shelves. The common name refers to the very short, silvery white hair on the leaf surfaces.

SHORT'S ASTER
Aster shortii

COMPOSITE FAMILY
Compositae
(Asteraceae)

The nearly 1"-wide flower heads with 10 to 15
violet-blue rays are arranged in a panicle on this
1' to 3' *Aster.* Lower to middle leaves are narrowly heart shaped, toothless or nearly so, and
have long, thin, smooth petioles. Upper leaves
are lanceolate, entire, and sessile, becoming
very tiny on the flowering branches. (Native)

September 10–October 22   Abundant

Leaf shape on this *Aster* varies greatly. An observation is that the broader and shorter leaves seem
to be found in limestone or calcareous areas, while
narrower and longer leaves appear in sandstone or acidic areas. This may or may
not be a valid observation, but would make an interesting scientific study.

WAVY-LEAVED ASTER
Aster undulatus

COMPOSITE FAMILY
Compositae
(Asteraceae)

Flower heads on this 1' to 3' plant are about $\frac{3}{4}$"
wide and have 8 to 15 pale-violet or blue rays.
The stem is somewhat rough and light hairy.
Lower leaves are wavy edged, lightly toothed,
pointed, and heart shaped with long, winged
petioles that widen abruptly at the base and
clasp the stalk. Middle leaves are entire, having
short, wide, winged petioles, and wavy edges.
Upper leaves are sessile and lanceolate. (Native)

September 19–October 6   Frequent

Some asters provide grazing for deer, horses, and sheep. A few are poisonous,
some have proposed medicinal qualities, some are good to eat, while many are
considered to have no practical value. Perhaps their beauty is there just to make
people feel good. After all, to the ancient Greeks asters were a talisman of love.

ELEPHANT'S FOOT
Elephantopus carolinianus

<small>COMPOSITE FAMILY</small>
Compositae
(Asteraceae)

Note the leafy bracts below compact heads of small, blue flowers
terminal on the flowering
branches. The flower heads are
without rays and the usually 3 tubular disk flowers are lobed and
cleft on one side. Leaves on this 1' to 3' plant are alternate and shallow
toothed. The lower leaves are broadly ovate and taper into winged petioles.
Upper leaves get progressively smaller, becoming nearly entire and sessile.
(Native)

August 6–September 30   Abundant

This is one of our most difficult plants to identify, with botanical keys being
nearly useless for the amateur. The genus name is from the Greek *elephas,* meaning elephant, and *pous,* meaning foot.

MISTFLOWER
Eupatorium coelestinum

<small>COMPOSITE FAMILY</small>
Compositae
(Asteraceae)

The flat-topped terminal clusters of $\frac{1}{4}$"-wide flower heads
are blue and somewhat fuzzy-
looking. The stem is very
finely hairy and only 1' to
$2\frac{1}{2}$' tall. The leaves are oppo-
site, toothed, petioled, and somewhat triangular, with heartshaped, straight,
or abruptly tapering bases. (Native)

August 15–October 22   Frequent

This plant may carpet low, damp fields with blue in late summer. Because of its
creeping underground stems, it spreads easily and is a favorite in perennial
flower beds. It is best known locally as Ageratum.

JOE-PYE-WEED
Eupatorium fistulosum

COMPOSITE FAMILY
Compositae
(Asteraceae)

The stem on this 4' to 10' plant is hollow, often purple, and smooth. Leaves are in whorls of 4 to 7 (usually 6) and are lanceolate, petioled, and toothed. Flower heads are in a large, spreading, domelike cluster. There are from 5 to 8 purplish, tubular flowers in each head. (Native)

August 10–September 24   Infrequent

From New England to the deep south, Native Americans used this plant to treat kidney and bladder problems. It was a good luck charm to one group, who carried the tops while gambling, feeling confident they would win big. The plant was also used in a poultice to treat burns.

BLUE LETTUCE
Lactuca floridana

COMPOSITE FAMILY
Compositae
(Asteraceae)

Flower heads on this stout, smooth, 3' to 7' plant are in a loose, open panicle. Heads are dandelion-like and about ½" wide with blue rays. Leaves are extremely variable, but generally are 4" to 12" long, deeply cut or lobed, toothed, and often wing petioled with a mostly triangular terminal segment. Note that the hairs behind the bracts are white. (Native)

August 1–September 24   Infrequent

The young leaves and stems may be cooked as a green or the young leaves used in salads. Past herbal use included a decoction of the plant as a lotion for sunburn, acne, or other inflammation of the skin.

IRONWEED
Vernonia altissima
(*Vernonia gigantea* ssp. *gigantea*)

COMPOSITE FAMILY
Compositae
(Asteraceae)

There are 15 to 30 bright, reddish purple, small, tubular florets on heads in a wide, flat-topped cluster on this 4' to 10' plant. Leaves are narrow lanceolate, tapering at both ends, sessile, alternate, sharp toothed, and finely hairy beneath. (Native)

August 6–September 24   Infrequent

This is usually a plant of open fields, where it is an indicator of overgrazing. Native Americans used Ironweed to control bleeding and to lessen pain after childbirth. Beekeepers hold the plant in high esteem and will argue forcefully against using the term "weed" in association with this plant.

IVY-LEAVED MORNING-GLORY
Ipomoea hederacea

MORNING-GLORY FAMILY
Convolvulaceae

The 1½"-long, flaring tubular blossoms on this climbing vine are similar to *I. purpurea,* but are mostly blue in color. Note the long, pointed, recurving tips on the hairy sepals. The leaves are deeply cut into 3 lobes with the 2 lateral lobes similar in shape to a butterfly wing. (Native)

August 3–September 6   Infrequent

Cursed as a weed by local tobacco farmers, this showy morning-glory is often grown as an ornamental vine in flower gardens. According to the ancient practice of plant symbolism, the sentiments of this plant are departure and farewell.

COMMON MORNING-GLORY
Ipomoea purpurea

MORNING-GLORY FAMILY
Convolvulaceae

Varying in color, the 5-pointed, funnel-shaped flowers may be purple, blue, pink, or even white and are about 2" long. This is a 5'- to 10'-long, twining or climbing vine with a hairy stem. The leaves are broadly heart shaped, petioled, entire, and finely hairy. (Introduced)

August 19–September 20   Infrequent

Geneticists frequently use this plant in studies because of it's obvious life cycle and its ease of growth indoors. It is also a serious pest in row-crop agriculture. The plant has been reportedly used to prepare a laxative.

SOAPWORT GENTIAN
Gentiana saponaria

GENTIAN FAMILY
Gentianaceae

The mostly smooth stems are 1' to 2' tall. Leaves are lanceolate, acute at both ends, nearly sessile, opposite, entire, 3-veined, and increase in length upward. Flowers are about 1 ½ " long, deep blue, and stay nearly closed. (Native)

October 18   Rare

Herbals suggest the chemical properties of the roots are almost identical to genus members found in Europe, where it is widely used as a tonic. Native Americans are reported to have used the roots to treat backache.

FALSE PENNYROYAL
Isanthus brachiatus
(Trichostema brachiatus)

MINT FAMILY
Labiatae
(Lamiaceae)

The stem is slender and smooth on this branching, 6" to 20" plant. Leaves are opposite, entire, parallel-veined, sessile, and lanceolate, tapering at both ends. Flowers are small, tubular, 5-lobed, blue, and on stems in the upper leaf axils. (Native)

September 4–October 5   Infrequent

Folk medicine in the eastern mountains of Kentucky has prescribed the boiling of a cup of False Pennyroyal leaves in a pint of water be taken internally to treat fever.

HORSE MINT
Perilla frutescens

MINT FAMILY
Labiatae
(Lamiaceae)

This 1' to 3' plant has a strong odor, purplish stem, and purplish tinged leaves. The tiny, white to pinkish flowers are in tall racemes growing from the leaf axils. Note that the 5-lobed, tubular flowers have a ring of fine hair in the throat and are mostly in single-sided pairs. Leaves are long petioled, broadly ovate, ragged toothed, and have somewhat wavy margins. (Introduced)

September 3–October 22   Abundant

In Asia, this plant is reportedly used to treat morning sickness. However, other reports say it should be avoided during pregnancy. Mountain folk medicine used a tea of this plant to treat colds. Certain oriental dishes specify the leaves of this plant and it does make a pleasant, if somewhat strong, tea.

MAD-DOG SKULLCAP
Scutellaria lateriflora

MINT FAMILY
Labiatae
(Lamiaceae)

Long, leafy, flowering stems
branch in pairs from the upper
leaf axils on this 1' to 2½' plant.
The small, ¼"-long, tubular flow-
ers with reduced hoods distinguish it from other genus members in the
park. Also note that flowers are in mostly single-sided racemes. Leaves are
opposite, pointed ovate, petioled, coarsely toothed, and size is reduced toward the summit. (Native)

August 10–October 5   Infrequent

Scutellaria nervosa, another small skullcap with single flowers in the leaf axils,
is unbranched and has ovate, toothed leaves.

Its common name comes from a 1773 claim heralding the belief that it could be
used successfully to treat rabies. Native Americans and folk medicine prescribed
a tea from this plant for use as a sedative, antispasmodic, and nerve tonic. Science has confirmed that chemicals in this plant will bring about these effects.

BLUE CURLS
Trichostema dichotomum

MINT FAMILY
Labiatae
(Lamiaceae)

This small, finely hairy, much-branched
plant is from 6" to 24" tall. Flowers are ½" to
¾" long, tubular, blue, and lobed with the
lower lip drooping. The filaments are blue
and distinctively arch up and over the flower.
Leaves are opposite, lanceolate, entire, and
petioled below to nearly sessile above.
(Native)

September 3–September 10   Rare

Bastard-Pennyroyal is another name given to this plant, which is sticky to the
touch. The plant is uncommon in the park and is usually found in a dry, sandstone, barren habitat.

TALL WHITE LETTUCE
Prenanthes altissima

COMPOSITE FAMILY
Compositae
(Asteraceae)

This 3' to 7' plant has a usually purplish stalk. Leaves are extremely variable in shape, but are mostly long petioled, lobed to some degree, and widely coarse toothed. Flower heads are bell-like, greenish or yellowish white, and hang in few-flowered clusters from the tips of the panicle branches. Note that there are only 5 bracts on this species. (Native)

September 13–October 2   Infrequent

Also known as Gall-of-the-Earth, this plant has a long history in folk medicine and among Native Americans as an antidote to the bite of the rattlesnake and other poisonous snakes.

CORAL-ROOT ORCHID
Corallorhiza odontorhiza

ORCHID FAMILY
Orchidaceae

This saprophytic orchid grows from 4" to 10" tall. It has a somewhat fleshy, smooth stem and may have 6 to 20 nodding flowers. The scalelike leaves and the stem are brownish purple, as are the flower parts except for the oval lower lip, which is white and spotted with purple. (Native)

September 6–October 5   Rare

Plants of this genus are dependent on soil fungus to supply them with food. Herbal medicine suggests this orchid is an effective treatment for fever, cramps, insomnia, and various skin diseases.

BEECHDROPS
Epifagus virginiana

BROOM-RAPE FAMILY
Orobanchaceae

There are no green parts to this smooth, yellowish brown, branching, 6" to 20" plant. The leaves are reduced to a few, small scales. The flowers are arranged spikelike on the branches, are tubular, about ½" long, whitish, tinged with yellowish brown, and the lower flowers are closed. (Native)

August 25–October 22   Frequent

These plants are parasitic and totally dependent on the roots of beech trees. Native American and herbal medicine describe this plant as an astringent and prescribe its use for wounds, cuts, bruises, skin irritations, mouth sores, and even dysentery.

APPENDICES

APPENDICES

APPENDIX A: OBSERVED FLOWERING PERIOD

		March		April		May		June	
		Week 1-2	Week 3-4	Week 1-2	Week 3-4	Week 1-2	Week 3-4	Week 1-2	Week 3-4
Dandelion	Taraxacum officinale	■	■	■	■	■	■	■	■ To October 22
Sessile Trillium	Trillium sessile				■	■	■		
Spring Beauty	Claytonia virginica	■	■	■	■	■			
Jacob's-Ladder	Polemonium reptans				■	■			
Early Saxifrage	Saxifraga virginiensis	■	■	■	■				
Cut-Leaf Toothwort	Dentaria laciniata	■	■	■	■	■	■		
Harbinger-of-Spring	Erigenia bulbosa	■	■	■					
Twinleaf	Jeffersonia diphylla	■	■						
Slender Toothwort	Dentaria heterophylla		■	■	■				
Roundleaf Ragwort	Senecio obovatus				■	■			
Hepatica	Hepatica acutiloba	■	■	■					
Pennywort	Obolaria virginica	■	■	■	■	■			
Yellow Corydalis	Corydalis flavula	■	■	■					
Common Blue Violet	Viola papilionacea	■	■	■	■	■			
Bloodroot	Sanguinaria canadensis	■	■						
Periwinkle	Vinca minor	■	■	■	■				
Rue Anemone	Anemonella thalictroides	■	■	■	■	■	■		
Common Chickweed	Stellaria media	■	■	■	■	■	■		
Ground-Ivy	Glechoma hederacea		■	■	■	■	■		
Plantain-Leaved Pussytoes	Antennaria plantaginifolia			■	■	■			
False Rue Anemone	Isopyrum biternatum		■	■	■	■			
Hepatica	Hepatica americana	■	■	■					
Purple Cress	Cardamine douglassii	■	■	■	■				
Two-Leaved Toothwort	Dentaria diphylla		■	■					
Wood-Betony	Pedicularis canadensis			■	■	■			

APPENDIX A, continued

		March		April		May		June	
		Week 1-2	Week 3-4	Week 1-2	Week 3-4	Week 1-2	Week 3-4	Week 1-2	Week 3-4
Toothwort	*Dentaria multifida*		▓	▓	▓				
Smooth Rock Cress	*Arabis laevigata*		▓	▓	▓				
Yellow Trout-Lily	*Erythronium americanum*		▓	▓					
Bluebells	*Mertensia virginica*		▓	▓	▓	▓			
May-Apple	*Podophyllum peltatum*		▓			▓	▓	▓	
Columbine	*Aquilegia canadensis*			▓	▓	▓	▓	▓	
Bluets	*Houstonia caerulea*			▓	▓	▓	▓		
Dutchman's-Breeches	*Dicentra cucullaria*		▓	▓	▓				
Blue Cohosh	*Caulophyllum thalictroides*		▓	▓	▓				
Solitary Pussytoes	*Antennaria solitaria*		▓	▓	▓				
Blue Phlox	*Phlox divaricata*					▓			
Wild Geranium	*Geranium maculatum*				▓	▓			
Hispid Buttercup	*Ranunculus hispidus*				▓	▓			
White Trout-Lily	*Erythronium albidum*		▓	▓					
Foamflower	*Tiarella cordifolia*		▓			▓	▓		
Star Chickweed	*Stellaria pubera*		▓		▓				
Early Spurge	*Euphorbia commutata*				▓				
Jack-in-the-Pulpit	*Arisaema atrorubens*					▓	▓		
Bent Trillium	*Trillium flexipes*				▓				
Celandine Poppy	*Stylophorum diphyllum*			▓	▓	▓			
Small Bluet	*Houstonia patens*			▓	▓				
Field Pansy	*Viola kitaibeliana*				▓				
Bishop's-Cap	*Mitella diphylla*			▓		▓			
Fire Pink	*Silene virginica*			▓		▓	▓	▓	
Wild Ginger	*Asarum canadense*			▓	▓	▓			▓

Common Name	Scientific Name	April Week 1-2	April Week 3-4	May Week 1-2	May Week 3-4	June Week 1-2	June Week 3-4	July Week 1-2	July Week 3-4
Kidneyleaf Buttercup	*Ranunculus abortivus*	■	■	■					
Squirrel-Corn	*Dicentra canadensis*	■	■						
Larkspur	*Delphinium tricorne*	■	■	■					
Pale Violet	*Viola striata*	■	■	■	■	■	■		
Common Cinquefoil	*Potentialla simplex*	■	■	■	■	■			
Lyre-Leaved Sage	*Salvia lyrata*	■	■	■	■				
Large Houstonia	*Houstonia purpurea*	■	■	■	■	■			
Appendaged Waterleaf	*Hydrophyllum appendiculatum*	■	■	■					
Goldenseal	*Hydrastis canadensis*	■	■	■					
False Solomon's-Seal	*Smilacina racemosa*		■	■	■				
Wild Hyacinth	*Camassia scilloides*		■						
Robin-Plantain	*Erigeron pulchellus*		■	■	■				
Cicely	*Osmorhiza longistylus*		■	■	■				
Violet Wood-Sorrel	*Oxalis violacea*	■	■	■	■				
Wild Yam	*Dioscorea quaternata*	■	■	■	■	■			
Squawroot	*Conopholis americana*	■	■	■	■	■			
Stonecrop	*Sedum ternatum*	■	■	■	■				
Cleavers	*Galium aparine*	■	■	■	■	■			
Houstonia	*Houstonia lanceolata*	■	■	■	■	■			
Wild Strawberry	*Fragaria virginiana*	■	■	■	■	■			
Blue-Eyed-Grass	*Sisyrinchium angustifolium*	■	■	■	■				
Dwarf Dandelion	*Krigia biflora*	■	■	■	■	■	■		
Alum-Root	*Heuchera americana*	■	■	■	■	■			
Wild Comfrey	*Cynoglossum virginianum*	■	■	■					
Early Spiderwort	*Tradescantia virginiana*	■	■	■					

APPENDIX A, continued

		April		May		June		July	
		Week 1-2	Week 3-4	Week 1-2	Week 3-4	Week 1-2	Week 3-4	Week 1-2	Week 3-4
Synandra	*Synandra hispidula*	▒	▒	▒	▒	▒	▒	▒	
Marsh Blue Violet	*Viola cucullata*	▒	▒	▒					
Sweet White Violet	*Viola blanda*	▒	▒						
Red Dead-Nettle	*Lamium purpureum*	▒	▒	▒					
Early Meadow Rue	*Thalictrum dioicum*	▒	▒	▒	▒				
Bellwort	*Uvularia perfoliata*		▒	▒	▒				
Large-Flowered Bellwort	*Uvularia grandiflora*		▒	▒	▒				
Coral-Root Orchid	*Corallorhiza wisteriana*		▒						
Hooked Crowfoot	*Ranunculus recurvatus*		▒						
Barren Strawberry	*Waldsteinia fragarioides*		▒						
Crested Dwarf Iris	*Iris cristata*		▒	▒					
White Baneberry	*Actaea pachypoda*		▒	▒					
Early Buttercup	*Ranunculus fascicularis*		▒	▒					
Hoary Puccoon	*Lithospermum canescens*		▒	▒	▒				
Garlic Mustard	*Alliaria officinalis*		▒	▒					
Woods Vetch	*Vicia caroliniana*		▒	▒					
Solomon's Seal	*Polygonatum biflorum*		▒	▒					
Birdfoot Violet	*Viola pedata*		▒	▒					
False Garlic	*Nothoscordum bivalve*		▒	▒	▒				
Shooting Star	*Dodecatheon media*		▒	▒	▒				
Yellow Lady's-Slipper	*Cypripedium calceolus*		▒	▒	▒				
Three-Lobed Violet	*Viola triloba*		▒	▒					
Baby's-Breath	*Arenaria patula*		▒	▒	▒	▒	▒	▒	
Yellow Wood-Sorrel	*Oxalis stricta*			▒	▒	▒	▒		
Yellow Stargrass	*Hypoxis hirsuta*			▒					

Common Name	Scientific Name	April Week 1-2	May Week 1-2	May Week 3-4	June Week 1-2	June Week 3-4	July Week 1-2	July Week 3-4	August Week 3-4
Golden Alexander	*Zizia aptera*	▓	▓	▓	▓	▓			
Wintercress	*Barbarea vulgaris*	▓							
Dwarf Dandelion	*Krigia dandelion*		▓	▓	▓				
Star-of-Bethlehem	*Ornithogalum umbellatum*	▓	▓						
Common Fleabane	*Erigeron philadelphicus*		▓	▓					
Early Scorpion-Grass	*Myosotis verna*	▓	▓						
American Columbo	*Swertia caroliniensis*		▓	▓	▓	▓			
Phacelia	*Phacelia purshii*		▓	▓					
Carrion-Flower	*Smilax ecirrata*			▓					
Large Yellow Wood-Sorrel	*Oxalis grandis*			▓	▓				
Purple Phacelia	*Phacelia bipinnatifida*		▓	▓					
Lance-Leaved Coreopsis	*Coreopsis lanceolata*			▓	▓	▓			
Showy Orchis	*Orchis spectabilis*		▓	▓					
Putty-Root Orchid	*Aplectrum hyemale*			▓					
Valerian	*Valeriana pauciflora*			▓	▓				
Ox-Eye Daisy	*Chrysanthemum leucanthemum*			▓	▓	▓	▓	▓	▓
Purple Rocket	*Iodanthus pinnatifidus*			▓	▓	▓			
Butterweed	*Senecio glabellus*		▓	▓	▓	▓	▓	▓	
Clustered Snakeroot	*Sanicula gregaria*			▓	▓	▓	▓		
Four-Leaved Milkweed	*Asclepias quadrifolia*				▓	▓	▓	▓	
Carrion-Flower	*Smilax herbacea*			▓	▓	▓			
Green Dragon	*Arisaema dracontium*			▓	▓	▓			
Lily-Leaved Twayblade	*Liparis liliifolia*			▓	▓	▓			
Golden Ragwort	*Senecio aureus*		▓	▓					
Foxglove Beard-Tongue	*Penstemon digitalis*				▓	▓	▓		

APPENDIX A, continued

Common Name	Scientific Name	May Week 1-2	May Week 3-4	June Week 1-2	June Week 3-4	July Week 1-2	July Week 3-4	August Week 1-2	August Week 3-4
Small's Ragwort	*Senecio smallii*	■	■	■	■	■			
White Bergamot	*Monarda russeliana*			■	■	■			
Rock Moss	*Sedum pulchellum*	■	■	■	■	■			
Horse-Gentian	*Triosteum angustifolium*						■		
Hop Clover	*Trifolium agrarium*	■	■	■	■	■	■		
Leonard's Skullcap	*Scutellaria parvula var. leonardii*	■	■						
Venus' Looking-Glass	*Specularia perfoliata*	■	■	■					
Sicklepod	*Arabis canadensis*	■	■	■	■	■			
Partridge-Berry	*Mitchella repens*		■	■	■	■			
Heal-All	*Prunella vulgaris*		■	■	■	■	■	■	■ To September 30
Purple Coneflower	*Echinacea pallida*		■	■	■	■	■		
Wild Garlic	*Allium canadense*		■	■	■	■			
Sampson's Snakeroot	*Psoralea psoralioides*		■	■	■	■			
Honewort	*Cryptotaenia canadensis*		■	■	■	■	■		
Yarrow	*Achillea millefolium*		■	■	■				
Slender-Flowered Beard-Tongue	*Penstemon tenuiflorus*		■	■					
Lance-Leaved Violet	*Viola lanceolata*		■						
White Milkweed	*Asclepias variegata*			■	■				
Ground-Cherry	*Physalis virginiana*		■	■	■	■	■	■	■ To October 4
Blackberry-Lily	*Belamcanda chinensis*			■	■	■	■	■	■
Daisy Fleabane	*Erigeron annuus*		■	■	■	■	■	■ To September 10	
Whorled Loosestrife	*Lysimachia quadrifolia*			■	■	■			
Indian Physic	*Gillenia stipulata*			■	■				
Angle-Pod	*Gonolobus shortii*				■	■	■		
Crown Vetch	*Coronilla varia*		■	■	■	■	■	■	■

Common Name	Scientific Name	May Week 1-2	June Week 3-4	June Week 1-2	July Week 3-4	July Week 1-2	August Week 3-4	August Week 1-2	September Week 3-4
Downy Wood-Mint	*Blephilia ciliata*								
Red Clover	*Trifolium patense*								
Heart-Shaped Skullcap	*Scutellaria ovata*								
Zigzag Spiderwort	*Tradescantia subaspera*							To September 16	
White Sweet Clover	*Melilotus alba*								
Japanese Honeysuckle	*Lonicera japonica*								
Alum-Root	*Heuchera villosa*								
White Clover	*Trifolium repens*								
Wild Rose	*Rosa carolina*								
Goat's-Rue	*Tephrosia virginiana*								
Indian Cucumber-Root	*Medeola virginiana*								
Wild Potato-Vine	*Ipomoea pandurata*								
White Bergamot	*Monarda clinopodia*								
Goat's-Beard	*Aruncus dioicus*								
Common Mullein	*Verbascum thapsus*								
Smooth Ruellia	*Ruellia strepens*								
Narrow-Leaved Vervain	*Verbena simplex*								
Hairy Skullcap	*Scutellaria elliptica*								
White Wild Licorice	*Galium circaezans*								
Western Daisy	*Astranthium integrifolium*								
Spotted Wintergreen	*Chimaphila maculata*								
Daylily	*Hemerocallis fulva*								
Large Coreopsis	*Coreopsis major*								
Nodding Thistle	*Carduus nutans*								
Horse-Nettle	*Solanum carolinense*								

APPENDIX A, continued

Common Name	Scientific Name	June Week 1-2	June Week 3-4	July Week 1-2	July Week 3-4	August Week 1-2	August Week 3-4	September Week 1-2	September Week 3-4
Swamp Rose	*Rosa palustris*		▓						
Moth Mullein	*Verbascum blattaria*			▓	▓				
Wild Hydrangea	*Hydrangea arborescens*			▓	▓	▓	▓		
Round-Leaved Fire Pink	*Silene rotundifolia*			▓	▓				
Ragged Fringed Orchis	*Habenaria lacera*		▓						
Yucca	*Yucca filamentosa*			▓					
Bergamot	*Monarda fistulosa*			▓	▓	▓			
Sundrops	*Oenothera fruticosa*		▓						
Crownbeard	*Verbesina helianthoides*		▓	▓	▓	▓			
Deptford Pink	*Dianthus armeria*		▓	▓	▓				
St. John's Wort	*Hypericum dolabriforme*		▓	▓	▓	▓			
Broadleaf Waterleaf	*Hydrophyllum canadense*		▓	▓	▓				
Black-Eyed Susan	*Rudbeckia hirta*		▓	▓	▓	▓	▓		
Sweet Pea	*Lathyrus odoratus*		▓	▓	▓				
Great Indian Plantain	*Cacalia muhlenbergii*		▓	▓	▓	▓	▓		
Butterfly Milkweed	*Asclepias tuberosa*		▓	▓	▓	▓			
Lance-Leaved Loosestrife	*Lysimachia lanceolata*		▓	▓	▓	▓	▓		
Prickly Pear Cactus	*Opuntia humifusa*		▓	▓	▓				
Wild Quinine	*Parthenium integrifolium*		▓	▓	▓	▓	▓	▓	
Prairie Coneflower	*Ratibida pinnata*		▓	▓	▓	▓			
Common St. John's Wort	*Hypericum perforatum*		▓	▓	▓	▓	▓		
Queen Anne's Lace	*Daucus carota*		▓	▓	▓	▓	▓	▓	
Smooth Phlox	*Phlox carolina var. triflora*		▓	▓	▓	▓	▓	▓	
Flowering Spurge	*Euphorbia corollata*		▓	▓	▓	▓	▓	▓	
Pale Spike Lobelia	*Lobelia spicata*		▓	▓	▓	▓	▓	▓	To October 7

		June		July		August		September	
		Week 1-2	Week 3-4	Week 1-2	Week 3-4	Week 1-2	Week 3-4	Week 1-2	Week 3-4
Common Milkweed	*Asclepias syriaca*		▓	▓	▓				
False Aloe	*Agave virginica*			▓	▓	▓	▓	▓	
Spotted Touch-Me-Not	*Impatiens capensis*		▓	▓	▓	▓	▓	▓	▓
Narrow-Leaf White-Top Aster	*Sericocarpus linifolius*		▓	▓	▓			▓	
Enchanter's Nightshade	*Circaea quadrisulcata*		▓	▓					
Tall Anemone	*Anemone virginiana*		▓	▓	▓	▓	▓		
White Avens	*Geum canadense*		▓	▓	▓				
Fragrant Bedstraw	*Galium triflorum*		▓	▓	▓				
Shining Bedstraw	*Galium concinnum*		▓	▓	▓	▓	▓		
Chicory	*Cichorium intybus*		▓	▓	▓	▓	▓	▓	▓
Ramp	*Allium tricoccum*		▓						
Trumpet Creeper	*Campsis radicans*			▓	▓				
Pointed-Leaf Tick-Trefoil	*Desmodium glutinosum*		▓	▓	▓				
Virginia Meadow-Beauty	*Rhexia virginica*		▓	▓	▓	▓		▓	
Hairy Ruellia	*Ruellia caroliniensis*		▓	▓	▓	▓	▓		
St. Andrew's Cross	*Ascyrum hypericoides*		▓	▓	▓		▓		
Fringed Loosestrife	*Lysimachia ciliata*			▓	▓				
Pencil Flower	*Stylosanthes biflora*			▓	▓			▓	
Slender Mountain-Mint	*Pycnanthemum flexuosum*			▓	▓	▓			
Water Hemlock	*Cicuta maculata*			▓	▓		▓		
Downy Skullcap	*Scutellaria incana*			▓	▓	▓			
Galinsoga	*Galinsoga ciliata*			▓	▓	▓			
Yellow Touch-Me-Not	*Impatiens pallida*			▓	▓	▓	▓	▓	▓
Wood Sage	*Teucrium canadense*			▓	▓	▓	▓		
Pinesap	*Monotropa hypopithys*					▓			▓

APPENDIX A, continued

Common Name	Scientific Name	July Week 1-2	July Week 3-4	August Week 1-2	August Week 3-4	September Week 1-2	September Week 3-4	October Week 1-2	October Week 3-4
Ginseng	*Panax quinquefolium*	░							
Button-Snakeroot	*Eryngium yuccifolium*								
Wild Lettuce	*Lactuca canadensis*	░	░	░					
Round-Leaved Thoroughwort	*Eupatorium rotundifolium*			░	░	░			
Virginia Knotweed	*Tovara virginiana*		░	░	░	░	░		
Orange-Grass	*Hypericum gentianoides*		░	░	░				
Shrubby St. John's Wort	*Hypericum spathulatum*	░	░	░					
White Vervain	*Verbena urticifolia*	░	░	░					
Indian Tobacco	*Lobelia inflata*		░	░	░	░	░		
Lopseed	*Phryma leptostachya*	░	░	░					
Green Milkweed	*Asclepias viridiflora*	░	░	░	░				
Michigan Lily	*Lilium michiganense*	░	░						
Dayflower	*Commelina communis*		░	░	░	░	░		
Whorled Milkweed	*Asclepias verticillata*		░	░	░				
Blazing Star	*Liatris squarrosa*	░	░	░	░	░	░		
Spotted Knapweed	*Centaurea maculosa*		░	░	░	░			
Early Ladies'-Tresses	*Spiranthes vernalis*	░	░						
Woodland Sunflower	*Helianthus divaricatus*	░	░	░		░			
Indian Pipe	*Monotropa uniflora*	░	░	░					
Angle-Pod	*Gonolobus gonocarpos*	░							
Naked-Flower Tick-Trefoil	*Desmodium nudiflorum*	░	░	░	░	░			
Agrimony	*Agrimonia rostellata*	░	░	░	░	░			
Starry Campion	*Silene stellata*	░	░	░	░	░			
Rosinweed	*Silphium integrifolium*	░	░	░	░	░		░	
Wood-Nettle	*Laportea canadensis*	░	░	░					

Common Name	Scientific Name	July Week 1-2	July Week 3-4	August Week 1-2	August Week 3-4	September Week 1-2	September Week 3-4	October Week 1-2	October Week 3-4
Hairy Angelica	Angelica venenosa		■	■					
Bear's Foot	Polymnia uvedalia			■	■				
Hoary Mountain-Mint	Pycnanthemum incanum		■	■	■	■			
Rattlesnake Plantain	Goodyeara pubescens			■	■				
Whorled Rosinweed	Silphium trifoliatum		■	■	■	■			
Tall Bellflower	Campanula americana		■	■	■	■	■	■	
False Sunflower	Heliopsis helianthoides		■	■	■	■	■		
Purple-Headed Sneezeweed	Helenium nudiflorum			■	■	■	■		
Fall Phlox	Phlox paniculata		■	■	■	■	■		
Rose Pink	Sabatia angularis		■	■	■				
Small-Flowered Leafcup	Polymnia canadensis		■	■	■	■			
Indian-Cup	Silphium perfoliatum		■	■	■				
Early Goldenrod	Solidagu juncea		■	■	■	■	■		
Green-Stemmed Joe-Pye-Weed	Eupatorium purpureum		■	■	■	■	■	■	
Tall Meadow Rue	Thalictrum polygamum		■	■					
White Tick-Trefoil	Desmodium pauciflorum			■	■				
Tall Coneflower	Rudbeckia laciniata		■	■	■	■			
Agrimony	Agrimonia parviflora		■	■	■	■			
False Foxglove	Gerardia virginica			■	■	■			
Trailing Wild Bean	Strophostyles helvola			■	■				
Monkey Flower	Mimulus alatus			■	■	■			
Eggert's Sunflower	Helianthus eggertii			■	■	■	■		
Crested Coral-Root Orchid	Hexalectris spicata			■					
Spider Lily	Hymenocallis occidentalis								
Spanish Needles	Bidens bipinnata						■		

APPENDIX A, continued

Common Name	Scientific Name	July Week 1-2	July Week 3-4	August Week 1-2	August Week 3-4	September Week 1-2	September Week 3-4	October Week 1-2	October Week 3-4
Cranefly Orchid	*Tipularia discolor*		■	■	■				
Alum-Root	*Heuchera parviflora var. rugelii*			■	■				
Passion-Flower	*Passiflora incarnata*			■	■				
Seedbox	*Ludwigia alternifolia*			■	■				
Small Green Wood Orchis	*Habenaria clavellata*		■	■					
Hairy Sunflower	*Helianthus mollis*			■	■				
Mullein Foxglove	*Seymeria macrophylla*			■	■				
Arrowhead	*Sagittaria latifolia*			■	■				
Coppery St. John's Wort	*Hypericum denticulatum*			■	■				
Whorled Milkwort	*Polygala verticillata*			■	■	■			
Blue Lettuce	*Lactuca floridana*			■	■	■	■		
Woodland Coneflower	*Rudbeckia umbrosa*			■	■	■	■	■	
Lance-Leaved Goldenrod	*Solidago graminifolia*			■	■	■	■		
Late Goldenrod	*Solidago gigantea*			■	■	■	■		
Orange Coneflower	*Rudbeckia fulgida*			■	■	■	■		
Partridge-Pea	*Cassia fasciculata*			■	■	■	■		
Elm-Leaved Goldenrod	*Solidago ulmifolia*			■	■	■			
Ivy-Leaved Morning-Glory	*Ipomoea hederacea*			■	■	■			
Thin-Leaved Coneflower	*Rudbeckia triloba*			■	■	■	■		
Culver's-Root	*Veronicastrum virginicum*								
Evening-Primrose	*Oenothera biennis*			■	■	■	■		
Tall Coreopsis	*Coreopsis tripteris*			■	■	■	■		
Pale Indian Plantain	*Cacalia atriplicifolia*			■	■	■	■		
Elephant's Foot	*Elephantopus carolinianus*			■	■	■	■		
Ironweed	*Vernonia altissima*			■	■	■	■		

		July		August		September		October	
		Week 1-2	Week 3-4	Week 1-2	Week 3-4	Week 1-2	Week 3-4	Week 1-2	Week 3-4
Ladies'-Tresses	*Spiranthes tuberosa*			▩	▩	▩	▩		
Wild Senna	*Cassia marilandica*			▩	▩				
Bugleweed	*Lycopus virginicus*			▩	▩	▩	▩		
Pink Wild Bean	*Strophostyles umbellata*			▩	▩	▩			
Sharp-Leaved Goldenrod	*Solidago arguta*			▩	▩	▩	▩		
Hairy Hawkweed	*Hieracium gronovii*			▩	▩	▩			
White Snakeroot	*Eupatorium rugosum*			▩	▩	▩	▩	▩	
Joe-Pye-Weed	*Eupatorium fistulosum*			▩	▩	▩	▩		
Cardinal Flower	*Lobelia cardinalis*			▩	▩	▩	▩	▩	
Mad-Dog Skullcap	*Scutellaria lateriflora*			▩	▩	▩	▩		
Small-Leaved Tick-Trefoil	*Desmodium ciliare*			▩	▩	▩			
Slender-Stalked Gaura	*Gaura filipes*			▩	▩	▩	▩		
Virginia Dayflower	*Commelina virginica*			▩	▩	▩			
Round-Leaf Tick-Trefoil	*Desmodium rotundifolium*			▩	▩	▩			
Small Wood Sunflower	*Helianthus microcephalus*			▩	▩	▩	▩		
Grey Goldenrod	*Solidago nemoralis*				▩	▩	▩	▩	
Wingstem	*Actinomeris alternifolia*			▩	▩	▩	▩		
Field Thistle	*Cirsium discolor*			▩	▩	▩	▩		
Tall Thistle	*Cirsium altissimum*			▩	▩	▩	▩	▩	▩
Wild Bean	*Phaseolus polystachios*			▩	▩	▩			
Groundnut	*Apios americana*				▩	▩	▩		
Downy Lobelia	*Lobelia puberula*					▩	▩	▩	
Smartweed	*Polygonum* spp.			▩	▩	▩	▩	▩	▩
Horseweed	*Erigeron canadensis*			▩	▩	▩	▩	▩	
Three-Seeded Mercury	*Acalypha virginica*			▩	▩	▩	▩	▩	▩

APPENDIX A, continued

Common Name	Scientific Name	July Week 1-2	July Week 3-4	August Week 1-2	August Week 3-4	September Week 1-2	September Week 3-4	October Week 1-2	October Week 3-4
Mistflower	*Eupatorium coelestinum*				▓	▓	▓	▓	▓
Blazing Star	*Liatris aspera*					▓	▓		
White Wingstem	*Verbesina virginica*				▓	▓	▓	▓	
Common Burdock	*Arctium minus*				▓	▓			
Blue-Stemmed Goldenrod	*Solidago caesia*					▓	▓	▓	
Virgin's-Bower	*Clematis virginiana*				▓				
Bull Thistle	*Cirsium vulgare*					▓	▓		
Western Sunflower	*Helianthus occidentalis*				▓	▓	▓		
Jimsonweed	*Datura stramonium*			▓	▓	▓			
Spearmint	*Mentha spicata*			▓	▓				
Large-Leaved Aster	*Aster macrophyllus*				▓	▓	▓		
Hog Peanut	*Amphicarpa bracteata*				▓	▓	▓		
Jerusalem Artichoke	*Helianthus tuberosus*				▓	▓	▓		
Common Morning-Glory	*Ipomoea purpurea*				▓	▓	▓	▓	
Hyssop-Leaved Thoroughwort	*Eupatorium hyssopifolium*				▓	▓	▓		
Small White Morning-Glory	*Ipomoea lacunosa*				▓	▓	▓		
Sericea Lespedeza	*Lespedeza cuneata*				▓	▓			
Late Flowering Thoroughwort	*Eupatorium serotinum*				▓	▓	▓	▓	
Prairie Dock	*Silphium terebinthinaceum*				▓	▓			
Erect Goldenrod	*Solidago erecta*				▓	▓	▓	▓	
Cornel-Leaf Aster	*Aster infirmus*				▓	▓	▓		
Bush-Clover	*Lespedeza intermedia*				▓	▓			
Large-Bracted Tick-Trefoil	*Desmodium cuspidatum*				▓	▓	▓		
False Goldenrod	*Solidago sphacelata*					▓	▓	▓	
Beechdrops	*Epifagus virginiana*								▓

		July		August		September		October	
		Week 1-2	Week 3-4	Week 1-2	Week 3-4	Week 1-2	Week 3-4	Week 1-2	Week 3-4
Horse-Balm	*Collinsonia canadensis*				▓	▓	▓	▓	
Bush-Clover	*Lespedeza violacea*					▓	▓		
Nodding Pogonia	*Triphora trianthophora*				▓				
Broad-Leaved Goldenrod	*Solidago flexicaulis*					▓	▓	▓	
Slender Ladies'-Tresses	*Spiranthes gracilis*				▓	▓	▓	▓	
Hoary Tick-Trefoil	*Desmodium canescens*				▓	▓			
Hairy Goldenrod	*Solidago hispida*					▓	▓	▓	
Panicled Tick-Trefoil	*Desmodium paniculatum*				▓	▓	▓		
White Wood Aster	*Aster divaricatus*				▓	▓	▓		
Silky Aster	*Aster sericeus*					▓	▓	▓	▓
Sweet Everlasting	*Gnaphalium obtusifolium*					▓	▓	▓	
Sticktight	*Bidens frondosa*					▓	▓		
Pilewort	*Erechtites hieracifolia*					▓	▓		
Blue Curls	*Trichostema dichotomum*					▓	▓	▓	
Horse-Mint	*Perilla frutescens*					▓	▓	▓	▓
Hairy Bush-Clover	*Lespedeza hirta*					▓	▓		
False Dragonhead	*Physostegia virginiana*					▓	▓	▓	
False Pennyroyal	*Isanthus brachiatus*					▓	▓		
Tickseed Sunflower	*Bidens aristosa*					▓	▓		
Late Purple Aster	*Aster patens*					▓	▓	▓	
Slender Gerardia	*Gerardia tenuifolia*					▓	▓	▓	
Arrow-Leaved Aster	*Aster sagittifolius*					▓	▓	▓	
Trailing Bush-Clover	*Lespedeza procumbens*					▓			
Tall Goldenrod	*Solidago altissima*					▓	▓	▓	
Coral-Root Orchid	*Corallorhiza odontorhiza*					▓	▓		

APPENDIX A, continued

		July		August		September		October	
		Week 1-2	Week 3-4	Week 1-2	Week 3-4	Week 1-2	Week 3-4	Week 1-2	Week 3-4
Sweet Goldenrod	Solidago odora					▓	▓		
Great Lobelia	Lobelia siphilitica					▓	▓	▓	
Short's Aster	Aster shortii					▓	▓	▓	▓
Nodding Ladies'-Tresses	Spiranthes cernua					▓	▓	▓	
Rough-Stemmed Goldenrod	Solidago rugosa					▓			
Tall White Lettuce	Prenanthes altissima						▓		
Japanese Mint	Mosla dianthera					▓	▓		
Frost-Weed Aster	Aster pilosus					▓	▓	▓	▓
Small White Aster	Aster vimineus					▓	▓	▓	
Stiff-Leaf Aster	Aster linariifolius						▓	▓	
Autumn Sneezeweed	Helenium autumnale					▓	▓	▓	
Smooth Aster	Aster laevis					▓	▓	▓	
Wavy-Leaved Aster	Aster undulatus					▓	▓	▓	
Heart-Leaved Aster	Aster cordifolius					▓	▓	▓	▓
New England Aster	Aster novae-angliae					▓	▓		
Crooked-Stemmed Aster	Aster prenanthoides						▓		
Ontario Aster	Aster ontarionis						▓	▓	
Rough Hawkweed	Hieracium scabrum						▓	▓	
Small-Flowered Ladies'-Tresses	Spiranthes ovalis						▓	▓	
Lowrie's Aster	Aster lowrieanus						▓		
Turtlehead	Chelone glabra						▓	▓	
Calico Aster	Aster lateriflorus						▓	▓	▓
Striped Gentian	Gentiana villosa							▓	▓
Field Milkwort	Polygala sanguinea							▓	
Soapwort Gentian	Gentiana saponaria								▓

APPENDIX B: FLOWER HUNTING PLANNING GUIDE

Legend:
- ■ Flower
- ▨ Foliage Only

Columns (left to right), by common name and scientific name:

1. Agrimony — *Agrimonia parviflora*
2. Agrimony — *Agrimonia rostellata*
3. Alum-Root — *Heuchera americana*
4. Alum-Root — *Heuchera parviflora var. rugelli*
5. Alum-Root — *Heuchera villosa*
6. American Columbo — *Swertia caroliniensis*
7. Angle-Pod — *Gonolobus gonocarpos*
8. Angle-Pod — *Gonolobus shortii*
9. Appendaged Waterleaf — *Hydrophyllum appendiculatum*
10. Arrowhead — *Sagittaria latifolia*
11. Arrow-Leaved Aster — *Aster sagittifolius*
12. Autumn Sneezeweed — *Helenium autumnale*
13. Baby's-Breath — *Arenaria patula*
14. Barren Strawberry — *Waldsteinia fragarioides*
15. Bear's Foot — *Polymnia uvedalia*
16. Beechdrops — *Epifagus virginiana*
17. Bellwort — *Uvularia perfoliata*
18. Bent Trillium — *Trillium flexipes*
19. Bergamot — *Monarda fistulosa*
20. Birdfoot Violet — *Viola pedata*
21. Bishop's-Cap — *Mitella diphylla*
22. Blackberry-Lily — *Belamcanda chinensis*
23. Black-Eyed Susan — *Rudbeckia hirta*
24. Blazing Star — *Liatris aspera*
25. Blazing Star — *Liatris squarrosa*

Location	1	2	3	4	5	6	7	8	9	10	11	12	13	14	15	16	17	18	19	20	21	22	23	24	25
White Oak	■	■			■														■	■			■		
Wet Prong/McCoy Hollow	■																		■						
Wet Prong	■					■	▨												■	■					
Ugly Creek Road	■		■	■												■			■	■			■		
Turnhole Bend South	■																		■						
Turnhole Bend	■		■		■														■				▨		
Sloan's Crossing	■																								
Sand Cave																									
Sal Hollow	■																								
Raymer Hollow		■																	■	■					
Park Ridge Road	■		■																				▨		
McCoy Hollow	■		■	■																▨					
Mammoth Cave Ferry Road			■																■	■			■		
Joppa Ridge	■																		■	■					
Houchins Ferry Road	■																		■	■			▨	■	
Highway 70/255																									
Heritage Trail																		■					■		
Green R. Bluffs/Styx/Dixon																		■					■		
Good Spring Loop																									
Ganter Cave			■							■									■	■			■		
Flint Ridge Road					■															■					
First Creek Hollow	■				■														■						
Echo River/Mammoth Dome			■	■		■		■				■							■						
Dennison Ferry Road			■		■		■			■									■						
Collie Ridge			■	■															■				■		
Cedar Sink																			■	■			■		
Campground			■					■											■						
Blair Spring Hollow	■																		■						

APPENDIX B, continued

■ Flower
▨ Foliage Only

Location	Bloodroot *Sanguinaria canadensis*	Bluebells *Mertensia virginica*	Blue Cohosh *Caulophyllum thalictroides*	Blue Curls *Trichostema dichotomum*	Blue-Eyed-Grass *Sisyrinchium angustifolium*	Blue Lettuce *Lactuca floridana*	Blue Phlox *Phlox divaricata*	Blue-Stemmed Goldenrod *Solidago caesia*	Bluets *Houstonia caerulea*	Broadleaf Waterleaf *Hydrophyllum canadense*	Broad-Leaved Goldenrod *Solidago flexicaulis*	Bugleweed *Lycopus virginicus*	Bull Thistle *Cirsium vulgare*	Bush-Clover *Lespedeza intermedia*	Butterfly Milkweed *Asclepias tuberosa*	Butterweed *Senecio glabellus*	Button-Snakeroot *Eryngium yuccifolium*	Calico Aster *Aster lateriflorus*	Cardinal Flower *Lobelia cardinalis*	Carrion-Flower *Smilax echirrata*	Carrion-Flower *Smilax herbacea*	Celandine Poppy *Stylophorum diphyllum*	Chicory *Cichorium intybus*	Cicily *Osmorhiza longistylus*	Cleavers *Galium aparine*
White Oak									■			■								■					■
Wet Prong/McCoy Hollow								■				■								■				■	
Wet Prong	■		▨		■		■	■	■		■	■		■					■	■					
Ugly Creek Road	■	■				■	■	■	■	■			■		■	■		■						■	■
Turnhole Bend South	■						■	■	■	■	■		■							■		■		■	■
Turnhole Bend		■					■		■			■								■					■
Sloan's Crossing									■			■													
Sand Cave								■	■									■			■				■
Sal Hollow							■	■	■															■	■
Raymer Hollow					■		■	■	■										■					■	■
Park Ridge Road									■																
McCoy Hollow	■		■				■	■	■	■										■				■	■
Mammoth Cave Ferry Road													■		■								■		
Joppa Ridge							■						■							■					
Houchins Ferry Road	■						■		■						■	■							■		■
Highway 70/255																									
Heritage Trail									■															■	
Green R. Bluffs/Styx/Dixon									■								■								
Good Spring Loop	■	■					■	■	■	■		■										■			
Ganter Cave	■		■				■												■	■		■		■	■
Flint Ridge Road						■	■		■									■					■	■	■
First Creek Hollow	■	■	■	■	■		■		■	■									■	■		■			■
Echo River/Mammoth Dome		■					■	■	■	■	■											■		■	■
Dennison Ferry Road						■	■	■	■	■					■							■	■		■
Collie Ridge						■		■	■										■	■			■	■	■
Cedar Sink							■		■	■	■				■			■		■		■		■	■
Campground	■	■					■	■	■	■	■									■		■		■	■
Blair Spring Hollow							■	■	■			■								■					

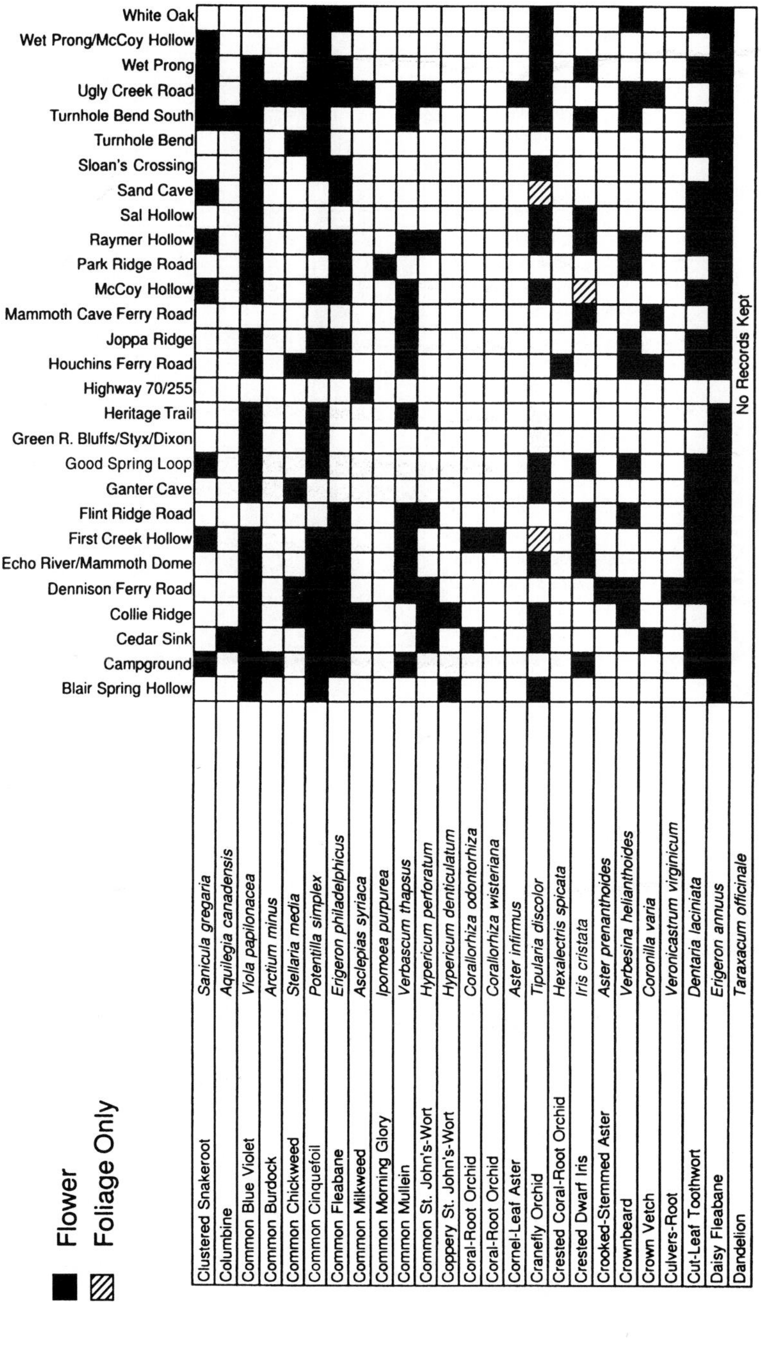
White Oak
Wet Prong/McCoy Hollow
Wet Prong
Ugly Creek Road
Turnhole Bend South
Turnhole Bend
Sloan's Crossing
Sand Cave
Sal Hollow
Raymer Hollow
Park Ridge Road
McCoy Hollow
Mammoth Cave Ferry Road
Joppa Ridge
Houchins Ferry Road
Highway 70/255
Heritage Trail
Green R. Bluffs/Styx/Dixon
Good Spring Loop
Ganter Cave
Flint Ridge Road
First Creek Hollow
Echo River/Mammoth Dome
Dennison Ferry Road
Collie Ridge
Cedar Sink
Campground
Blair Spring Hollow
No Records Kept
Clustered Snakeroot *Sanicula gregaria*
Columbine *Aquilegia canadensis*
Common Blue Violet *Viola papilonacea*
Common Burdock *Arctium minus*
Common Chickweed *Stellaria media*
Common Cinquefoil *Potentilla simplex*
Common Fleabane *Erigeron philadelphicus*
Common Milkweed *Asclepias syriaca*
Common Morning Glory *Ipomoea purpurea*
Common Mullein *Verbascum thapsus*
Common St. John's-Wort *Hypericum perforatum*
Coppery St. John's-Wort *Hypericum denticulatum*
Coral-Root Orchid *Corallorhiza odontorhiza*
Coral-Root Orchid *Corallorhiza wisteriana*
Cornel-Leaf Aster *Aster infirmus*
Cranefly Orchid *Tipularia discolor*
Crested Coral-Root Orchid *Hexalectris spicata*
Crested Dwarf Iris *Iris cristata*
Crooked-Stemmed Aster *Aster prenanthoides*
Crownbeard *Verbesina helianthoides*
Crown Vetch *Coronilla varia*
Culvers-Root *Veronicastrum virginicum*
Cut-Leaf Toothwort *Dentaria laciniata*
Daisy Fleabane *Erigeron annuus*
Dandelion *Taraxacum officinale*
Flower
Foliage Only

APPENDIX B, continued

■ Flower
▨ Foliage Only

	Dayflower *Commelina communis*	Daylily *Hemerocallis fulva*	Deptford Pink *Dianthus armeria*	Downy Lobelia *Lobelia puberula*	Downy Skullcap *Scutellaria incana*	Downy Wood-Mint *Blephilia ciliata*	Dutchmans-Breeches *Dicentra cucullaria*	Dwarf Dandelion *Krigia biflora*	Dwarf Dandelion *Krigia dandelion*	Early Buttercup *Ranunculus fascicularis*	Early Goldenrod *Solidago juncea*	Early Ladies'-Tresses *Spiranthes vernalis*	Early Meadow Rue *Thalictrum dioicum*	Early Saxifrage *Saxifraga virginiensis*	Early Scorpion-Grass *Myosotis verna*	Early Spiderwort *Tradescantia virginiana*	Early Spurge *Euphorbia commutata*	Eggert's Sunflower *Helianthus eggertii*	Elephant's Foot *Elephantopus carolinianus*	Elm-Leaved Goldenrod *Solidago ulmifolia*	Enchanter's Nightshade *Circaea quadrisulcata*	Erect Goldenrod *Solidago erecta*	Evening Primrose *Oenothera biennis*	Fall Phlox *Phlox paniculata*	False Aloe *Agave virginica*
White Oak						■		■	■										■						
Wet Prong/McCoy Hollow	■		■	■	■	■		■	■		■		■	■		■			■	■	■	■	■	■	
Wet Prong				■		■		■			■					■			■	■	■	■			
Ugly Creek Road	■			■	■	■		■					■	■		■	■	■		■		■	■	■	
Turnhole Bend South	■			■				■							■					■		■			
Turnhole Bend				■	■	■								■					■	■	■		■		
Sloan's Crossing	■			■															■	■					
Sand Cave				■							■								■	■	■				
Sal Hollow				■		■		■						■	■	■			■	■		■			
Raymer Hollow				■	■			■			■					■			■	■	■	■		■	
Park Ridge Road		■		■				■			■							■							
McCoy Hollow				■		■		■						■		■			■					■	
Mammoth Cave Ferry Road		■			■	■		■			■									■			■		
Joppa Ridge				■	■	■		■		■	■			■					■	■			■		
Houchins Ferry Road						■		■			■			■									■		■
Highway 70/255											■	■						■					■		
Heritage Trail									■							■			■			■			
Green R. Bluffs/Styx/Dixon	■			■		■		■						■					■	■	■	■		■	
Good Spring Loop					■	■								■					■		■	■			
Ganter Cave		■		■		■		■			■		■	■					■			■	■		■
Flint Ridge Road				■		■	■	■	■					■					■	■	■	■			
First Creek Hollow						■				■				■		■				■	■				
Echo River/Mammoth Dome						■		■		■	■			■					■	■		■	■	■	■
Dennison Ferry Road	■			■	■	■		■			■								■	■	■	■		■	
Collie Ridge			■	■	■	■		■			■			■			▨		■		■			■	
Cedar Sink		■		■	■	■		■			■		■	■					■	■		■			
Campground						■																			■
Blair Spring Hollow				■	■			■												■	■	■			

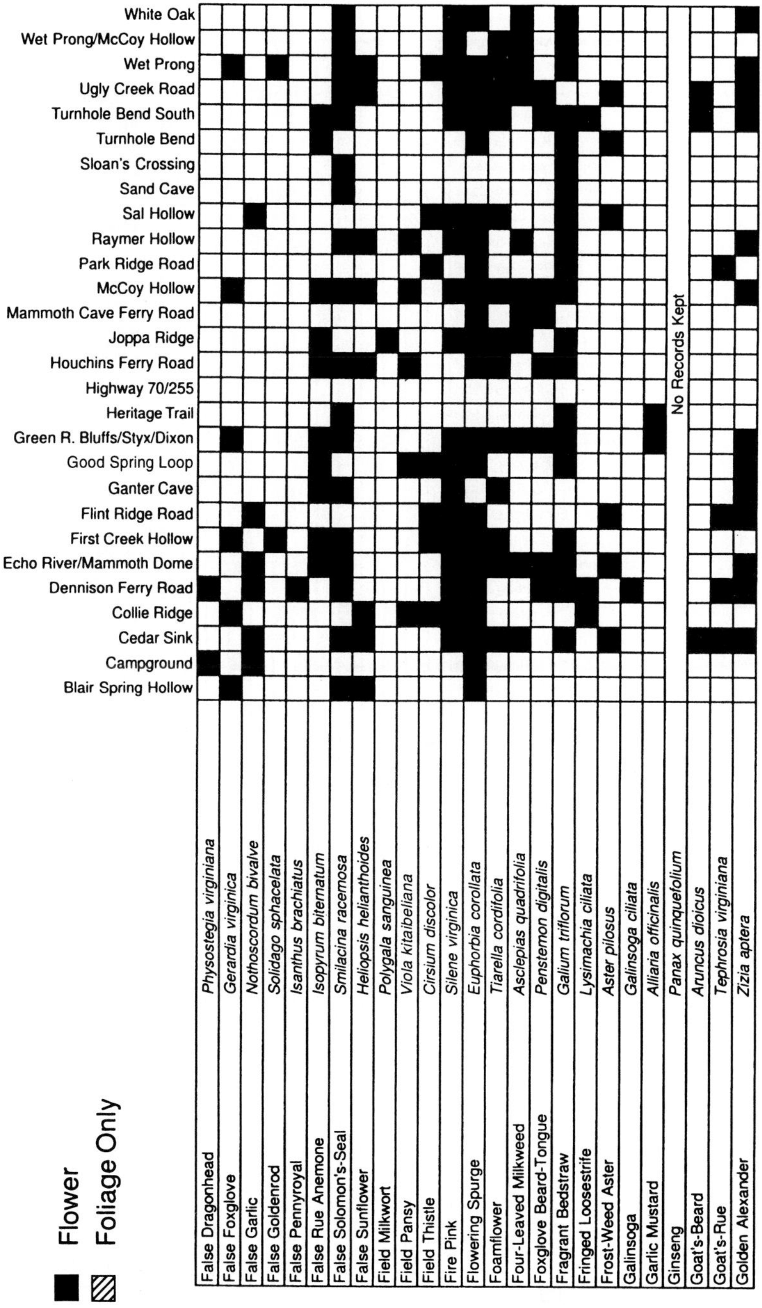
White Oak
Wet Prong/McCoy Hollow
Wet Prong
Ugly Creek Road
Turnhole Bend South
Turnhole Bend
Sloan's Crossing
Sand Cave
Sal Hollow
Raymer Hollow
Park Ridge Road
McCoy Hollow
Mammoth Cave Ferry Road
Joppa Ridge
Houchins Ferry Road
Highway 70/255
Heritage Trail
Green R. Bluffs/Styx/Dixon
Good Spring Loop
Ganter Cave
Flint Ridge Road
First Creek Hollow
Echo River/Mammoth Dome
Dennison Ferry Road
Collie Ridge
Cedar Sink
Campground
Blair Spring Hollow
No Records Kept
False Dragonhead Physostegia virginiana
False Foxglove Gerardia virginica
False Garlic Nothoscordum bivalve
False Goldenrod Solidago sphacelata
False Pennyroyal Isanthus brachiatus
False Rue Anemone Isopyrum biternatum
False Solomon's-Seal Smilacina racemosa
False Sunflower Heliopsis helianthoides
Field Milkwort Polygala sanguinea
Field Pansy Viola kitaibeliana
Field Thistle Cirsium discolor
Fire Pink Silene virginica
Flowering Spurge Euphorbia corollata
Foamflower Tiarella cordifolia
Four-Leaved Milkweed Asclepias quadrifolia
Foxglove Beard-Tongue Penstemon digitalis
Fragrant Bedstraw Galium triflorum
Fringed Loosestrife Lysimachia ciliata
Frost-Weed Aster Aster pilosus
Galinsoga Galinsoga ciliata
Garlic Mustard Alliaria officinalis
Ginseng Panax quinquefolium
Goat's-Beard Aruncus dioicus
Goat's-Rue Tephrosia virginiana
Golden Alexander Zizia aptera
Flower
Foliage Only

APPENDIX B, continued

■ Flower
▨ Foliage Only

	Golden Ragwort *Senecio aureus*	Goldenseal *Hydrastis canadensis*	Great Indian Plantain *Cacalia muhlenbergii*	Great Lobelia *Lobelia siphilitica*	Green Dragon *Arisaema dracontium*	Green Milkweed *Asclepias viridiflora*	Green-Stemmed Joe-Pye-Weed *Eupatorium purpureum*	Grey Goldenrod *Solidago nemoralis*	Ground Cherry *Physalis virginiana*	Ground-Ivy *Glechoma hederacea*	Groundnut *Apios americana*	Hairy Angelica *Angelica venenosa*	Hairy Bush-Clover *Lespedeza hirta*	Hairy Goldenrod *Solidago hispida*	Hairy Hawkweed *Hieracium gronovii*	Hairy Ruellia *Ruellia caroliniensis*	Hairy Skullcap *Scutellaria elliptica*	Hairy Sunflower *Helianthus mollis*	Harbinger-of-Spring *Erigenia bulbosa*	Heal-All *Prunella vulgaris*	Heart-Leaved Aster *Aster cordifolius*	Heart-Leaved Skullcap *Scutellaria ovata*	Hepatica *Hepatica acutiloba*	Hepatica *Hepatica americana*	Hispid Buttercup *Ranunculus hispidus*
White Oak								■		■					■	■	■			■					■
Wet Prong/McCoy Hollow	■			■	▨			■							■		■			■	■		■	■	■
Wet Prong	■	▨															■			■			■		■
Ugly Creek Road	■		■	■			■	■	■						■	■	■			■	■		■		■
Turnhole Bend South								■		■			■		■	■	■			■					■
Turnhole Bend										■					■	■	■		■	■	■		■		■
Sloan's Crossing											■				■					■					
Sand Cave					■			■								■			■	■			■		
Sal Hollow		▨						■							■	■	■			■					■
Raymer Hollow	■	▨	■	■			■	■	■						■					■			■	■	■
Park Ridge Road								■								■				■					
McCoy Hollow	■	■				■		■							■		▨			■			■	■	■
Mammoth Cave Ferry Road						■		■								■									
Joppa Ridge		■						■		■					■	■	■			■					■
Houchins Ferry Road								■		■					■	■	■			■		■	■		
Highway 70/255																		■		■					
Heritage Trail																				■					
Green R. Bluffs/Styx/Dixon	■	▨	■		■		■	■							■	■	■		■	■	■			■	■
Good Spring Loop				■						■							■		■				■		
Ganter Cave						■		■				■				■	■			■					
Flint Ridge Road		■		■				■		■							■		■	■					■
First Creek Hollow		■								■				■		■	■		■	■	■	■	■		■
Echo River/Mammoth Dome						■	■	■		■					■	■			■	■	■				■
Dennison Ferry Road								■				■	■		■	■	■	■		■	■				
Collie Ridge			■		■		■	■						■	■	■				■	■		■		
Cedar Sink						■		■							■	■				■					
Campground		▨					■			■					■	■	■		■	■	■	■	■		
Blair Spring Hollow								■							■		■			■	■		■		■

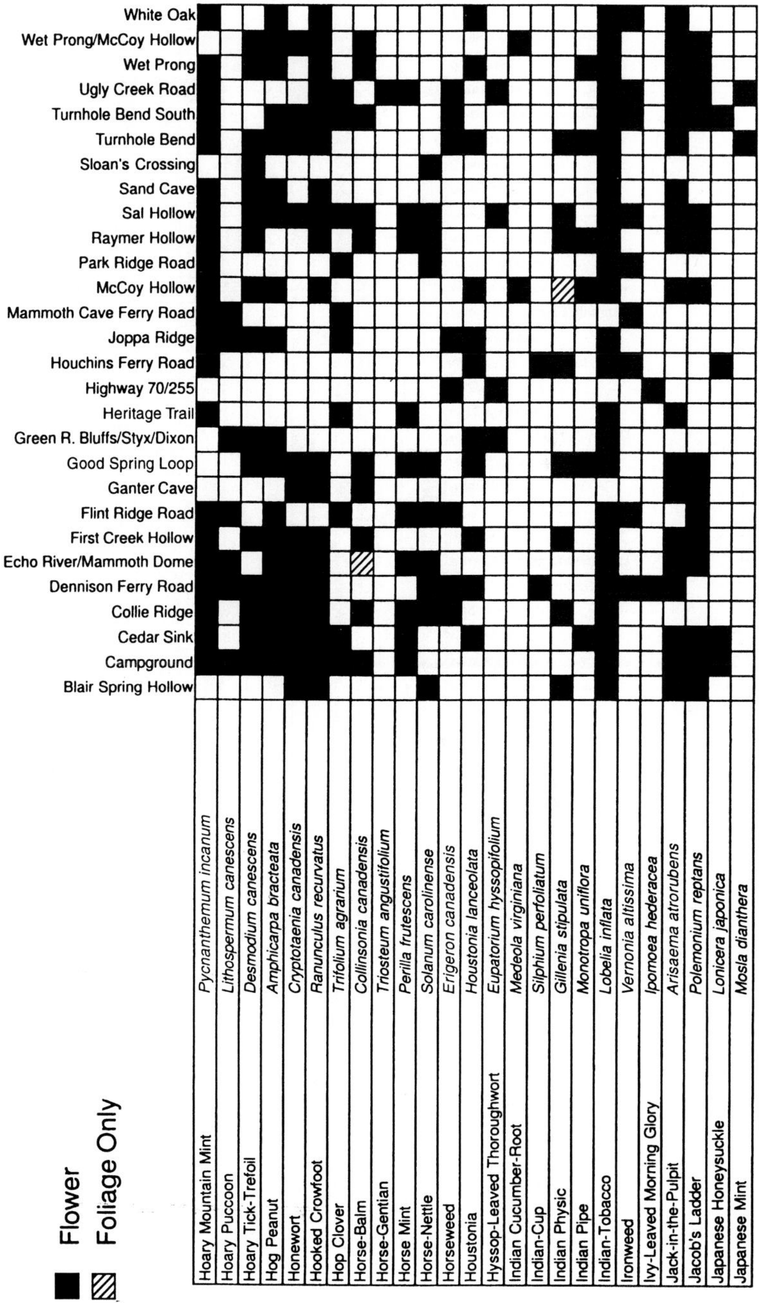
White Oak
Wet Prong/McCoy Hollow
Wet Prong
Ugly Creek Road
Turnhole Bend South
Turnhole Bend
Sloan's Crossing
Sand Cave
Sal Hollow
Raymer Hollow
Park Ridge Road
McCoy Hollow
Mammoth Cave Ferry Road
Joppa Ridge
Houchins Ferry Road
Highway 70/255
Heritage Trail
Green R. Bluffs/Styx/Dixon
Good Spring Loop
Ganter Cave
Flint Ridge Road
First Creek Hollow
Echo River/Mammoth Dome
Dennison Ferry Road
Collie Ridge
Cedar Sink
Campground
Blair Spring Hollow
Hoary Mountain Mint *Pycnanthemum incanum*
Hoary Puccoon *Lithospermum canescens*
Hoary Tick-Trefoil *Desmodium canescens*
Hog Peanut *Amphicarpa bracteata*
Honewort *Cryptotaenia canadensis*
Hooked Crowfoot *Ranunculus recurvatus*
Hop Clover *Trifolium agrarium*
Horse-Balm *Collinsonia canadensis*
Horse-Gentian *Triosteum angustifolium*
Horse Mint *Perilla frutescens*
Horse-Nettle *Solanum carolinense*
Horseweed *Erigeron canadensis*
Houstonia *Houstonia lanceolata*
Hyssop-Leaved Thoroughwort *Eupatorium hyssopifolium*
Indian Cucumber-Root *Medeola virginiana*
Indian-Cup *Silphium perfoliatum*
Indian Physic *Gillenia stipulata*
Indian Pipe *Monotropa uniflora*
Indian-Tobacco *Lobelia inflata*
Ironweed *Vernonia altissima*
Ivy-Leaved Morning Glory *Ipomoea hederacea*
Jack-in-the-Pulpit *Arisaema atrorubens*
Jacob's Ladder *Polemonium reptans*
Japanese Honeysuckle *Lonicera japonica*
Japanese Mint *Mosla dianthera*
Flower
Foliage Only

APPENDIX B, continued

Locations (rows):

- White Oak
- Wet Prong/McCoy Hollow
- Wet Prong
- Ugly Creek Road
- Turnhole Bend South
- Turnhole Bend
- Sloan's Crossing
- Sand Cave
- Sal Hollow
- Raymer Hollow
- Park Ridge Road
- McCoy Hollow
- Mammoth Cave Ferry Road
- Joppa Ridge
- Houchins Ferry Road
- Highway 70/255
- Heritage Trail
- Green R. Bluffs/Styx/Dixon
- Good Spring Loop
- Ganter Cave
- Flint Ridge Road
- First Creek Hollow
- Echo River/Mammoth Dome
- Dennison Ferry Road
- Collie Ridge
- Cedar Sink
- Campground
- Blair Spring Hollow

Species (columns):

- Jerusalem Artichoke — *Helianthus tuberosus*
- Jimsonweed — *Datura stramonium*
- Joe-Pye-Weed — *Eupatorium fistulosum*
- Kidneyleaf Buttercup — *Ranunculus abortivus*
- Ladies'-Tresses — *Spiranthes tuberosa*
- Lance-Leaved Coreopsis — *Coreopsis lanceolata*
- Lance-Leaved Goldenrod — *Solidago graminifolia*
- Lance-Leaved Loosestrife — *Lysimachia lanceolata*
- Lance-Leaved Violet — *Viola lanceolata*
- Large-Bracted Tick-Trefoil — *Desmodium cuspidatum*
- Large Coreopsis — *Coreopsis major*
- Large-Flowered Bellwort — *Uvularia grandiflora*
- Large Houstonia — *Houstonia purpurea*
- Large-Leaved Aster — *Aster macrophyllus*
- Large Yellow Wood-Sorrel — *Oxalis grandis*
- Larkspur — *Delphinium tricorne*
- Late Flowering Thoroughwort — *Eupatorium serotinum*
- Late Goldenrod — *Solidago gigantea*
- Late Purple Aster — *Aster patens*
- Leonard's Skullcap — *Scutellaria parvula var. leonardii*
- Lily-Leaved Twayblade — *Liparis liliifolia*
- Loopseed — *Phryma leptostachya*
- Lowrie's Aster — *Aster lowrieanus*
- Lyre-Leaved Sage — *Salvia lyrata*
- Mad-Dog Skullcap — *Scutellaria lateriflora*

Legend:

 Flower

 Foliage Only

Legend:

■ Flower

▨ Foliage Only

Location	Viola cucullata (Marsh Blue Violet)	Podophyllum peltatum (May-Apple)	Lilium michiganense (Michigan Lily)	Eupatorium coelestinum (Mistflower)	Mimulus alatus (Monkey Flower)	Verbascum blattaria (Moth Mullein)	Seymeria macrophylla (Mullein Foxglove)	Desmodium nudiflorum (Naked-Flowered Tick-Trefoil)	Sericocarpus linifolius (Narrow-Leaf White-Top Aster)	Verbena simplex (Narrow-Leaved Vervain)	Aster novae-angliae (New England Aster)	Spiranthes cernua (Nodding Ladies'-Tresses)	Triphora trianthophora (Nodding Pogonia)	Carduus nutans (Nodding Thistle)	Aster ontarionis (Ontario Aster)	Rudbeckia fulgida (Orange Coneflower)	Hypericum gentianoides (Orange-Grass)	Chrysanthemum leucanthemum (Ox-Eye Daisy)	Cacalia atriplicifolia (Pale Indian Plaintain)	Lobelia spicata (Pale Spike Lobelia)	Viola striata (Pale Violet)	Desmodium paniculatum (Panicled Tick-Trefoil)	Mitchella repens (Partridge-Berry)	Cassia fasciculata (Partridge-Pea)	Passiflora incarnata (Passion-Flower)
White Oak	■			■				■														■		■	
Wet Prong/McCoy Hollow	■			■				■														■		■	
Wet Prong				■				■											■			■			■
Ugly Creek Road				■		■		■			■								■			■		■	
Turnhole Bend South								■				■							■			■		■	
Turnhole Bend								■											■			■			
Sloan's Crossing												■								■		■		■	
Sand Cave	▨							■														■			
Sal Hollow				■				■											■			■			
Raymer Hollow	■			■				■		■									■			■			
Park Ridge Road	■			■				■											■			■			■
McCoy Hollow	■			■				■											■			■	▨	■	■
Mammoth Cave Ferry Road				■		■		■											■			■			■
Joppa Ridge				■				■											■			■			
Houchins Ferry Road				■		■		■											■			■			
Highway 70/255				■								■							■			■			■
Heritage Trail				■				■			■								■			■			
Green R. Bluffs/Styx/Dixon				■				■											■			■		■	
Good Spring Loop				■				■														■			
Ganter Cave				■				■											■			■			■
Flint Ridge Road				■		■		■			■								■			■			
First Creek Hollow				■				■				■							■			■		■	
Echo River/Mammoth Dome				■				■											■			■			■
Dennison Ferry Road				■				■											■			■		■	
Collie Ridge	■			■				■											■			■			■
Cedar Sink								■								■						■			
Campground				■				■														■			
Blair Spring Hollow				■				■								■						■			

APPENDIX B, continued

■ Flower
▨ Foliage Only

	Pencil-Flower *Stylosanthes biflora*	Pennywort *Obolaria virginica*	Periwinkle *Vinca minor*	Phacelia *Phacelia purshii*	Pilewort *Erechtites hieracifolia*	Pinesap *Monotropa hypopithys*	Pink Wild Bean *Strophostyles umbellata*	Plantain-Leaved Pussytoes *Antennaria plantaginifolia*	Pointed-Leaf Tick-Trefoil *Desmodium glutinosum*	Prairie Coneflower *Ratibida pinnata*	Prairie Dock *Silphium terebinthinaceum*	Prickly Pear Cactus *Opuntia humifusa*	Purple Coneflower *Echinacea pallida*	Purple Cress *Cardamine douglassii*	Purple-Headed Sneezeweed *Helenium nudiflorum*	Purple Phacelia *Phacelia bipinnatifida*	Purple Rocket *Iodanthus pinnatifidus*	Putty-Root Orchid *Aplectrum hyemale*	Queen Anne's Lace *Daucus carota*	Ragged Fringed Orchis *Habenaria lacera*	Ramp *Allium tricoccum*	Rattlesnake Plantain *Goodyera pubescens*	Red Clover *Trifolium pratense*	Red Dead Nettle *Lamium purpureum*	Robin-Plantain *Erigeron puchellus*
White Oak		■													■			▨	■	■		■			■
Wet Prong/McCoy Hollow	■	■			■			■	■					■				▨	■			■			■
Wet Prong					■				■					■				▨							
Ugly Creek Road		■	■		■			■	■									▨	■			■	■		■
Turnhole Bend South		■		■	■			■	■										■						■
Turnhole Bend	■				■		■		■										■			■	■		■
Sloan's Crossing		■																		■		■			
Sand Cave		■																	■						■
Sal Hollow		■	■		■			■										▨	■			▨	■		
Raymer Hollow		■	■		■	■		■	■					■	■			▨	■			▨			■
Park Ridge Road		■						■	■										■				■		■
McCoy Hollow		■						■	■					■											■
Mammoth Cave Ferry Road											■		■						■				■		■
Joppa Ridge		■						■	■										■			■	■		■
Houchins Ferry Road			■	■				■									■	■	■				■		■
Highway 70/255							■																	■	
Heritage Trail																			■				■		
Green R. Bluffs/Styx/Dixon		■	■		■	■		■	■									▨	■			■		■	■
Good Spring Loop		■												■		■									■
Ganter Cave	■	■	■		■			■		■			■	■					■				■		■
Flint Ridge Road		■	■		■			■				■							■		■	▨			
First Creek Hollow					■			■	■			■		■				▨	■			■			■
Echo River/Mammoth Dome	■						■	■	■	■			■	■			■		■				■	■	■
Dennison Ferry Road		■	■		■			■	■			■							■				■		■
Collie Ridge	■						■	■	■						■			■	■				■		■
Cedar Sink	■									■			■												
Campground	■			■	■	■		■	■							■	■	▨	■			■		■	■
Blair Spring Hollow					■				■					■											

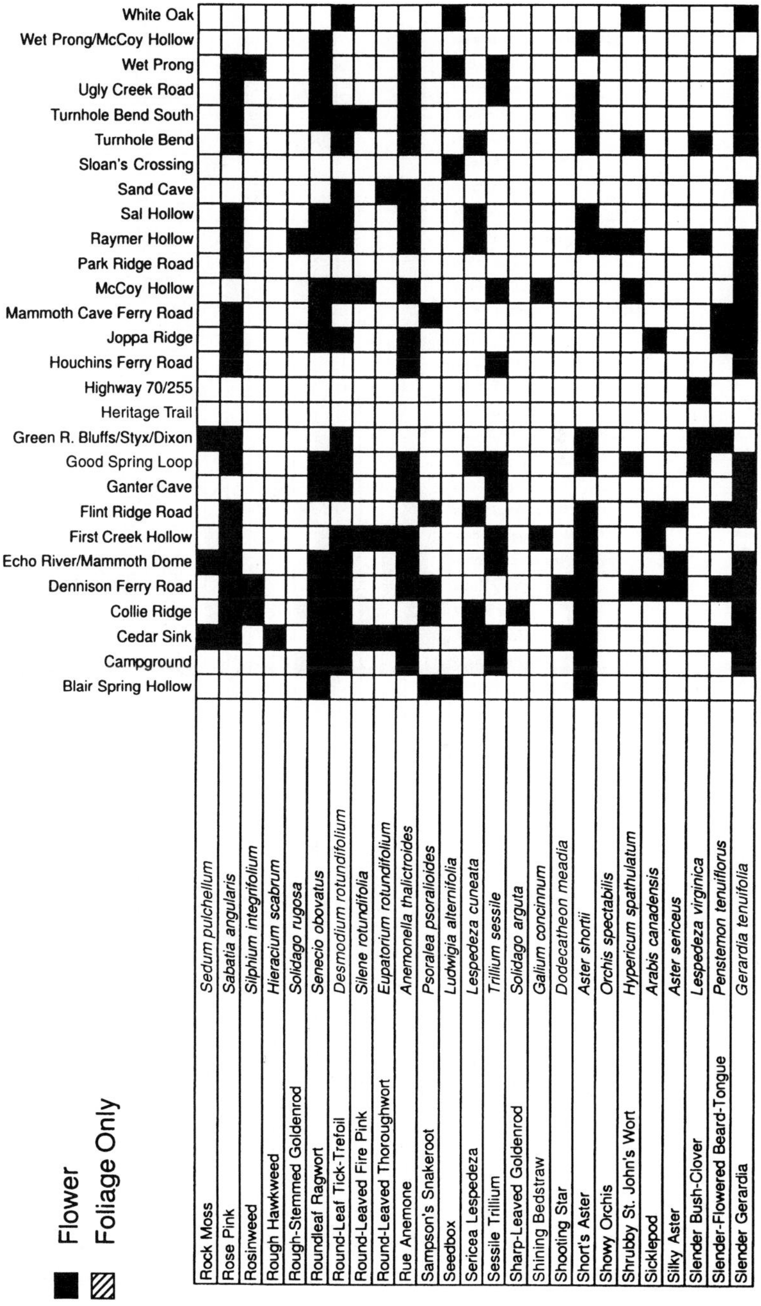
White Oak
Wet Prong/McCoy Hollow
Wet Prong
Ugly Creek Road
Turnhole Bend South
Turnhole Bend
Sloan's Crossing
Sand Cave
Sal Hollow
Raymer Hollow
Park Ridge Road
McCoy Hollow
Mammoth Cave Ferry Road
Joppa Ridge
Houchins Ferry Road
Highway 70/255
Heritage Trail
Green R. Bluffs/Styx/Dixon
Good Spring Loop
Ganter Cave
Flint Ridge Road
First Creek Hollow
Echo River/Mammoth Dome
Dennison Ferry Road
Collie Ridge
Cedar Sink
Campground
Blair Spring Hollow
Rock Moss *Sedum pulchellum*
Rose Pink *Sabatia angularis*
Rosinweed *Silphium integrifolium*
Rough Hawkweed *Hieracium scabrum*
Rough-Stemmed Goldenrod *Solidago rugosa*
Roundleaf Ragwort *Senecio obovatus*
Round-Leaf Tick-Trefoil *Desmodium rotundifolium*
Round-Leaved Fire Pink *Silene rotundifolia*
Round-Leaved Thoroughwort *Eupatorium rotundifolium*
Rue Anemone *Anemonella thalictroides*
Sampson's Snakeroot *Psoralea psoralioides*
Seedbox *Ludwigia alternifolia*
Sericea Lespedeza *Lespedeza cuneata*
Sessile Trillium *Trillium sessile*
Sharp-Leaved Goldenrod *Solidago arguta*
Shining Bedstraw *Galium concinnum*
Shooting Star *Dodecatheon meadia*
Short's Aster *Aster shortii*
Showy Orchis *Orchis spectabilis*
Shrubby St. John's Wort *Hypericum spathulatum*
Sicklepod *Arabis canadensis*
Silky Aster *Aster sericeus*
Slender Bush-Clover *Lespedeza virginica*
Slender-Flowered Beard-Tongue *Penstemon tenuiflorus*
Slender Gerardia *Gerardia tenuifolia*
Flower
Foliage Only

APPENDIX B, continued

Legend:
- ■ Flower
- ▨ Foliage Only

Species (column headers):

Common Name	Scientific Name
Slender Ladies'-Tresses	*Spiranthes gracilis*
Slender Mountain Mint	*Pycnanthemum flexuosum*
Slender-Stalked Gaura	*Gaura filipes*
Slender Toothwort	*Dentaria heterophylla*
Small Bluet	*Houstonia patens*
Small-Flowered Ladies'-Tresses	*Spiranthes ovalis*
Small-Flowered Leafcup	*Polymnia canadensis*
Small Green Wood Orchid	*Habenaria clavellata*
Small-Leaved Tick-Trefoil	*Desmodium ciliare*
Small's Ragwort	*Senecio smallii*
Small White Aster	*Aster vimineus*
Small White Morning-Glory	*Ipomoea lacunosa*
Small Wood Sunflower	*Helianthus microcephalus*
Smartweed	*Polygonum spp.*
Smooth Aster	*Aster laevis*
Smooth Phlox	*Phlox carolina var. triflora*
Smooth Rock Cress	*Arabis laevigata*
Smooth Ruellia	*Ruellia strepens*
Soapwort Gentian	*Gentiana saponaria*
Solitary Pussytoes	*Antennaria solitaria*
Solomon's Seal	*Polygonatum biflorum*
Spanish Needles	*Bidens bipinnata*
Spearmint	*Mentha spicata*
Spider Lily	*Hymenocallis occidentalis*
Spotted Knapweed	*Centaurea maculosa*

Locations (row labels):

- White Oak
- Wet Prong/McCoy Hollow
- Wet Prong
- Ugly Creek Road
- Turnhole Bend South
- Turnhole Bend
- Sloan's Crossing
- Sand Cave
- Sal Hollow
- Raymer Hollow
- Park Ridge Road
- McCoy Hollow
- Mammoth Cave Ferry Road
- Joppa Ridge
- Houchins Ferry Road
- Highway 70/255
- Heritage Trail
- Green R. Bluffs/Styx/Dixon
- Good Spring Loop
- Ganter Cave
- Flint Ridge Road
- First Creek Hollow
- Echo River/Mammoth Dome
- Dennison Ferry Road
- Collie Ridge
- Cedar Sink
- Campground
- Blair Spring Hollow

	Spotted Touch-Me-Not *Impatiens capensis*	Spotted Wintergreen *Chimaphila maculata*	Spring Beauty *Claytonia virginica*	Squawroot *Conopholis americana*	Squirrel-Corn *Dicentra canadensis*	St. Andrew's Cross *Ascyrum hypericoides*	Star Chickweed *Stellaria pubera*	Star-of-Bethlehem *Ornithogalum umbellatum*	Starry Campion *Silene stellata*	Sticktight *Bidens frondosa*	Stiff-Leaf Aster *Aster linariifolius*	St. John's-Wort *Hypericum dolabriforme*	Stonecrop *Sedum ternatum*	Striped Gentian *Gentiana villosa*	Sundrops *Oenothera fruticosa*	Swamp Rose *Rosa palustris*	Sweet Everlasting *Gnaphalium obtusifolium*	Sweet Goldenrod *Solidago odora*	Sweet Pea *Lathyrus odoratus*	Sweet White Violet *Viola blanda*	Synandra *Synandra hispidula*	Tall Anemone *Anemone virginiana*	Tall Bellflower *Campanula americana*	Tall Coneflower *Rudbeckia laciniata*	Tall Coreopsis *Coreopsis tripteris*
White Oak	■	■	■			■	■															■			
Wet Prong/McCoy Hollow	■	■	■	■		■	■		■				■							■		■	■	■	
Wet Prong		■	■	■		■	■															■			
Ugly Creek Road	■	■	■				■		■	■								■				■	■		■
Turnhole Bend South	■	▨	■			■	■	■		■							■	■							
Turnhole Bend		■	■	■		■	■		■			■	■				■					■			■
Sloan's Crossing		■												■		■						■			
Sand Cave		■					■							■			■					■			
Sal Hollow	■		■	■			■			■			■				■					■	■		
Raymer Hollow	■	■	■	■		■	■						■				■					■	■		
Park Ridge Road	■									■						■	■					■			■
McCoy Hollow		■	■	■		■	■		■				■									■	■		
Mammoth Cave Ferry Road							■									■						■	■		■
Joppa Ridge							■															■	■		
Houchins Ferry Road			■		■		■					■	■									■			
Highway 70/255	■																		■						
Heritage Trail		■	■														■	■							
Green R. Bluffs/Styx/Dixon		■	■			■	■			■			■			■						■	■		
Good Spring Loop	■		■				■						■					■			■		■		
Ganter Cave							■			■	■	■			■							■	■		■
Flint Ridge Road	■	■	■	■		■	■	■					■					■		■	■	■	■		
First Creek Hollow			■	■			■					■	■				■				■		■		
Echo River/Mammoth Dome	■	■	■	■			■					■	■									■	■	■	■
Dennison Ferry Road	■	■	■			■			■	■		■					■	■				■		■	
Collie Ridge	■	■	■				■		■	■		■	■	■			■					■	■		■
Cedar Sink												■													
Campground		■	■	■		■	■		■				■					■			■	■	■		
Blair Spring Hollow	■	■	■			■	■			■		■	▨					■							

■ Flower
▨ Foliage Only

APPENDIX B, continued

Legend:

■ Flower
▨ Foliage Only

Location	Tall Goldenrod (*Solidago altissima*)	Tall Meadow Rue (*Thalictrum polygamum*)	Tall Thistle (*Cirsium altissimum*)	Tall White Lettuce (*Prenanthes altissima*)	Thin-Leaved Coneflower (*Rudbeckia triloba*)	Three-Lobed Violet (*Viola triloba*)	Three-Seeded Mercury (*Acalypha virginica*)	Tickseed Sunflower (*Bidens aristosa*)	Toothwort (*Dentaria multifida*)	Trailing Bush-Clover (*Lespedeza procumbens*)	Trailing Wild Bean (*Strophostyles helvola*)	Trumpet Creeper (*Campsis radicans*)	Turtlehead (*Chelone glabra*)	Twinleaf (*Jeffersonia diphylla*)	Two-Leaved Toothwort (*Dentaria diphylla*)	Valerian (*Valeriana pauciflora*)	Venus' Looking-Glass (*Specularia perfoliata*)	Violet Wood-Sorrel (*Oxalis violacea*)	Virginia Dayflower (*Commelina virginica*)	Virginia Knotweed (*Tovara virginiana*)	Virginia Meadow-Beauty (*Rhexia virginica*)	Virgin's-Bower (*Clematis virginiana*)	Water Hemlock (*Cicuta maculata*)	Wavy-Leaved Aster (*Aster undulatus*)	Western Daisy (*Astranthium integrifolium*)
White Oak																			■	■					
Wet Prong/McCoy Hollow	■																		■	■					
Wet Prong				■																■					
Ugly Creek Road	■			■															■	■			■		
Turnhole Bend South																				■					
Turnhole Bend				■					■										■	■		■			
Sloan's Crossing																			■	■					
Sand Cave				■															■	■					
Sal Hollow				■	■	■													■	■					
Raymer Hollow		■																	■	■		■			
Park Ridge Road		■																	■	■		■			
McCoy Hollow				■															■	■					
Mammoth Cave Ferry Road				■															■	■				■	
Joppa Ridge								■											■		■	■		■	
Houchins Ferry Road												■							■		■			■	
Highway 70/255	■											■							■						
Heritage Trail																			■						
Green R. Bluffs/Styx/Dixon		■	■	■	■														■		■	■			
Good Spring Loop																			■						
Ganter Cave																			■						
Flint Ridge Road				■	■	■	■	■											■	■					
First Creek Hollow																			■						
Echo River/Mammoth Dome		■	■	■															■	■					
Dennison Ferry Road		■		■															■					■	
Collie Ridge				■				■	■	■									■	■					
Cedar Sink		■																							
Campground		■		■										■	■			■						■	
Blair Spring Hollow		■		■															■					■	

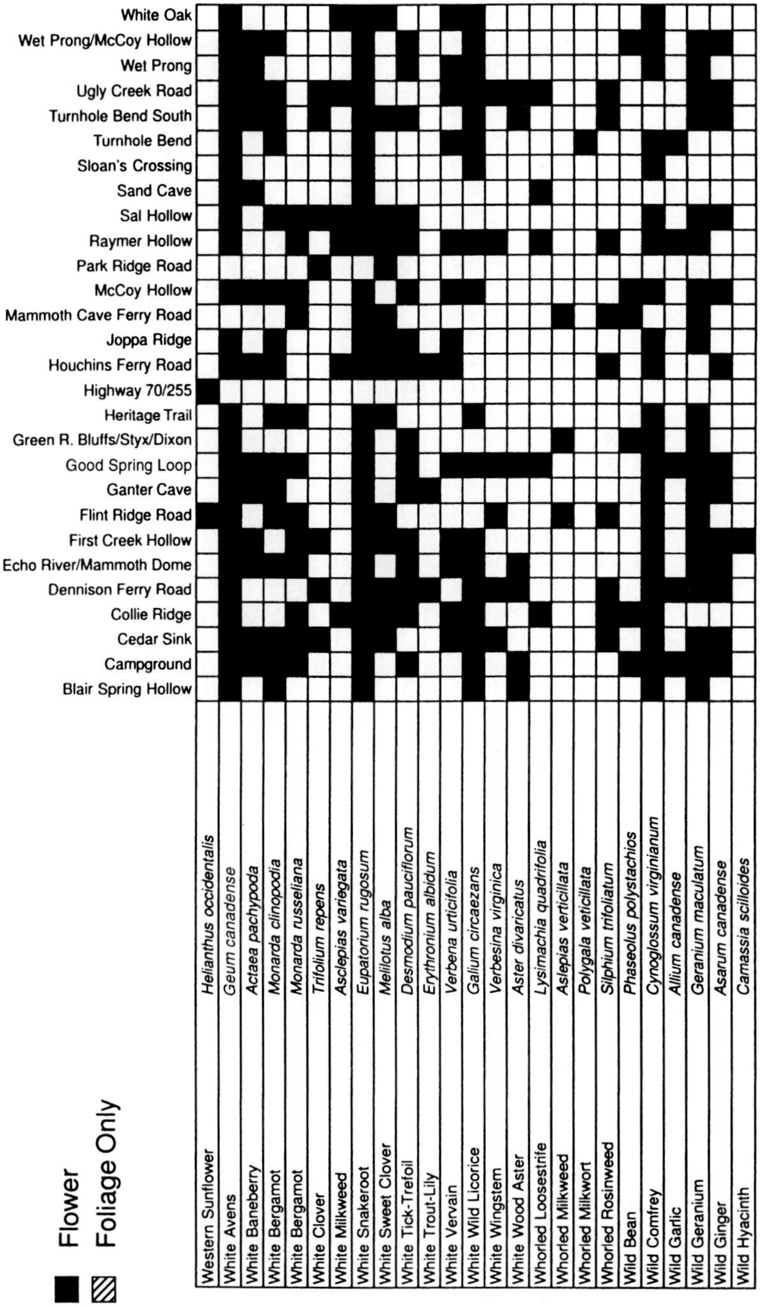
White Oak
Wet Prong/McCoy Hollow
Wet Prong
Ugly Creek Road
Turnhole Bend South
Turnhole Bend
Sloan's Crossing
Sand Cave
Sal Hollow
Raymer Hollow
Park Ridge Road
McCoy Hollow
Mammoth Cave Ferry Road
Joppa Ridge
Houchins Ferry Road
Highway 70/255
Heritage Trail
Green R. Bluffs/Styx/Dixon
Good Spring Loop
Ganter Cave
Flint Ridge Road
First Creek Hollow
Echo River/Mammoth Dome
Dennison Ferry Road
Collie Ridge
Cedar Sink
Campground
Blair Spring Hollow
Western Sunflower *Helianthus occidentalis*
White Avens *Geum canadense*
White Baneberry *Actaea pachypoda*
White Bergamot *Monarda clinopodia*
White Bergamot *Monarda russeliana*
White Clover *Trifolium repens*
White Milkweed *Asclepias variegata*
White Snakeroot *Eupatorium rugosum*
White Sweet Clover *Melilotus alba*
White Tick-Trefoil *Desmodium pauciflorum*
White Trout-Lily *Erythronium albidum*
White Vervain *Verbena urticifolia*
White Wild Licorice *Galium circaezans*
White Wingstem *Verbesina virginica*
White Wood Aster *Aster divaricatus*
Whorled Loosestrife *Lysimachia quadrifolia*
Whorled Milkweed *Aslepias verticillata*
Whorled Milkwort *Polygala veticillata*
Whorled Rosinweed *Silphium trifoliatum*
Wild Bean *Phaseolus polystachios*
Wild Comfrey *Cynoglossum virginianum*
Wild Garlic *Allium canadense*
Wild Geranium *Geranium maculatum*
Wild Ginger *Asarum canadense*
Wild Hyacinth *Camassia scilloides*
Flower
Foliage Only

APPENDIX B, continued

■ Flower
▨ Foliage Only

	Wild Hydrangea *Hydrangea arborescens*	Wild Lettuce *Lactuca canadensis*	Wild Potato-Vine *Ipomoea pandurata*	Wild Quinine *Parthenium integrifolium*	Wild Rose *Rosa carolina*	Wild Senna *Cassia marilandica*	Wild Strawberry *Fragaria virginiana*	Wild Yam *Dioscorea quaternata*	Wingstem *Actinomeris alternifolia*	Wintercress *Barbarea vulgaris*	Wood-Betony *Pedicularis canadensis*	Wood-Nettle *Laportea canadensis*	Woodland Coneflower *Rudbeckia umbrosa*	Woodland Sunflower *Helianthus divaricatus*	Wood Sage *Teucrium canadense*	Woods Vetch *Vicia caroliniana*	Yarrow *Achillea millefolium*	Yellow Corydalis *Corydalis flavula*	Yellow Lady's-Slipper *Cypripedium calceolus*	Yellow Stargrass *Hypoxis hirsuta*	Yellow Touch-Me-Not *Impatiens pallida*	Yellow Trout-Lily *Erythronium americanum*	Yellow Wood-Sorrel *Oxalis stricta*	Yucca *Yucca filamentosa*	Zigzag Spiderwort *Tradescantia subaspera*
White Oak								■	■					■				■							
Wet Prong/McCoy Hollow	■	■			■			■	■		■	■	■	■								■	■		■
Wet Prong								■			■	■													
Ugly Creek Road	■	■	■		■	■	■	■	■					■	■								■		■
Turnhole Bend South									■									■							
Turnhole Bend	■	■			■				■								■	■	■	■			■		■
Sloan's Crossing							■																		
Sand Cave	■																■					■			
Sal Hollow						■		■	■														■		
Raymer Hollow							■	■	■													■			■
Park Ridge Road		■	■	■	■					■				■			■								
McCoy Hollow	■							■			■			■				■				■			■
Mammoth Cave Ferry Road				■	■				■					■			■								
Joppa Ridge				■	■			■	■					■	■	■									
Houchins Ferry Road	■		■	■	■	■								■	■		■	■				■	■		
Highway 70/255		■								■															
Heritage Trail																									
Green R. Bluffs/Styx/Dixon					■			■	■	■	■	■		■								■	■		■
Good Spring Loop								■	■									■				■			■
Ganter Cave			■	■	■				■					■		■							■	■	
Flint Ridge Road	■							■	■		■			■				■	■				■		■
First Creek Hollow	■							■	■		■		■			■		■				■			■
Echo River/Mammoth Dome	■		■	■			■		■					■						■	■	■	■		
Dennison Ferry Road		■	■	■	■		■	■						■			■						■		
Collie Ridge	■		■				■	■	■	■				■			■	■				■	■		■
Cedar Sink								■						■											
Campground	■					■		■	■					■		■		■		■	■	■	■		■
Blair Spring Hollow		■		■							■		■	■											■

APPENDIX C: INDEX OF FLOWERS BY TRAIL

TRAIL	Number of Species Found			Flowering Period	
	This Trail	This Trail Only		Number of Species Observed in Flower	
Blair Spring Hollow	88	0		March 1	6
Campground	54	1		March 15	23
Cedar Sink	170	1		April 1	36
Collie Ridge	154	4		April 15	41
Dennison Ferry Road	172	6		May 1	77
Echo River/Mammoth Dome Sink	134	3		May 15	54
First Creek Hollow	161	7		June 1	43
Flint Ridge Road	132	5		June 15	61
Ganter Cave	82	0		July 1	76
Good Spring Loop	149	1		July 15	84
Green River Bluffs/River Styx/Dixon Cave	152	0		August 1	88
Heritage Trail	43	0		August 15	96
Highway 70/255	27	4		September 1	92
Houchins Ferry Road	111	2		September 15	96
Joppa Ridge Road	98	1		October 1	51
Mammoth Cave Ferry Road	69	1		October 15	14
McCoy Hollow	133	1			
Park Ridge Road	66	2			
Raymer Hollow	153	2			
Sal Hollow	115	0			
Sand Cave	62	1			
Sloan's Crossing Pond	50	3			
Turnhole Bend	100	2			
Turnhole Bend South	139	0			
Ugly Creek Road	175	4			
Wet Prong	154	2			
Wet Prong/McCoy Hollow	84	0			
White Oak	88	0			

BIBLIOGRAPHY

Angier, Bradford. *Free for the Eating.* Harrisburg, Penn.: Telegraph Press, 1966.
———. *Field Guide to Edible Wild Plants.* Harrisburg, Penn.: Stackpole Books, 1974.
Birdseye, Clarence G. and Eleanor Birdseye. *Growing Woodland Plants.* 1951. Reprint, New York: Dover Publications, 1972.
Britton, Nathaniel, and Addison Brown. *An Illustrated Flora of the Northern United States and Canada,* 3 vols. 1913. Reprint, New York: Dover Publications, 1970.
Campbell, Carlos C., William F. Huston, and Aaron J. Sharp. *Great Smoky Mountains Wildflowers.* Knoxville: University of Tennessee Press, 1968.
Coon, N. *Using Wayside Plants.* New York: Hearthside Press, 1957.
Craighead, John J., Frank C. Craighead, and Ray J. Davis. *A Field Guide to Rocky Mountain Wildflowers.* Boston: Houghton Mifflin, 1963.
Davies, Adrian. *Wildflowers of America.* New York: Archcape Press, 1989.
Deganawidan. *The Rangers Guide to Useful Plants of Eastern Wilds.* Boston: Christopher Publishing House, 1964.
Erichsen-Brown, Charlotte. *Medicinal and Other Uses of North American Plants.* 1979. Reprint, New York: Dover Publications, 1989.
Fernald, M.L. *Gray's Manual of Botany,* 8th ed. New York: Van Nostrand Reinhold, 1950.
Fernald, Merritt L., and Alfred C. Kinsey. *Edible Wild Plants of Eastern North America,* rev. ed. New York: Harper and Rowe, 1958.
Foster, Steven, and A. James Duke. *Medicinal Plants.* Boston: Houghton Mifflin, 1990.
Gibbons, Euell. *Stalking the Healthful Herbs.* Putney, Vt.: Alan C. Hood, 1966.
Gleason, Henry A., and Arthur Cronquist. *Manual of Vascular Plants of Northeastern United States and Adjacent Canada,* 2d ed. Bronx: New York Botanical Garden, 1991.
Greene, Wilhelmina, and Hugo L. Blomquist. *Flowers of the South.* Chapel Hill: University of North Carolina Press, 1968.
Grieve, M. *A Modern Herbal.* 1931. Reprint, New York: Dover Publications, 1971.
Grimm, William C. *How to Recognize Flowering Wild Plants.* Harrisburg, Penn.: Stackpole Company, 1968.
Hall, A. *The Wild Food Trail Guide.* New York: Holt, Rinehart and Winston, 1973.
Haragan, Patricia D. *Weeds of Kentucky and Adjacent States.* Lexington: University Press of Kentucky, 1991.
Hutchens, Alma R. *Indian Herbalogy of North America.* Boston: Shambhala Publications, 1991.
Justice, William S., and Ritchie C. Bell. *Wildflowers of North Carolina.* Chapel Hill: University of North Carolina Press, 1968.
Kartesz, John T. *A Synonymized Checklist of the Vascular Flora of the United States, Canada, and Greenland,* 2d ed. Portland, Ore.: Timber Press, 1994.
Kreig, M. B. *Green Medicine.* Chicago: Rand McNally, 1964.

Lehner, Ernst, and Johanna Lehner. *Folklore and Symbolism of Flowers, Plants, and Trees.* New York: Tudor Publishing, 1960.

Lust, John. *The Herb Book.* New York: Bantam Books, 1974.

Mabey, Richard. *The New Age Herbalist.* New York: Macmillan, 1988.

Martin, Alexander C., Herbert S. Zim, and Arnold L. Nelson. *American Wildlife and Plants: A Guide to Wildlife Food Habits.* Toronto: General Publishing, 1951.

Martin, Laura C. *Wildflower Folklore.* Charlotte, N.C.: East Woods Press, Fast and MacMillan, 1984.

————. *Southern Wildflowers.* Marietta, Ga.: Longstreet Press, 1989.

Meuninck, J. *The Basic Essentials of Edible Wild Plants and Useful Herbs.* Merrillville, Ind.: ICS Books, 1988.

Mooney, James. *Myths of the Cherokee and Sacred Formulas of the Cherokees.* 1900. Reprint, Nashville: Charles and Randy Elder, 1982.

Muenscher, Walter C. *Poisonous Plants of the United States.* New York: Macmillan, 1951.

Palmer, E. Laurence. *Fieldbook of Natural History,* rev. ed. New York: McGrawHill, 1975.

Patterson, David, ed. *Culpepper's Color Herbal.* New York: Sterling Publishing, 1983.

Peterson, Lee A. *Edible Wild Plants.* Boston: Houghton Mifflin, 1977.

Peterson, Roger T., and Margaret McKenny. *A Field Guide to Wildflowers of Northeastern and Northcentral North America.* Boston: Houghton Mifflin, 1968.

Readers Digest. *Magic and Medicine of Plants.* Pleasantville, N.Y.: Readers Digest Association, 1986.

Rickett, H.W. *The Odyssey Book of American Wildflowers.* New York: Western Publishing, 1964.

Schmutz, Ervin M., and Lucretia B. Hamilton. *Plants That Poison.* Flagstaff, Ariz.: Northland Publishing, 1979.

Selsam, M. E. *Plants That Heal.* New York: William Morrow, 1959.

Strausbaugh, P.D., and Earl L. Core. *Flora of West Virginia,* 2d ed. Morgantown, W. Va.: Seneda Books, 1978.

Weiner, Michael A. *Earth Medicine, Earth Food.* New York: Ballantine Books, 1972.

Wharton, Mary E., and Roger W. Barbour. *A Guide to the Wildflowers and Ferns of Kentucky.* Lexington: University Press of Kentucky, 1971.

Wigginton, Eliot. *The Foxfire Book.* Garden City, N.Y.: Anchor Books, 1972.

————. *Foxfire 3.* Garden City, N.Y.: Anchor Books, 1975.

INDEX OF GENERA BY FAMILY

---

* Now in Agavaceae

---

* Now in Smilaceae
** Now in Agavaceae

---

* Now in Hydrangeaceae

INDEX OF SCIENTIFIC AND COMMON SPECIES NAMES

Flower Structure and Terminology

Parts

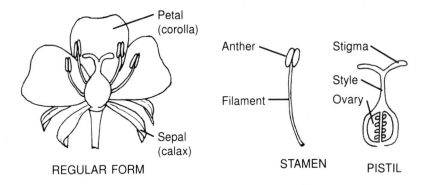

Petal
(corolla)

Sepal
(calax)

REGULAR FORM

Anther

Filament

STAMEN

Stigma

Style

Ovary

PISTIL

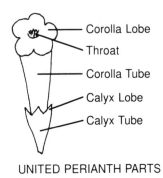

Corolla Lobe

Throat

Corolla Tube

Calyx Lobe

Calyx Tube

UNITED PERIANTH PARTS

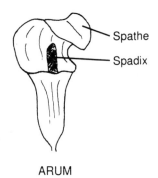

Spathe

Spadix

ARUM

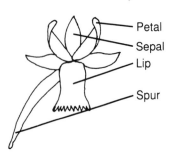

Petal

Sepal

Lip

Spur

ORCHID

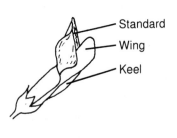

Standard

Wing

Keel

PEA-TYPE